NEONATOLOGY AND LABORATORY MEDICINE

Sarah Heap, PhD, FRCPath
Consultant in Clinical Biochemistry, Birmingham Children's and Women's Hospitals, Birmingham, UK

Jim Gray, MB ChB, MRCP (UK), FRCPath
Consultant Microbiologist, Birmingham Children's and Women's Hospitals, Birmingham, UK

Andrew Ewer, MD, MRCP , FRCPCH
Consultant Neonatologist, Birmingham Women's Hospitall and Professor of Neonatal Medicine, Birmingham University

Editor
Helen C Losty BSc, MSc, FRCPath
Clinical Biochemist, South West Pathology Services, Taunton, Somerset,UK

Guest Editor
Valerie Walker BSc, MD, MBChB, FRCPath FRCPCH
Honorary Consultant Chemical Pathologist, University Hospital, Southampton, UK

ACB VENTURE PUBLICATIONS

ACB VENTURE PUBLICATIONS
Managing Editor - Roy Sherwood

British Library Cataloguing in Publication Data

A catalogue record for the book is available from the British Library

ISBN 978-0-902429-57-4, EAN 9780902429574, ACB Venture Publications

Printed by

Cover design by Aspire Design Studios, London

Important notice
Although ACB Venture Publications has made every effort to ensure the accuracy of the information contained in this book, the responsibility for the patient is ultimately that of the medical practitioner ordering or performing/supervising the investigations. All drugs and intravenous fluids must be prescribed by a registered medical practitioner and administered by an individual authorised to do so. The publishers, authors and editors do not assume any liability for any injury and/or damage to persons or property arising from this publication.

Preface

In this third edition of Neonatal Laboratory Medicine, the content has been updated to ensure its continued relevance. Since the last edition, there have been many important developments in laboratory and clinical practice, and in the UK both Neonatal Units and laboratories have developed networks to ensure consistency of approach and to promote good practice. There have been significant changes in the provision of laboratory services, arising both from a drive for improved efficiency and important technological advances. The scope and methodology of newborn screening has changed, there is a greater focus on infection prevention and control, and especially on antibiotic stewardship, and important clinical guidelines have been published by NICE that emphasise the importance of timely access to laboratory test results in informing neonatal care.

As in previous editions the book is intended as a basic guide for junior doctors, laboratory scientists and neonatal nurses – hopefully to enable the consideration, identification and management of common neonatal problems. The text provides brief background information, discussion of the practical aspects of diagnosis and management and references for further detailed reading should a more in depth knowledge be required.

Many clinical and scientific colleagues at both Birmingham Children's Hospital (Pippa Goddard, Mary Anne Preece, Paul Griffiths) and Birmingham Women's Hospital (Ian Mills) have helped with detail and advised on content during the review process. Special thanks go to Dr Alice Norton, Consultant Haematologist for her extensive updating and rewriting of the chapter on haematological disorders and to Dr Gemma Holder, Consultant Neonatologist for updating the chapter on parenteral nutrition.

Finally we thank ACB Venture Publications for providing us with the opportunity for this final edition. We extend thanks to Helen Losty (Editor) for her help, support, direction and editorial skill throughout the process and to Professor Roy Sherwood (Managing Editor) for his skillful assembly of text and illustrations. In particular we are grateful to Dr Valerie Walker (Guest Editor) for her significant contribution to the revision of the chapters on fluid and electrolytes, jaundice and glucose.

Jim Gray
Sarah Heap
Andrew Ewer

January 2017

Contents

Chapter 1
Overview: Neonatal care and biochemistry

Summary

- The majority of newborns require no routine laboratory testing apart from a blood sample for the the the neonatal screening programme.

- A minority (around 11% in the UK) of newborn babies have problems that require admission to a neonatal unit (NNU). The majority are born preterm.

- The complexity of care required covers a broad spectrum. NNUs are classified according to their capacity to provide this.

- All NNUs should have immediate access to a range of laboratory services at all times.

- The use of laboratory tests to investigate, and monitor the progress of sick babies needs to be weighed against the discomfort and blood loss caused by repeated blood sampling.

- The need for repeated blood sampling can be minimised by careful timing of investigations ensuring that good quality samples are sent to the laboratory, and avoiding over-investigation of babies.

- The results of laboratory tests need to be interpreted in the context of the baby's gestational and postnatal age using robust, locally applicable reference data.

Definitions

Gestational age: weeks + 1-6 days from conception.
Postnatal age: weeks + 1-6 days from birth; the day of birth is day 1.
Term birth: gestational age of 37 weeks and 0 days to 42 weeks and 0 days.
Neonate: a newborn infant under 28 days of age.
Preterm (premature) birth: gestational age 36 weeks and six days or less.
Low birth weight (LBW): birth weight less than 2,500g.
Very low birth weight (VLBW): birth weight less than 1,500g.
Small for gestational age (SGA): all babies with birth weight less than the 10th percentile for gestational age. This includes babies who are constitutionally small but have achieved their growth potential.
Intrauterine growth restriction (IUGR): SGA babies who have been unable to achieve their genetic growth potential *in utero.*
Stillbirth: a baby born dead after 24 completed weeks of pregnancy.
Miscarriage or late fetal loss: a fetus who died before 24 completed weeks of pregnancy.
Apgar score: a clinical score used to assess the vital signs of a baby one and five minutes after birth: assesses heart rate, respiration, muscle tone, response to stimulation, colour. Scores ≥ 7, usually normal; ≤ 3 critically low.

Perinatal (birth) asphyxia: the clinical disturbance that results from an inadequate supply of oxygen to the brain and other organs immediately prior to, during, or just after, delivery.

Introduction

The majority of babies are born at term after an uncomplicated pregnancy and labour, are well post-partum, and are discharged home with their mothers within a few hours of birth. These babies require no routine laboratory testing other than a heel prick blood sample collected in the community at five to eight days of age for the NHS Newborn Blood Spot Screening Programme (see Chapter 9). In spite of their prematurity, many preterm babies of ≥ 34 weeks of gestation also have an uneventful course post-partum and are discharged within 48 hours of birth after no, or minimal, laboratory investigations. Other babies who do not require close monitoring, have tests undertaken on the postnatal wards or in the community if there are concerns, for example about jaundice, hypoglycaemia or sepsis. In the UK around 11% of newborn babies develop more serious problems that require admission to a neonatal unit (NNU). Many of these have transient disorders and can be discharged quickly but some, particularly those who are very premature, have extremely complex problems that need intensive management with close biochemical monitoring.

Common minor neonatal problems requiring laboratory support

Jaundice

About one third of babies will develop visible jaundice (equivalent to a plasma bilirubin of ≥ 80 µmol/L). This appears on the second day or later and usually resolves by day 10, or later than this in breast-fed babies. In a well infant, in the first fourteen days, no investigation is indicated.

If the baby is unwell, or the jaundice is thought to be severe, or if the baby is clinically jaundiced on day one or after day 14, then clinical examination is required, plasma total and conjugated bilirubin should be measured, and other investigations may be indicated (see Chapter 6).

Hypoglycaemia

Certain groups of babies are at risk of postnatal hypoglycaemia – the biochemical definition is a plasma glucose ≤2.6 mmol/L (Figure 1.1). When hypoglycaemia is asymptomatic other energy sources (such as ketones) are available to, and used by, the baby's brain; this stage is not thought to be harmful. By contrast, symptomatic hypoglycaemia (see Chapter 7) is an emergency requiring prompt treatment. Surveillance monitoring, from birth, of blood glucose in at-risk babies is used to detect low concentrations (<2 mmol/L) so that management can be initiated – ranging from early or more frequent feeds to immediate correction if blood sugar is very low or the baby is symptomatic (see Chapter 7). Three hourly measurements of blood glucose before feeds using a point of care (POC) glucose meter is used for surveillance monitoring.

- Birth weight below 10th centile.

- Preterm <37 weeks of gestation.

- Low Apgar score (≤ 3) at one minute.

- Hypothermia (axillary temperature < 36.5°C).

- Infants of diabetic mothers.

- Suspicion or evidence of infection acquired *in utero* or during delivery.

Figure 1.1. Risk factors for hypoglycaemia.

Suspected infection

There is frequently concern about the possibility of early-onset neonatal infection, although its actual occurrence is uncommon. As a result, around 10% of newborn babies are commenced on intravenous antibiotics (Chapter 12). Laboratories have an important role in undertaking, and communicating the results of tests to exclude infection and thus expedite discontinuation of antibiotic therapy.

Babies requiring neonatal unit (NNU) care

Babies with specialised nursing or medical requirements in the newborn period are cared for in neonatal units (NNUs).

Organisation of NNU services

NNUs are categorised according to the level of care they can provide (Figure 1.2). They are organised into local Neonatal Networks where hospitals work together to ensure that a baby has access to appropriate care as close to home as possible. Babies who require observation and relatively simple interventions can be managed in Special Care Baby Units in the local maternity hospitals. However it may be necessary to transfer those, with more complex needs, to an NNU in another hospital specially equipped and staffed to provide the highly skilled, high dependency or intensive care required (Figure 1.3)

Where the need for NNU care is anticipated antenatally, women will have their obstetric care transferred to a hospital with an appropriate NNU. Where a sick baby is born without immediate access to an NNU it will have to be resuscitated and stabilised locally, before being collected by a transport team and taken to a tertiary service with appropriate and available facilities. Although a neonate is defined as a baby in the first four weeks of life, NNU care covers a much wider age range than this. Very ill or preterm babies may have an NNU stay of three to four months, and after discharge may continue to require specialist support and treatment at home, such as medication or oxygen (for the management of chronic lung disease).

The severity and complexity of disorders, particularly of premature babies who require care on an NNU, cover a broad spectrum as listed in Figure 1.4. These disorders will be discussed in greater detail in individual chapters.

Category	Type of care provided
Special Care Unit (SCBU)	• Monitoring, oxygen therapy, phototherapy, tube feeding, recovery or convalescence
Local Neonatal Unit (LNU)	• Short-term intensive care • Non-invasive respiratory support such as continuous positive airways pressure (CPAP)
Neonatal Intensive Care Unit (NICU)	• Care of extremely premature infants (<27 weeks) • Invasive long-term respiratory support (ventilation) • Care of babies with complex conditions • Care of babies requiring emergency surgery
Transitional Care	• Care of babies who are well and almost ready to go home but have additional needs

Figure 1.2. Levels of NNU categorised according to complexity of care.

Intensive care (Babies who are most unwell or unstable)	High-dependency care (Babies requiring care from highly skilled staff)	Special care (Additional care but not intensive or high-dependency care)
• Invasive ventilation • Non-invasive ventilation combined with parenteral nutrition • Undergoing surgery • Umbilical arterial catheter, peripheral arterial line or chest drain • Procedures such as therapeutic hypothermia, dialysis or exchange transfusion • Insulin or prostaglandin infusion • Babies on the day of death	• Non-invasive ventilation • Babies receiving parenteral nutrition and/or continuous infusion of drugs (not insulin or prostaglandin) • Convulsions or undergoing cerebral function monitoring* • Tracheostomy or nasal airway • Urinary catheter	• Oxygen by nasal cannula • Tube feeding • Peripheral intravenous cannula • Phototherapy • Observations of physiological variables at least four hourly • Stoma care

* cerebral function monitoring: monitoring of the background electrical activity of the brain with a bedside electroencephalogram (EEG)

Figure 1.3. Conditions and procedures requiring different levels of NNU care.

Condition	Origin	Management
Anaemia – chapter 15	Repeated venepunctures Marrow unresponsive Increased blood volume with growth	Replace losses by transfusion (taking care to minimise donor exposure)
Chronic lung disease	Barotrauma, volutrauma and oxygen toxicity in the extreme preterm with respiratory distress syndrome	Prolonged oxygen requirement Supportive monitoring, nutritional and diuretic therapy
Hyponatraemia – chapter 4	Renal tubular immaturity	Adequate replacement of urinary losses
Dehydration/ Hypernatraemia – chapter 4	Transdermal water losses in the extreme preterm Polyuria in recovering tubular necrosis	Humidified environment Monitor urinary losses Adequate water and salt intake
Hypoglycaemia – chapter 7	Inadequate intake Low glycogen stores	Monitor glucose as per local protocol IV dextrose
Hyperglycaemia – chapter 7	Diabetogenic effect of parenteral nutrition ± steroid therapy	May require insulin infusion
Hypocalcaemia – chapter 8	Immature parathyroid regulation	Adequate calcium supplementation
Hypothermia	Large surface area Poor insulation Immature skin structure Nursed naked	Plastic bag at delivery Thermoneutral environment (e.g. incubator) Consider added humidity Clothing
Infection – chapter 12	Invasive management Immature immune defences	High index of suspicion Prophylactic parenteral antibiotics
Irregular respiration/ apnoea of prematurity	Immature respiratory centre	Monitor respiration Caffeine Seek pathological cause
Jaundice – chapter 6	Hepatic immaturity Bruising Delayed feeding	Phototherapy Exchange transfusion

Figure 1.4. Major medical problems in preterm babies (Cont..).

Condition	Origin	Management
Malnutrition – chapter 14	Low energy stores Undernutrition Energy expenditure can be large	Minimal enteral feeding as soon as tolerated Parenteral nutrition and fortified milks
Metabolic acidosis – chapter 5	Renal immaturity (in presence of protein load)	May need to reduce protein intake Sodium bicarbonate transfusion
Necrotising enterocolitis	Inadequate perfusion of gut Hypoxic insults Formula fluids	Parenteral nutrition Supportive Surgical resection of infarcted tissue may be required
Nephrocalcinosis	Oliguria, poor acidification, hypercalciuria Use of frusemide	Avoid prolonged use of loop diuretics
Osteopenia of prematurity – chapter 8	Demineralisation of bones if nutrition inadequate	Adequate mineral content (particularly phosphate) of feeds
Periventricular haemorrhage	Immaturity Cerebrovascular instability	Supportive care Rarely progresses to hydrocephalus
Periventricular leucomalacia	Cerebral white matter infarction after ischaemic insult	Supportive care Minimise hypocapnia Avoid hypotension
Persistent patent ductus arteriosus	Immaturity Hypoxia Acidosis	Ibuprofen Diuretics and fluid restriction Surgical ligation
Respiratory distress syndrome	Surfactant deficiency	Exogenous surfactant Respiratory support IV fluids/nutrition
Retinopathy of prematurity	Local oxygen toxicity affects retinal vasculature	Screening of at risk babies (<31 weeks) Monitor oxygen saturation Laser treatment
Unable to suck	Immature suck/swallow coordination	Nasogastric tube feeds if well

Figure 1.4 (Cont..). Major medical problems in preterm babies.

Outcomes of NNU babies

Mortality and long-term morbidity amongst survivors is seen mainly in those babies born before 27 weeks gestation and/or with birth weight less than 1 kg. Most deaths are in the first week, with an excess on the first day. The commonest cause of death in premature babies remains complications of respiratory disease, despite the use of prenatal steroids and post-natal exogenous surfactant.

Both the number of extremely premature babies admitted for NNU care, and the proportion surviving, has increased in the past two decades. The EPICure 2 study in 2006 of maternity units across the UK and Ireland found that:

- 2,000 births in England (0.3% of all births) were of 23 to 25+6 weeks gestation. This represents an increase of 44% compared with the first EPICure study in 1995.

- Survival for these babies improved by 13%, from 40% to 53% and more so at 24 and 25 weeks; survival of babies born before 23 weeks remains very rare.

- Despite these improvements, the number of babies leaving NNUs with abnormalities on their brain ultrasound scans, and with lung, bowel and eye problems was little changed.

Ethics and consent

In the UK, explicit consent from parents for intensive neonatal care treatment, including most laboratory investigations, is not usually required. Informed signed consent is required if the baby is to undergo an invasive procedure (skin, liver, or muscle biopsy) or surgery, genetic or HIV testing. It is important that parents are kept informed about all aspects of their baby's care, including circumstances where continuation of neonatal intensive care is not in the baby's best interests. This is best done by regular discussions, the content of which are recorded in the case notes. An explanatory booklet can also be used to help parents under-stand, in general terms, the investigations and treatments their baby will or may require. Parents will usually be guided by healthcare professionals on what is in the baby's best inter-ests. However, problems can arise where one or both parents decline an investigation or treat-ment that is considered essential for the baby, or where a test result is of such sensitivity (e.g. detection of a sexually-transmitted pathogen in the baby) that it should only be disclosed to the mother. Depending on the circumstances, the Neonatologists may need to seek expert advice. Ultimately the clinician must be assured that any decisions taken are in the baby's best interests and that the interests being protected are important.

Laboratory support for neonatal care

All levels of NNU must have immediate access at all times to laboratory facilities equipped to analyse very small samples. Investigations include blood gas analysis, electrolytes, creatinine, glucose, bilirubin and liver function tests, ammonia and lactate, coagulation (fibrinogen, PT, APTT) and full blood count analysis, microscopy and culture of CSF and blood cultures. Some of these investigations may be undertaken at the point of care (Chapter 2). They must also have protocols for collection of acute samples when an inherited biochemical disorder is suspected (Chapter 10 and Appendix B).

Blood samples from neonates for laboratory tests

Volume of blood samples

The blood volume of a term neonate is about 275 mL, while a premature baby weighing 1kg will have a blood volume of only 80 mL. The high neonatal haematocrit means that the plasma yield (for testing) from a given blood volume is up to 30% lower for a neonate than for an older child or adult. These observations have implications, particularly for a very low birth weight baby, for the number and size of blood samples that can safely be taken, and the number of analyses that can be performed per sample.

- The volume of blood collected should be minimised by careful selection of tests, with priority given to the most important; most routine monitoring tests can be undertaken on 500-600 µL.

- For babies undergoing regular blood testing in intensive care, volumes of blood taken should be monitored, and blood replaced by transfusion if the haemoglobin falls below 110 g/L or if more than 10% of the circulating volume has been removed.

Collection of blood samples (Appendix A)

Blood collection from neonates is a skilled process that should be undertaken by trained and competent staff who understand the technical difficulties involved.

A uniform sampling technique is important to reduce pain and psychological trauma. This involves swaddling the infant and offering routine analgesia such as oral sucrose or breast milk – see below.

A number of types of blood samples may be taken from neonates.

CORD BLOOD SAMPLES FROM THE UMBILICAL ARTERY AND VEIN

- These are often taken after high-risk or difficult deliveries to identify respiratory or metabolic acidosis (see Chapter 5, Acid-base disorders).

- They are useful for urgent investigation of conditions such as haemophilia, or as a baseline to measure the rate of increase in bilirubin in haemolytic disorders.

- They are not useful for diagnosis of neonatal viral infections (e.g. HIV), because they may be contaminated with maternal blood.

VENEPUNCTURE

- This is the preferred method of blood sampling for an uncontaminated sample where blood cultures are required, and for tests that require larger specimen volumes.

CAPILLARY PUNCTURE

- Providing the baby is well perfused, this is suitable for collecting the small volumes of liquid blood (500-600 µL) required for most routine tests, however collection requires skill and may take up to 10 minutes.

- Poor technique, such as squeezing the heel and scraping the tube over the skin, is unacceptable. It will be painful for the baby and produce a grossly haemolysed sample, possibly contaminated with tissue fluid, so that reliable results are not obtained. Results from such specimens may have elevated potassium and magnesium (released from red cells), falsely low sodium and albumin (from tissue fluid contamination), or elevated ammonia or amino acids from sweat.

- Plasma potassium will be on average 1-1.5 mmol/L higher than in arterial blood, even without visible haemolysis.

SAMPLES FROM ARTERIAL LINES

Arterial access allows regular measurement of blood gases and acid base status (see Chapter 5) and pain-free collection of routine samples. When blood is collected from an arterial line, particular care is needed to avoid the aspiration of infusion fluid otherwise erroneous results can occur due to dilution with the infusate. Collection of blood for measurement of drug concentrations through the same line as a drug has been administered is not recommended.

CAPILLARY BLOOD SPOTS

Increasingly, analyses for hormones and metabolites are now being undertaken on capillary blood which has been spotted directly on to absorbent card or even on to reagent strips. These may require as little as 6 µL of blood per spot.

REDUCING STRESS ASSOCIATED WITH BLOOD SAMPLE COLLECTION

It is important to remember that neonates in an NNU undergo a vast number of uncomfortable or frankly painful procedures and treatments, for example having an endotracheal tube sucked out, having an intravenous cannula inserted and undergoing heel pricks for blood tests. Studies have shown that babies of less than 30 weeks' gestation may have up to 2000 painful procedures during their care. The associated distress may lead to well documented physiological changes including crying, altered breathing, apnoeas (pauses in breathing), increased blood pressure, increased risk of intracranial haemorrhage and increased pulmonary pressures leading to right-left circulatory shunting. Repeated experience of pain can lead to sensitisation, so that simple touch in future can lead to a 'pain' response. Anatomical studies have confirmed the presence of pain pathways to cortical and subcortical levels even in the most immature babies cared for on neonatal units.

MEASURES TO REDUCE DISCOMFORT INCLUDE:

- Confining tests to those that are deemed necessary for the baby's care at that time.

- Collection of blood from an indwelling arterial line, if there is one *in situ*, instead of by venepuncture or heel prick.

- Restriction of blood collection to trained competency-assessed staff. This will not only protect the baby from avoidable distress, but also ensure that good quality samples are obtained.

- Grouping of potentially painful handling and procedures together in time, so the baby can then have a rest period.

- Providing comfort to the baby to reduce the physiological reactions to pain, for example sucking a dummy, comfort touch, or swaddling.

- Giving sucrose solution or expressed breast milk orally. Sucrose can act as an effective analgesic and is widely employed in NNUs.

- Use of local anaesthesia provided this will not make the procedure more difficult (and hence prolong it). Note that EMLA (eutectic mixture of local anaesthetics) cream is contraindicated in the neonate.

Neonatal reference intervals

Immaturity, the birth process and the adjustment of the newborn to independent life have a major effect on laboratory analytes. Consequently reference intervals in neonates differ significantly from those for infants and older children and also change markedly within the first four weeks of life. Different reference intervals are required at different ages during the neonatal period. A more detailed discussion of the factors that affect neonatal reference intervals is included with Appendix D. It is also important to note that neonatal reference intervals are often derived from limited data, sometimes from poor quality samples, and that the distribution of data may be skewed due to the ethical and logistical constraints of procuring blood samples for testing from well babies. As in all other age groups, reference intervals are also affected by pre-analytical factors such as stress, type of feeds and time since the last feed, by instrument technology and methodology, and by sample type. Thus any reference intervals given in this book are intended as a guide only, and are not a substitute for good data provided by the local laboratory.

Further reading

British Association of Perinatal Medicine. Service standards for hospitals providing neonatal care, 3rd edn, August 2010.

EPICure population based studies of survival and later health status in extremely premature infants. http://www.epicure.ac.uk.

Royal College of Pathologists. Code of practice for clinical biochemists/chemical pathologists and clinical biochemistry services, March 2011.

Royal College of Pathologists. Guidance on consent for the processing and analysis of clinical samples following an initial consultation, November 2008.

Chapter 2
Requirements for laboratory services

Summary

- Provision of a relevant, robust, laboratory diagnostic service around the clock is central to the management of sick newborns.

- This must respond appropriately to a very broad spectrum of clinical needs from simple monitoring to diagnosis of complex inherited disorders.

- The demands are met by a combination of point of care testing analyses undertaken at the local on-site hospital laboratories and testing in off-site specialist laboratories. Analyses from different sites must be harmonised to produce comparable results.

- Readily accessible, knowledgeable, staff must be available to advise about tests and interpretation.

- Laboratories must be closely involved in, and/or, responsible for collection, transport and pre-analytical processing of blood samples.

- Laboratories must be closely involved in, and/or, responsible for procurement and maintenance of point of care equipment, training ward staff in its use, monitoring quality control and responding quickly to poor performance.

- Laboratories must supply appropriate reference intervals for neonates.

- Laboratories must supply, or assist in producing, protocols for laboratory investigations of clinical disorders.

- Signed parental consent must be obtained before taking biopsy samples, undertaking genetic and HIV testing, and consent from the Coroner for analysis of samples from dead babies.

Introduction

Neonatal Units (NNUs) require timely round the clock access to laboratory services that can analyse small samples and provide access to specialist advice. Most NNUs obtain their laboratory results from a combination of point of care testing (POCT), testing undertaken at the local on-site general hospital laboratory and testing in off-site specialist laboratories. The choice of the site where testing is undertaken is determined by factors such as:

- The required turnaround time for a test result. Figure 2.1 indicates the maximum turnaround times which would be acceptable generally for neonatal tests.

- Availability of a laboratory with appropriate equipment and skills.

- Availability of suitable POCT (see later).

- IT links between the NNU and laboratories.

Analysis	Recommended maximum turnaround times for requests that are:	
	Routine	Urgent
Clinical Biochemistry		
Acylcarnitine	5 working days	1 working day
Albumin	4 hours	Rarely required
Amino acids	5 working days	1 working day
Ammonia	All requests are urgent	Analysed immediately
Bilirubin	1-2 hours	<1 hour
Blood gases	All requests are urgent	Analysed immediately
Calcium	4 hours	30 minutes
Creatinine, urea	4 hours	<1 hour
Glucose	1-2 hours	30 minutes
Lactate	All requests are urgent	1-2 hours
Liver enzymes	Same day	Rarely required
Magnesium	4 hours	<1 hour
Organic acids (urine)	5 working days	1 working day
Phosphate	Same working day	Rarely required
Sodium, potassium	1-2 hours	30 minutes
17OH-progesterone	1 working day	Same day
CRP	Same working day	4 hours
Haematology		
Full blood count	1-2 hours	30 minutes
PT & APTT	1-2 hours	30 minutes
Cross-match	4 hours	1 hour
Microbiology		
Antibiotic assays	Same day	<1 hour
CSF microscopy	All requests are urgent	<1 hour
Endotracheal tube aspirate microscopy	<4 hours	<1 hour
Urine microscopy	<4 hours	<1 hour
HIV antibodies	1-2 working days	<4 hours
Hepatitis screen	1-2 working days	Same working day
Blood cultures	Preliminary negative cultures reported after 18 h incubation	Gram stain ideally undertaken & reported within 1 hour of culture signalling positive
MRSA screen	All requests are urgent	1 working day
Bacterial & fungal culture	Set up in <4 hours	Set up at same time as microscopy
Direct immunofluorescence: respiratory secretions	Same day	<2 hours
Viral PCR (enterovirus, herpes simplex, CMV)	1-2 working days	1 working day

Figure 2.1. Suggested specification for turnaround times for routine and urgent requests.

Test requesting, sample collection, transport and processing

The events which precede the analysis of samples ('pre-analytical' events) are critical for producing valid and useful laboratory results for neonates, with the minimum of stress for the babies. Failure to diagnose promptly a range of neonatal conditions can result in death or serious life-long morbidity. Unnecessary sampling needs to be avoided because it is distressing for babies and their families; in particular, repeated venepuncture can quickly lead to anaemia.

Test requestiing

Laboratories should assist with the production of protocols and pathways for the investigation and monitoring of common and/or important neonatal diseases.

Electronic test ordering is preferred, to streamline and improve the quality of test requesting. Among the benefits are:

- Reduction in transcription error rates.
- Easy, legible and accurate labelling of request forms and sample containers.
- Assistance for the test requester, which can include:
    - Giving information about sample types and volumes needed.
    - Showing which tests have already been requested and when.
    - Providing information about the indications for tests on screen to help with their selection and interpretation of results.
    - Linking test groups to protocols or pathways.

Collection of samples

Laboratories may be required to provide support for specimen collection by supplying sample collection devices and sample containers, training clinical staff to take blood samples and providing a phlebotomy service. Chapter 1 addresses the means, and difficulties, of obtaining acceptable blood samples from neonates.

Storage and transport of samples

Laboratories will be required to provide, or advise on, the safe storage of samples before transport to the laboratory (for example specimen refrigerators, incubators). They will also need to ensure that specimens are transported quickly, reliably and safely to the on-site laboratory and to specialist referral laboratories. In addition, their remit may include management or support for vacuum-tube transport or portering systems. It is the responsibility of the laboratory to record, process and store received samples correctly prior to analysis.

Analysis of samples

There needs to be a robust system for appropriate prioritisation of NNU work, especially in large laboratories. Procedures must be in place to allow same day diagnosis of serious conditions that may present in the neonatal period, including inherited metabolic disorders, clotting problems and haemolytic disease of the newborn (see Chapters 10 and 11).

Analysers

Essential requirements for analysers and manual procedures in clinical biochemistry and haematology, and ward based point of care devices are:

- The ability to handle and analyse small sample volumes, with minimal losses from evaporation.

- Use of assays/methodologies that are sufficiently accurate and precise to measure neonatal values across analytical ranges that are lower (for example creatinine) or higher (for example bilirubin) than in other age groups.

- Operational spectral indices may require revision to allow for the accurate provision of clinical biochemistry results from haemolysed, lipaemic and/or icteric samples.

- Use of procedures that have been validated for specimens with a low or high haematocrit.

Microbiological analyses for neonates

Because of the heavy use of broad spectrum antibiotics on NNUs and the poor immunological defences of neonates due to immaturity, there are important differences in the spectrum and pathogenicity of infective organisms prevalent on NNUs from other hospital units. It is essential that microbiological investigations:

- are tailored to maximise detection of common and/or important neonatal pathogens,

- recognise that microorganisms usually dismissed as contaminants in other age groups may be important neonatal pathogens (e.g. coagulase-negative staphylococci isolated from blood cultures),

- provide antibiotics susceptibility testing that reflects NNU antimicrobial prescribing policy.

Issuing results of analyses – the post-analytical phase

It is crucial that the results of analyses are issued to responsible NNU staff accurately, safely (with minimal or no opportunity for transcription errors), within an appropriate time for the clinical urgency, and with reference intervals and interpretative advice when needed.

Clinically acceptable turnaround times for results must be achieved (see Figure 2.1). This is greatly facilitated by electronic transmission of results to the NNU, because it gives clinicians immediate access to authorised results.

Where applicable, results should be reported with appropriate reference intervals (see Appendix D). Many reference intervals in the neonate differ considerably from other paediatric age groups.

There should be agreed protocols for liaison, with full 24 hour cover, over potentially serious abnormal results. Examples of results that justify immediate communication, verbally as well as by electronic alert (if this facility is available), are shown in Figures 2.2 to 2.4.

Appropriately experienced senior staff must take responsibility for providing clinical advice and liaison. For grossly abnormal results this must be with a consultant Neonatologist.

Test	Value	Possible symptoms/complications
Ammonia	>100 µmol/L	Seizures, coma
Bilirubin	>300 µmol/L	Kernicterus
Calcium	<1.5 & >3.5 mmol/L	Heart problems
Glucose	<2.0 & >20.0 mmol/L	Heart problems
Magnesium	<0.5 & >3.0 mmol/L	Heart problems
Phosphate	<0.3 & >4.0 mmol/L	Myocardial dysfunction, respiratory failure, muscle weakness, seizures, death
Potassium	<2.5 & >7.5 mmol/L	Cardiac dysrhythmias, death
Sodium	<130 mmol/L	Seizures
	>150 mmol/L	Seizures

Figure 2.2. Clinical biochemistry laboratory test results that should be notified immediately to the responsible clinician.

Test	Value	Possible symptoms/complications
Fibrinogen	Elevated concentrations	Suggestive of infection
Haemoglobin	<80 g/ L	Anaemia, cardiac failure
Neutrophils	$<1.0 \times 10^9$/L	Risk of infection
Platelets	$<50 \times 10^9$/L	Risk of bleeding
PT/APTT	Prolonged	Risk of bleeding

Figure 2.3. Haematology laboratory test results that should be notified immediately to the responsible clinician.

Test	Results	Rationale
Antibiotic assays	All results >20% outside target range	Low levels sub-therapeutic High levels toxic
Antibiotic susceptibility tests	Unexpected antibiotic resistances, e.g. MRSA; multidrug-resistant, extensively drug-resistant and pandrug-resistant bacteria Gram-negative bacteria	To optimise therapy and implement infection control precautions, where indicated
Blood cultures	All positive results All negative results at 36-48 h	To optimise therapy To facilitate discontinuing antibiotic therapy and earlier discharge from hospital in some cases
CSF microscopy and culture	All microscopy results All positive culture results	To optimise therapy
Respiratory tract samples microscopy and culture	All positive Gram stain results, especially those showing Gram-negative bacteria or yeasts	To optimise therapy
Detection of microorganisms that may cause outbreaks of infection (see also Chapter 12)	All positive results	To implement infection control precautions
Detection of N. gonorrhoeae or C. trachomatis	All positive results	To optimise therapy of infant and parents
Microbial serology or PCR	All results consistent with recent infection	To expedite patient management
Urine microscopy and culture	All microscopy results All positive culture results	To optimise therapy

Figure 2.4. Microbiology laboratory test results that should be notified immediately to the responsible clinician.

Point of care testing

Rapid developments in medical electronics and analytical technology now make it feasible to conduct many diagnostic and monitoring tests at the point of care. The main reason for moving analytical procedures to the bedside is to expedite rapid adjustments to patients' management. Miniaturisation of Point of Care Testing (POCT) processes often allows tests to be undertaken on reduced sample volumes, which is better for babies and easier for the phlebotomist. There are no international standards for the use of POCT. Different countries have different approaches to assessment:

- In the US, diagnostic tests are categorised by the FDA into three groups according to complexity: waived, moderate or high complexity. Waived tests account for the vast majority of POCT in the US; these are non-critical tests that employ methodologies that are so simple and accurate that the likelihood of an erroneous result is minimal, so that they are approved for use with no routine regulatory oversight.

- In the UK guidance produced by organisations such as the Medicines and Healthcare Products Regulatory Agency (MHRA), the Royal College of Pathologists and the Institute of Biomedical Science focus more on how to ensure the accuracy and clinical safety of POCT, rather than on defining tests that can and cannot be undertaken at the POC according to their complexities.

POCT or laboratory analyses?

Many factors must be considered when deciding which bedside tests are appropriate for a NNU. These include:

- the urgency with which results are required,

- the demand for the test,

- the proximity and working hours of the laboratory, which are important determinants of result turnaround times,

- the reliability and accuracy of results obtained with the equipment available,

- whether the equipment is robust and easy to use,

- the cost of equipment and consumables necessary to perform the test,

- whether there are resources to ensure that clinically-based staff have sufficient time and training to operate POCT equipment safely, reliably and competently,

- the availability of space on the NNU to accommodate POCT equipment.

Quality considerations in POCT

POCT must be performed to the same standard as laboratory-based tests. The laboratory must be closely involved in its operation, even if not in overall control. In some Trusts this falls within the remit of a medical devices committee or similar. Whatever the local arrangement, the laboratory must be closely involved in:

- evaluation and procurement of suitable equipment,

- ensuring that equipment is appropriately and safely sited,

- production of policies and protocols relating to the use of the equipment,

- training, certification of competence, and revalidation of operators,

- equipment maintenance and troubleshooting,

- quality assurance monitoring.

They will need to provide backup testing in the event of equipment failure, and to confirm unexpectedly high or low results and, where appropriate, to ensure that results from POCT are comparable with those from laboratory based testing. Interfacing of POCT analysers to the laboratory information system assists with quality assurance and maintains a permanent record of tests undertaken.

POCT in clinical biochemistry

The most common POCT on NNUs are clinical biochemistry tests. POCT blood glucose and arterial blood gas measurements are now routine. Equipment is also readily available for other tests, including sodium, potassium, lactate, ionised calcium concentrations, creatinine and bilirubin. There is also increasing interest in measurement of acute phase reactants (for example C-reactive protein or procalcitonin), driven by the need to improve antibiotic stewardship.

POCT in haematology

Use of POCT in haematology has grown in popularity in recent years with improvements in technology. Measurement of haemoglobin concentration has been possible for some time. New devices are also available for red cell indices, white blood cell count and platelets. However, POCT for testing of neonatal coagulation remains of limited value.

POCT in microbiology

At present there is little use of POCT for microbiology in NNUs. Current candidate tests (often based on detection of microbial antigens) have poor sensitivity and specificity, and in any case are not directed towards common neonatal pathogens. However, there have been rapid developments of real-time nucleic acid amplification techniques for detecting important neonatal pathogens such as group B streptococci and herpes simplex virus. These techniques have the potential to expand rapidly into POCT in the near future.

Out of hours service

NNUs have a significant round-the-clock requirement for laboratory support. Most laboratories now operate an extended working day or 24 hour shift system, but some will continue to deal with out of hours work on an on-call basis. If a local on-site (satellite) laboratory provides daytime services, but another laboratory provides the out of hours service, it is essential that the laboratories use the same methodology which gives comparable results and the same reference ranges. The harmonisation of methodology and reference data should be regularly reviewed. This is especially important when following trends in measurements such as sodium, bilirubin, alkaline phosphatase and other plasma enzymes or haematological parameters.

Whilst not all specimens collected out of hours require immediate analysis, a significant number of samples will at least require laboratory processing. These include the majority of specimens for biochemical analysis. Separation from red cells is required prior to analysis of potassium or prior to freezing for future analysis as for insulin and c-peptide. Blood cultures also require immediate handling; these should be incubated immediately to obtain the greatest and most rapid yield of positive results.Those specimens that do not require to be sent directly to the laboratory should be stored in a ward refrigerator designated for specimen storage. Clinical users must be clear about the local laboratory arrangements for sample handling and 24 hour laboratory support, to ensure that valuable samples are not lost or compromised, and that urgent work is processed appropriately.

Quality assurance and accreditation

Quality is paramount in all aspects of laboratory work. Laboratories should have a comprehensive internal quality control programme and should be able to provide evidence of satisfactory performance in all relevant external quality assurance schemes, such as those organised by the National External Quality Assessment Service (NEQAS) in the UK. There should be a programme of departmental audit, and also a willingness to participate with users in multidisciplinary audits. Accreditation by a relevant professional body is a good indication that quality standards are adequate, and all laboratories should be accredited, or at least actively working towards obtaining accreditation. In the UK, the United Kingdom Accreditation Service (UKAS) has recently superseded Clinical Pathology Accreditation (CPA (UK) Ltd.) as the main accreditation body.

External reporting

Microbiology departments play an important role in contributing to national statistics on infection. In the UK, a range of important infections, including bacteraemia, meningitis and viral infections, are reported to national public health agencies. Liaison with local health protection units is important to ensure that statutorily notifiable diseases and important hospital-acquired infections are reported locally. In addition laboratories should be able to assist NNUs that participate in national or international infection surveillance programmes. Laboratories can also provide data to national disease registries, such as those administered by the British Paediatric Surveillance Unit.

Teaching and research

Laboratory personnel have an important role in training users on all aspects of use of the laboratories. Especially in larger centres, laboratories should be able to support clinical research projects, as well as initiating laboratory-based research.

Ethical issues for laboatory testing

Consent is assumed for routine investigations on blood, urine and CSF that are essential for care. However, many parents are grateful to know what is going on and why. It is important to ensure that they understand the reasons for, and the possible implications of, tests carried out to diagnose chronic diseases, or conditions where the diagnosis may be sensitive (for example a sexually-transmitted infection). Written, informed, consent is required before taking biopsies and surgical samples, genetic analyses and HIV testing (see Chapter 1). It is normally the responsibility of the doctor treating the patient to obtain consent for testing for diagnostic purposes. Laboratories must check that consent has been given for the tests that are requested.

Laboratories should not initiate tests that have not been requested, unless they are closely related to the original request, and in the direct interest of the patient. Sometimes it may be in the best interests of the child to undertake an investigation that has been refused by the parents. This may be because of concerns about the implications of a diagnosis such as HIV infection, or because of an attempt to conceal a diagnosis of fabricated or induced illness. Where parents initially refuse consent for a test to be undertaken it is best, where time allows, to have further discussion with the parents and give them further opportunity to agree to the test. Where agreement with parents cannot be reached, the laws relating to sample collection and testing vary from country to country, even within the UK. However, as a general principle anyone seeking to collect or test a sample in such circumstances should feel able to justify their decision in the courts, or to their professional body. Prior discussion with experienced colleagues, hospital managers and/or legal advisors is advisable, and where a suitable sample that has been collected previously is available, it is preferable to test this, rather than collecting a further sample under duress.

Important samples from patients may be stored for possible further use. This should be explained to parents at the time of sampling. Subsequent testing on stored samples for clinical reasons, for example in inherited conditions where technological advances allow new genetic information to be ascertained, should not be undertaken unless consent has been obtained. For any research using clinical material, approval must be obtained from a Research Ethics Committee, and specific consent obtained from the parents of each infant.

Examination of specimens collected from the patient immediately after death may help to determine the cause of sudden unexplained death. Only a coroner (or equivalent) has the authority to consent to such investigations, which are best undertaken under the aegis of an agreed routine protocol (see Appendix C).

Future trends

Whatever changes occur in the organisation of laboratory services, there will continue to be a need for on-site provision of core laboratory support for NNUs. However there is likely to be greater centralisation of more specialised tests, both to achieve economy of scale and to ensure that there is adequate expertise in performing and interpreting the results of such tests.

Developments continue to be made in improving the quality of, and increasing the number of rare disorders tested for as part of the newborn blood spot screening programme for the UK. Diagnostic molecular biology is developing very rapidly. Tests are being developed that can rapidly detect several different biomarkers, whilst closed, self-contained, fully integrated and automated platforms allow testing to be carried out on-demand and nearer to the patient. Only the cost of these tests is likely to slow their adoption into mainstream practice.

The growing threat posed by antibiotic resistance is likely to be one of the main drivers of changes to microbiology laboratory work: likely changes will be better means of detecting antibiotic resistance, increased use of surveillance cultures and of epidemiological typing, and the development of tests that can rapidly diagnose or exclude infection to allow better targeting of antibiotic therapy.

Further reading

BS EN ISO 15189 Medical laboratories. Requirements for quality and competence. British Standards Institution, London, UK, 2012

General Medical Council. Consent: patients and doctors making decisions together. GMC, London, UK, 2008.

http://newbornbloodspot.screening.nhs.uk/

Chapter 3
Pregnancy and delivery

Summary

- Pregnancy is a normal physiological process and for the majority does not require extensive 'medicalisation'.

- Routine screening procedures during pregnancy help identify those that require further assessment or intervention.

- Specific maternal conditions can affect fetal wellbeing and pregnancies complicated by these require more investigation and assessment than normal low-risk pregnancies.

- Laboratory tests have little place in the management of labour and delivery.

The uncomplicated pregnancy

Antenatal care in the UK recognises that pregnancy is a normal physiological process and that, as such, any interventions offered should have known benefits and be acceptable to pregnant women. The majority of pregnant women are cared for in the community by family doctors and midwives, in liaison with an appropriate obstetric unit.

Delivery is still mainly hospital based with only 2% of deliveries in the UK occurring in the mother's home. Currently, 21% of labours in the UK are 'induced' and up to 25% of babies in the UK are now delivered by Caesarean section, of which 60% are performed as an emergency. A further 12% of babies are delivered instrumentally with the aid of ventouse suction cup or forceps.

At the booking appointment (usually by 10 weeks of pregnancy), the need for additional care (such as risk factors for diabetes or pre-eclampsia, maternal health or social problems, past medical or obstetric complications or family history of a potentially recurrent condition) is identified. Maternal medical problems managed through hospital clinics include diabetes, epilepsy, cardiac, endocrine, metabolic or renal disease in which obstetricians may work in conjunction with an appropriate specialist physician. Examples of joint clinics where close cooperation with the biochemistry laboratory is required are obstetric/endocrine clinics and obstetric/metabolic clinics.

A number of screening investigations are offered to the mother and include blood tests and an early ultrasound scan to confirm gestational age and the number of fetuses present. Further monitoring of fetal health during 'low-risk' pregnancy includes listening to the fetal heart, assessing uterine size using fundal height measurement and maternal attention to fetal movements from the second half of pregnancy onwards. An example of an antenatal schedule for a low-risk pregnancy in the UK is presented in Figure 3.1.

Gestation	Events	Aims
6-12 weeks	Booking	Identify need for additional care
		Dating, viability, multiplicity
	Ultrasound scan	Fix expected date of delivery
	Screening tests	Routine blood tests
16 weeks		Results of screening tests
		Check BP and urinalysis
18- 20 weeks	Mid trimester ultrasound scan	Structural anomaly screen
25 weeks	Community	BP, urinalysis, fundal height
28 weeks	Community	BP, urinalysis, fundal height, Check for anaemia and screen for antibodies
34 weeks	Community/hospital	BP, urinalysis, fundal height, Birth plan including information on Caesarian section
36 weeks	Community	As above Assess presentation
38 and 40 weeks		BP, urinalysis, fundal height,
41 weeks	Hospital visit	Assessment for post dates review and indication for induction

Figure 3.1. Antenatal schedule for a low-risk, primiparous pregnancy.

Screening tests in pregnancy

All women are offered a routine surveillance screening programme as outlined in the antenatal schedule. Minimum routine surveillance screening comprises:

- General medical examination, weight, blood pressure, urinalysis.

- Abdominal examination.

- Full blood count (to identify anaemia, blood group, red cell alloantibody status and screen for haemoglobinopathy (sickle and thalassaemia).

- Infection screen for syphilis, hepatitis B, rubella susceptibility, and HIV. Women younger than 25 should be encouraged to be tested for chlamydia under the National Chlamydia Screening Programme.

- Anomaly detection screening (after counselling). Anomaly detection comprises a combination of blood tests (for the aneuploides: Down [trisomy 21], Patau [trisomy 13] and Edward [trisomy 18] syndromes) and ultrasound screening. This should be undertaken only after full explanation to the mother of the purpose of the screening tests involved. Unwillingness to consider termination of pregnancy in any circumstance is not necessarily a reason for an informed woman not to have anomal screening; some families have derived great benefit from being able to plan for the birth of a baby with problems. Screening for aneuploides usually employs a combined screen between 11 and 14 weeks involving:
  - ultrasound assessment of nuchal translucency (measurement of the pocket of fluid at the back of the fetus' neck) and
  - measurement of two hormones – PAPP-A (pregnancy associated plasma protein) and free beta HCG (human chorionic gonadotrophin). If combined screening is not available or testing takes place after 14+1 weeks then quadruple (alpha fetoprotein [AFP], HCG, unconjugated oestriol [UE3] and inhibin A) hormone test is offered up until 20+0 weeks gestational age. Maternal age is incorporated into the results of the above tests to give the risk of an individual having an affected fetus. If screening shows an increased risk (> 1 in 150) of aneuploidy then one of two diagnostic tests can be offered – chorionic villus sampling (CVS) or amniocentesis (see below). Only 80-85% of fetuses with Testing for the presence of fetal DNA in maternal serum (also referred to as NIPT – non-invasive prenatal testing) is now available privately. This has been reported to detect trisomy 21 in around 99% of cases, but has yet to complete large scale clinical trials. Ultrasound examination to screen for abnormality is usually carried out around the 20th week of gestation. Some structural abnormalities, such as defects of the anterior abdominal wall or major spinal abnormalities, are readily detected; others, such as some potentially major heart defects, are much harder to see and detection rates are lower. Assessment of aortic and pulmonary outflow tracts in addition to a 'four chamber' view of the heart improves detection. A scan in which no abnormality is detected does not guarantee that the baby is normal and careful postnatal assessment is vital. Only 80-85% of fetuses with Down syndrome are detected prenatally by screening methods currently offered in the UK. This is dependent on the testing undertaken and the test strategy employed.

Immunisation in pregnancy

Pregnant women who contract influenza are at increased risk from complications. Influenza during pregnancy may also be associated with premature birth and smaller birth size and weight.

It is recommended that all pregnant women, regardless of their stage of pregnancy, should receive the influenza vaccine during the usual vaccination period which, in the UK, is between October and January.

Vaccination during pregnancy provides passive immunity against influenza to infants in the first few months of life. This strategy of immunising mothers to protect newborns, before they can commence routine immunisation, is known as cocooning. It may also be undertaken with the combined pertussis, tetanus, diphtheria and polio vaccine.

The high-risk pregnancy

Invasive prenatal diagnosis

CHORIONIC VILLUS SAMPLING OR PLACENTAL BIOPSY.

This early test, usually carried out trans-cervically at 11 weeks of pregnancy, or shortly after, provides trophoblastic cells, which are a source of fetal DNA for chromosomal, DNA or metabolic investigations in women with a fetus at high risk of chromosomal abnormality or with a family history of selected genetic diseases (see Chapter 10). Results from direct genetic analysis are usually available within a week, so that if termination of pregnancy is required, it can be carried out within the first trimester. If cell culture is required prior to analysis, results will not be available for at least 3 to 4 weeks. Risks of pregnancy loss after the procedure are about 2%, twice that for amniocentesis.

AMNIOCENTESIS

Amniocentesis is a simpler procedure, involving removal of liquor from the amniotic sac under ultrasound guidance. The earliest time at which the test can be done is the 14th week of pregnancy; the risk of pregnancy loss is between 0.5 to 1%.

Fetal cells (amniocytes) can be used for chromosomal DNA analysis, fetal sexing, and enzyme assay in cultured cells. The fluid can also be analysed for bilirubin concentrations in blood group alloimmunisation. Cultures take at least 2-3 weeks but sometimes may fail completely.

FETAL BLOOD SAMPLING

Cordocentesis, or fetal blood sampling, provides rapidly available direct fetal information including:
- rapid karyotyping,
- fetal haemoglobin in isoimmunisation or hydrops fetalis (see below),
- infection investigations in a very growth-restricted fetus or one with intracranial abnormality (e.g. CMV, toxoplasma, parvovirus, rubella),
- fetal blood group,
- DNA analysis,
- fetal blood gases or blood biochemistry,
- diagnosis of haemoglobinopathy,
- diagnosis of some inborn errors of metabolism.

This procedure is done in larger centres with appropriate technical expertise and laboratory and cytogenetic support. There is a risk of sudden fetal compromise or death during the procedure if there is bleeding from the cord.

Fetal monitoring

In high-risk pregnancies, whether because of maternal disease, past obstetric history, or a detected problem such as poor growth or developing maternal hypertension, more detailed surveillance of the fetus is undertaken.

- Fetal growth can be followed ultrasonically (fetal biometry). Measurements include femur length, (useful in dating a pregnancy from 12 weeks on), biparietal diameter (the distance across the widest diameter of the fetal skull – used in the second trimester), fetal head circumference and abdominal circumference – used in the late second and early third trimester.

- Amniotic fluid measurements. The liquor volume around the fetus is also important, as it reflects fetal renal function and placental function. This is assessed by measuring the depth in centimetres of pools of liquor and will be reduced (oligohydramnios) when there is reduced fetal urine production.

- Doppler assessment of the diastolic flow velocity in the umbilical artery is increasingly used as a risk predictor in the small fetus for whom early delivery may be the best option. Absent or reversed end-diastolic flow is associated with 40% perinatal mortality and high perinatal morbidity without intervention.

- Fetal fibronectin.

Maternal disorders affecting the baby

With an increasing number of women with underlying endocrine and particularly, disorders of intermediary metabolism, requiring specialised antenatal care, there has been an increase in specialised obstetric clinics with joint care – obstetric/endocrine clinics and obstetric/metabolic clinics.

Maternal diabetes

The achievement of good diabetic control usually becomes more difficult in the diabetic pregnancy owing to effects on carbohydrate metabolism. Additionally glucose tolerance can become abnormal for the first time during pregnancy and return to normal postnatally i.e. gestational diabetes. In these situations the fetus receives an increased glucose load and becomes hyperinsulinaemic. This predisposes to macrosomia, the severity of which is related to the adequacy of third trimester maternal glycaemic control. Optimisation of maternal blood glucose control can reduce the incidence of fetal malformations, particularly congenital heart disease, and the risk of sudden fetal death in late pregnancy. This involves intensive biochemical monitoring with POCT glucose and glycated haemoglobin measurements. Macrosomia can lead to intrapartum hypoxia or birth trauma, particularly shoulder dystocia with its associated risks of fractured clavicle and brachial plexus nerve injury (Erb's palsy, phrenic nerve palsy). The infant of a diabetic mother, in whom the control of glucose is poor, is at risk of early hypoglycaemia, particularly if macrosomic (see Chapter 7).

Maternal thyroid disorders

Both pre-existing hypothyroidism and hyperthyroidism may lead to a number of complications. Untreated hypothyroidism can cause miscarriage, pregnancy-induced hypertension, preterm delivery, low birth weight, stillbirth, anaemia and post-partum haemorrhage. The majority of hypothyroid patients require significant increases in thyroxine dose during the first few weeks of pregnancy to maintain thyroid status. This should be monitored with four weekly thyroid function tests. With adequate thyroxine replacement complication rates can be reduced to that of the normal population. It is important that trimester specific reference intervals are used for interpretation and that these are specific for the methodology used. Untreated subclinical hypothyroidism is associated with an increased risk of miscarriage and increased rates of assisted delivery and caesarean section.

Hyperthyroidism, although rarer than hypothyroidism amongst women of child-bearing age, may, depending on the aetiology, have more severe consequences for the fetus and neonate. Neonatal thyrotoxicosis due to the transplacental passage of thyroid stimulating antibodies is a medical emergency and can be avoided by knowledge of the mother's thyroid history and determination of the presence of thyroid stimulating antibodies antenatally.

Inherited metabolic disease

Improvements in diagnosis and treatment have allowed girls with disorders of intermediary metabolism to reach child-bearing age. In general, strict dietary adherence prior to conception (to ensure optimal metabolic control) results in improved outcome. This is best exemplified in respect of management of pregnancy in women with phenylketonuria. Pregnant women with phenylketonuria, who are not on a strictly controlled diet, are at risk of severe fetal damage. Without treatment, learning difficulties resulting in severe handicap will occur in a large percentage (95%) and there is also a high risk of microcephaly, intra-uterine growth restriction and congenital heart disease. The risk of these congenital abnormalities can be greatly reduced by strictly controlling plasma phenylalanine pre-conception and throughout pregnancy.

The same approach is adopted for other rarer inherited metabolic disorders. Throughout pregnancy close monitoring of protein and dietary supplementation should be undertaken to ensure adequacy in relation to increasing demands. A number of factors may predispose IMD patients to metabolic decompensation:

- Reduced nutritional intake   - Hyperemesis, labour, delivery
- Increased catabolism   - Post-partum
- Increased energy demands   - Breastfeeding

Thrombocytopenia

In the vast majority of cases where the mother has thrombocytopenia (platelets $<100 \times 10^9$/L), the baby is unaffected or has only mild thrombocytopenia at birth. There is no correlation between maternal and neonatal platelet counts. Treatment of the baby is with group-compatible platelet infusion or intravenous immunoglobulin if there is active bleeding or if the platelet count is less than 20×10^9/L.

The exception is alloimmune thrombocytopenia which is a rare and potentially serious condition. The mother's platelet count is normal but she has IgG anti-platelet antibodies that may cross the placenta and produce fetal intracerebral bleeding or death. First pregnancies can be affected. Where the diagnosis is known in pregnancy, fetal platelet transfusions and early delivery are indicated.

Blood group alloimmunisation

This is a serious problem of blood group incompatability responsible for a number of complications including hydrops fetalis and severe neonatal jaundice. Further discussion is in Chapter 11.

Fetal complications

Hydrops fetalis

This condition is characterised by soft tissue oedema *plus* fluid within at least one body cavity, such as pleural or pericardial effusions or abdominal ascites. Diagnosis is by ultrasound examination.

Hydrops fetalis can be divided into two types according to aetiology. The immune type is usually due to haematological causes, mainly Rhesus isoimmunisation. The non-immune type has many causes and an overall worse prognosis.

When the affected baby is delivered they often need vigorous and effective resuscitation which may include immediate drainage of ascites and/or pleural effusions. Appropriate investigations for both immune and non-immune hydrops, which should be performed in a specialised centre, should be undertaken before any transfusion. Inborn errors of metabolism are a relatively rare cause and it is important to exclude some of the more common causes of non-immune hydrops before embarking on a detailed investigative work-up.

Guidance on the biochemical investigation of hydrops fetalis are provided in a MetBionet guideline. http://www.metbio.net/

Labour and delivery

Monitoring in labour

Where delivery of the baby is planned at home or in a low technology setting, monitoring of fetal wellbeing during labour is by direct auscultation of the fetal heart rate. In hospitals generally, intrapartum cardiotocography is the mainstay of fetal monitoring in labour.

For high risk cases, including presence of meconium, breech presentation, preterm, post-term, maternal diabetes, intrauterine growth retardation, antepartum haemorrhage, previous Caesarian section, poor obstetric history, and multiple pregnancy, continuous cardiotocographic monitoring is usually employed.

If fetal distress is suspected, the fetal condition is first optimised prior to the collection of a fetal blood sample. A low pH in the fetal scalp sample is an indication of lactate accumulation and developing acidosis which may reflect fetal compromise and may help to guide further clinical decision-making such as need and urgency for Caesarean section.

Cord gases at delivery

Cord gases will give an assessment of the acid-base status of the baby *at the moment of birth*. This may be very useful in attributing possible causes to a baby who has respiratory depression at birth or behaves abnormally afterwards. In all complex deliveries – instrumental or operative deliveries, breech or twin deliveries, after fetal distress in labour, when there is concern about fetal growth, or if the one minute Apgar score for the baby is three or less – cord gases should be measured and the results recorded.

Paired samples from one of the umbilical arteries and from the umbilical vein should be taken as soon as practical after delivery from a section of cord which has been clamped at both ends (double clamping). These processes mean that a blood gas analyser should be constantly available on, or directly adjacent to, the delivery suite.

Acidosis at birth is only a reflection of the situation at that time, and the duration or severity of any problem cannot be deduced from this measure alone. Umbilical arterial pH of less than 7.00 is an indication for active resuscitation of the baby at birth. Low cord pH is neither a sensitive nor a specific indicator of poor neonatal outcome unless combined with other factors such as prolonged depression of neonatal Apgar score (<6 at five minutes).

Most babies with severe acidosis at birth do not go on to develop cerebral palsy. The vast majority of children with cerebral palsy have normal cord gases and are in good condition at birth.

Preterm delivery

Preterm labour is often secondary to underlying pathology which will affect the outcome. Such processes include systemic or local genital infection, placental abruption, fetal or uterine abnormalities, multiple pregnancy, polyhydramnios, ruptured membranes and pre-eclampsia. Prior to 32 weeks, tocolytics are sometimes used to prolong pregnancy, in order to allow the administration of steroids. If delivery is anticipated between 24 and 36 weeks gestation, antenatal steroids given within the seven days preceding delivery improve neonatal survival.

Measurement of fetal fibronectin, to assess the risk of preterm delivery, is now increasingly undertaken in women with signs and symptoms of preterm labour where there are intact membranes and minimal cervical dilatation.

Many preterm births are elective, induced either to protect the wellbeing of the mother – e.g. uncontrolled pre-eclampsia, or the baby – e.g. poor fetal growth, oligohydramnios, and absent end-diastolic flow on umbilical artery Doppler monitoring.

The care of the preterm baby is complex, involving close monitoring and attention to temperature, fluid balance, energy supply, and circulatory stability, as well as management of the specific problems of prematurity. The major medical problems of preterm babies have already been summarised in Chapter 1. Further chapters in this book discuss the specific biochemical aspects of the diagnosis and management of these problems.

Mortality and morbidity increase as gestation and size at birth decrease. Knowledge of local survival figures at given gestations and birthweights is useful in counselling parents both before and after delivery. In the UK, prematurity is the leading cause for 55% of deaths in the first week of life, other causes being congenital abnormality (26%), intrapartum events (9%), and other specific events (11%).

Infections in the delivery suite

The delivery presents significant risks of infection for the mother and her baby. Both general infection control precautions and specific interventions can greatly reduce these risks.

INFECTION IN THE MOTHER

Puerperal sepsis is a life threatening condition where Streptococcus pyogenes (group A streptococcus – GAS) invades local tissues around the time of delivery, leading to endometritis and septicaemia. The infection can also be transmitted to the baby, who may also get a life-threatening invasive infection.

GAS carriers may be symptomatic or asymptomatic; carriage sites include the throat, genital tract and skin. In at least half of cases the organism originates from the mother herself. However, the possibility of nosocomial transmission from healthcare workers or other patients, or even from the hospital environment, must always be considered, especially if there is evidence of clustering of cases.

INFECTION IN THE NEONATE

During delivery, the neonate may acquire infection with microorganisms present in the maternal genital tract, including commensals of the maternal genital tract (most commonly group B streptococci – GBS); sexually-acquired pathogens (e.g. Neisseria gonorrhoeae, Chlamydia trachomatis), herpes simplex virus); and blood-borne viruses (e.g. hepatitis B virus, HIV). This is discussed in more detail in Chapter 12.

Specific preventative measures used to protect neonates from these infections are outlined in Figure 3.2.

Infection	Risk factors	Preventative measures
Neonatal early-onset group B streptococcus infection	Maternal GBS colonisation at any time during pregnancy GBS infection in a previous baby	High-dose intravenous penicillin (clindamycin for penicillin-allergic women) given to mother from onset of labour
Neonatal sepsis (any cause)	Pyrexia (>38°C) in labour Chorioamnionitis	Give broad-spectrum intravenous antibiotics to include GBS cover
Ophthalmia neonatorum	Maternal gonorrhoea or chlamydial infection at time of delivery	Test infants for gonorrhoea and chlamydial infection: treat as appropriate
Herpes simplex infection	High risk of neonatal infection where primary genital herpes at the time of, or within six weeks of, delivery	Caesarean section
	Low risk of neonatal infection where recurrent genital herpes present at onset of labour	Caesarean section **not** mandatory; mode of delivery should be individualised, taking account of mother's preference
Hepatitis B	Risk of mother-to-baby transmission related to maternal eAg and anti-eAb status	Vaccination of neonate (+ administration of immunoglobulin if maternal infectivity high)
HIV infection	Risk of mother-to-baby transmission related to maternal viral load; with anti-retroviral treatment during pregnancy viral load usually undetectable	Anti-retroviral treatment given to mother and neonate Delivery by Caesarean section if viral load not adequately suppressed

Figure 3.2. Specific measures used to prevent intrapartum transmission of infections from mother to infant.

Further reading

Best Practice Guidelines for the Biochemical Investigation of Patients with Foetal and Neonatal Hydrops
http://www.metbio.net/docs/MetBio-Guideline-FAFU703461-28-01-2013.pdf

Diabetes in pregnancy: management from preconception to the postnatal period https://www.nice.org.uk/guidance/ng3 NICE guidelines [NG3] Published date: February 2015

HTA - 10/130/01: Rapid fetal fibronectin (fFN) testing to predict pre-term birth in women with symptoms of premature labour: A systematic review and cost-effectiveness analysis.
http://www.nets.nihr.ac.uk/projects/hta/1013001

Lazarus JH. Thyroid function in pregnancy Br Med Bull (2011) **97**: 137-148.

NHS Fetal Anomoly Screening Programme http://fetalanomaly.screening.nhs.uk/

NIPT for Down syndrome evaluation study
http://www.rapid.nhs.uk/about-rapid/evaluation-study-nipt-for-down-syndrome/

Stagnaro-Green A, Abalovich M, Alexander E *et al.* American Thyroid Association Taskforce on Thyroid Disease During Pregnancy and Postpartum. Guidelines of the American Thyroid Association for the diagnosis and management of thyroid disease during pregnancy and post-partum. Thyroid. 2011; **21**: 1081-125.

UK Guidelines for the Use of Thyroid Function Tests http://www.british-thyroid-association.org/info-for patients/Docs/TFT_guideline_final_version_July_2006.pdf

Chapter 4
Sodium, potassium and water; renal dysfunction

Summary

- The newborn baby is vulnerable to large water losses which can lead to hypovolaemia and electrolyte disturbances.

- Hyponatraemia is usually caused by renal loss of sodium. Excessive administration or retention of free water is another common cause, as is inadequate sodium intake. Intestinal losses and rarely endocrine disorders are other causes.

- Sodium depletion can also arise from inadequate intake and intestinal losses.

- Hypernatraemia is usually a reflection of dehydration. Sodium excess is invariably iatrogenic.

- Plasma sodium is normal in some disorders with excessive salt retention.

- Hypokalaemia can be secondary to renal tubular dysfunction, diuretic therapy, hypovolaemia or gastrointestinal disorders.

- Hyperkalaemia in neonates is frequently artefactual or iatrogenic but endocrine and renal causes should not be overlooked. It occurs more often in extremely preterm infants; hypocalcaemia and hypomagnesaemia increase the risk of arrhythmias in hyperkalaemia.

- Diagnosis of renal impairment and its management is complicated by renal immaturity and by the small size of the neonatal kidneys.

Introduction

At birth, babies are removed suddenly from an environment in which the plasma volume, electrolytes and temperature have been tightly controlled. They become dependent on their carers and their own homeostatic mechanisms for maintenance of body temperature, normal hydration and circulatory volume.

Water balance

Distribution

At term, about 75% of body weight is accounted for by water (30% intracellular and 45% extracellular). A greater proportion of body weight is due to water in premature babies although the intra-/extracellular distribution remains approximately constant. A 32 week baby comprises about 85% water at birth.

Body water falls – mainly as a reduction in extracellular fluid – in all babies after birth, accounting for the frequently observed 5-10% weight loss that occurs in the first week of life. The mechanism is a diuresis related to altered renal perfusion and increasing glomerular filtration rate. This fluid loss represents isotonic contraction of body fluids, that is, loss of water and electrolytes together. A high fluid intake during this period can overcome this loss, but is thought to be disadvantageous, and is associated with increased frequency of both necrotising enterocolitis and symptomatic patent ductus arteriosus in preterm infants.

Homeostasis

Body water is regulated through several feedback systems. These result in control of both the amount of water in the body and the osmolality of plasma, that is, the concentration of solute particles in plasma, which is maintained at 275-295 mmol/kg. Gains in body water derived from intake and from oxidation of protein, fat and carbohydrate must balance losses from the kidneys, lungs, skin and gastrointestinal tract. Intake in the suckling infant is regulated by thirst, mainly in response to an increase in plasma osmolality, detected by osmoreceptors in the hypothalamus. Thirst is also stimulated by hypovolaemia, through the activation of volume and baroreceptors in the cardiac atria and blood vessels, and an increase in the secretion of renin which, in turn, increases production of angiotensin II. This acts on the hypothalamus to stimulate thirst.

Fine, continuous, control of body water is regulated through plasma osmolality by altering the amount of water lost through the kidneys. When there is water depletion, the increase in plasma osmolality is sensed by neurons (osmoreceptors) in the supraoptic and paraventricular nuclei of the hypothalamus which synthesise vasopressin (AVP, the antidiuretic hormone). AVP is transported along their axons to the posterior pituitary gland from which it is released into the bloodstream when the osmoreceptors are activated. Secretion of AVP increases linearly with increasing plasma osmolality. AVP binds to receptors in the renal collecting ducts, and by activating water pores (aquaporin 2) increases the duct permeability to water and hence conserves water.

A fall in blood volume of ≥ 10% also increases AVP secretion by increased secretion of angiotensin II and through stimulation of volume receptors and baroreceptors in the cardiac atria and great veins, and carotid sinuses and aortic arch, respectively. As hypovolaemia develops it causes an exponential increase in AVP secretion and shifts the AVP osmotic response curve to the left, that is, it reduces the osmotic threshold for the secretion of vasopressin. Hence in severe hypovolaemia, water is retained avidly in an attempt to restore plasma volume but this is at the expense of a fall in plasma sodium and osmolality.

Obligatory water losses

Obligatory losses of water are higher in neonates than in older infants. They include losses via the lungs, skin, kidneys and intestine.

From the lungs: losses are increased because of rapid breathing (tachypnoea) and when inhaled air is not humidified.

From the skin: The surface area of the skin of neonates is large relative to body size. This ratio may be around five times higher in a small preterm baby than in adults. The skin is thin and poorly keratinised and allows easy transudation of water and increased heat and water losses and evaporation. In addition, preterm babies have poor control of their body temperature coupled with a reduced ability to regulate blood flow to the skin. Vasodilatation occurs at a rectal temperature above 37°C and sweating above about 37.2°C. Evaporative insensible water loss can be significant. Average losses of 2.4 g/kg/h have been described in low birth weight babies under radiant warmers, increasing to 3.5 g/kg/h if phototherapy is added. Body temperature and water loss from the skin and lungs may be controlled by nursing very preterm babies at a constant warm environmental temperature: by placing under radiant warmers immediately after delivery, using humidified air in incubators (to 80-90% relative humidity), use of appropriate clothing (particularly hats) and blankets and ensuring adequate humidification of inspired warmed gases in headboxes, CPAP (continuous positive airways pressure) and ventilator circuits.

From the kidneys: By 36 weeks of gestation the fetus has the full adult complement of glomeruli but they are small and, at birth, their diameter is only around half that of adults. At birth, there is also a high resistance to blood flow through the kidneys. The glomerular filtration rate (GFR) is low (average 1 mL/kg/min). This resistance falls rapidly, renal blood flow doubles within days and GFR has doubled by three weeks of life. The renal tubules are short at birth (proximal tubules only around 10% of adult length), and glomerular filtration may exceed the reabsorptive capacity of the renal tubules, particularly in very preterm babies. Neonates are able to produce very dilute urine, but they have a limited capacity to concentrate urine, up to a maximum osmolality of only 800 mmol/kg. Hence even with extreme dehydration, they may continue to pass inappropriately dilute urine. This is explained largely by their reduced ability to produce a high cortico-medullary osmotic gradient in the renal interstitium which is necessary for urine concentration; the loops of Henle, responsible for producing the gradient, do not extend deeply into the medulla and, in addition, because neonates are intensely anabolic and use amino acids for growth, they produce only small amounts of urea. Urea contributes to the osmotic gradient. In very preterm babies poor renal response to AVP also reduces concentrating ability.

From the bowel: Necrotising enterocolitis, other intestinal disorders or surgery may lead to large losses of water in the stools.

Fluid requirements

The fluid volume normally offered to bottle fed infants is indicated in Figure 4.1. These volumes are also appropriate for a standard parenteral nutrition regimen, provided that there is neither fluid deficit nor overload, nor ongoing increased losses.

Sodium balance

Distribution

Sodium is the main cation in extracellular fluid, 40% of total body sodium residing in plasma and interstitial fluid. Intracellular sodium concentration is generally low (about 10 mmol/L) while extracellular concentration is maintained at around 140 mmol/L. Sodium ions are the major osmotically active species in the extracellular fluid and because of the primacy of the control of osmolality through the mechanisms described above, body sodium content is the major determinant of extracellular fluid volume.

Homeostasis

Sodium homeostasis depends on the maintenance of a balance between input, sodium retained as the ECF volume expands with growth, and output. In a healthy infant, relatively little sodium loss occurs through the skin and gut. The kidneys provide the major route for controlled excretion.

Intake

Figure 4.1 shows the sodium requirements of healthy neonates. Breast milk supplied at 150 mL/kg/24h will provide only 1 mmol/kg/24h each of sodium and chloride. Enteral salt intake can be increased by adding salt to breast milk, e.g. 0.25 mL of 1 mmol/L NaCl added to 25 mL of breast milk for all babies less than the equivalent of 34 weeks gestation (e.g. a 32 week gestation baby up to two weeks old), a proprietary breast milk fortifier, or by use of a preterm formula milk. Adequacy of supplementation in well, preterm, orally fed babies can be monitored by weekly checks of $[Na^+])/[K^+]$ molar ratio on a spot urine sample, however this is now rarely undertaken except in babies with a stoma.

Day	Fluid volume mL/kg	Sodium mmol/kg (30% NaCl = 5 mmol/mL)	Potassium mmol/kg (as 15% KCl = 2 mmol/mL)
1	60	0	0
2	90 (1)	2-3 (2)	2-3 (3)
3	120	3-4	2-3
4	150	3-4	2-3
5	180	3-4	2-3

(1) Restrict to 60 in babies with respiratory distress, asphyxia or infection
(2) In babies below 32 weeks requirements are sometimes higher; check plasma sodium concentration daily
(3) Start potassium only after urine output of at least 1 mL/kg/h is established
An additional 30 mL/kg should be given to babies under a radiant warmer
NB. Beyond the first week requirements should be calculated on actual or birth weight (whichever is greater).

Figure 4.1. Fluid and mineral requirements for a healthy neonate based on birth weight.

Renal excretion

On a normal sodium intake, the kidneys reabsorb over 99% of filtered sodium by the renal tubules. This is a two stage process:
- reabsorption of a constant proportion of the filtered load
  - proximal tubules (about 67%)
  - loops of Henle (about 20%)
- variable reabsorption regulated by aldosterone
  - distal tubules (7%)
  - collecting ducts (5%).

Production of aldosterone is regulated by the renin-angiotensin system:

- Renin is an enzyme released from the juxtaglomerular apparatus, a cluster of specialised cells in the afferent arterioles, in response to hypovolaemia via the baroreceptor reflex and activation of the sympathetic nervous system, to intrarenal blood pressure, and to intrarenal sensing of sodium excretion. Renin secretion is inhibited by hyperkalaemia.

- Renin catalyses the synthesis of angiotensin I from its inactive precursor angiotensinogen, synthesised in the liver.

- Angiotensin I is converted to angiotensin II by angiotensin converting enzyme. Angiotensin II stimulates aldosterone production by the adrenal cortex.

- Aldosterone acts on the distal convoluted tubules and proximal collecting ducts to promote sodium reabsorption and potassium excretion.

Potassium also stimulates aldosterone secretion from the adrenal zona glomerulosa directly. This protects against hyperkalaemia.

Urinary sodium and water excretion are *increased* by atrial natriuretic peptides produced in cardiac muscle: ANP in the atria, B-type natriuretic peptide (BNP) in the ventricles. They are released when the atria and ventricles are stretched by an increase in blood volume. Both peptides suppress renin and aldosterone production. ANP increases the GFR. Renal conservation of sodium is impaired in the immediate post-delivery period, in immature infants, in sick infants and when loop diuretics have been used. Obligatory renal loss can be estimated by calculating fractional sodium excretion, the value varying from less than 1% to over 15% in a sick, very preterm baby:

$$\text{Fractional excretion Na}^+ = \frac{\text{Urine [Na}^+]}{\text{Urine [creatinine]}} \quad \text{x} \quad \frac{\text{Plasma [creatinine] x 100}}{\text{Plasma [Na}^+]}$$

Disturbances of sodium and water balance

Hyponatraemia

Small decreases in plasma sodium below the reference interval of 135-145 mmol/L are common, generally not clinically significant and not pursued. Causes of decreases to less than 130 mmol/L are explained by:

- decreased extracellular sodium content
- an increase in body water
- a combination of the above.

Symptoms of hyponatraemia depend upon its severity, rate of development and whether it is due primarily to sodium depletion with a low blood volume, or to water retention with a normal or expanded ECF volume. In the former, the greatest risk is for circulatory collapse and hypovolaemic shock. In the latter, if hyponatraemia develops rapidly with an abrupt fall (<48h) in plasma sodium to below 125 mmol/L the risk is for cerebral oedema, and in severe hypona-traemia raised intracranial pressure, seizures, brain stem compression and death. However, if water retention is a chronic process the brain is able to adapt to the low osmolality and even plasma sodium concentrations < 120 mmol/L may not cause overt symptoms.

In immature infants, the most frequent cause of hyponatraemia is excess renal loss due to immature tubular function and consequently reduced ability to conserve sodium. Babies receiving parenteral fluids should be provided with at least 3 mmol sodium/kg/24h. In some preterm babies, even this will be insufficient. An increase in body water is most likely to occur when AVP secretion is excessive and/or uncontrolled.

The causes, clinical features and principles of management of hyponatraemia are listed in Figure 4.2. Some of the rarer biochemical causes are discussed below.

Congenital adrenal hyperplasia (CAH)

This term refers to a group of autosomal recessive disorders of adrenal steroid hormone biosynthesis resulting in deficiency of cortisol or aldosterone or both (see the biochemical pathway in Figure 4.3). Cortisol deficiency leads to:

- stimulation of the hypothalamo-pituitary axis,
- adrenocortical hyperplasia,
- overproduction of cortisol precursors and androgens.

The presentation depends on which enzymatic step is deficient, and whether the genetic mutation is severe or mild. Hyponatraemia occurs when aldosterone and other mineralocor-ticoid steroids are deficient. This may present with a severe salt-wasting crisis with circulatory collapse. In less severe cases there may be no signs of extracellular fluid volume depletion. In addition to hyponatraemia, there may be:

- virilisation of the affected female (ambiguous genitalia),
- excessive pigmentation of the genitalia at birth,
- incomplete virilisation of the affected male (ambiguous genitalia),
- neonatal hypoglycaemia secondary to cortisol deficiency.

The key diagnostic features of these disorders are shown in Figure 4.4

Aetiology	Condition	Presentation	Management
Excess of water			
Maternal water excess	Large volumes of salt-poor fluids during labour	Low sodium concentration for 48 hours	Recovers spontaneously
Iatrogenic water excess	Prolonged parenteral administration of dextrose without sodium; excessive infusion rates	Laboratory results	Add NaCl to fluid, restrict volume
Excess AVP secretion	Intracranial bleeding or space occupying lesions, birth injury, systemic sepsis, positive pressure ventilation, surgery	Weight gain/oedema, respiratory problems, cerebral oedema, poor urine output, plasma osmolality reduced, urine osmolality >100 mmol/kg, low plasma creatinine	Restrict fluids to 40-60 mL/kg/24h if acute and symptoms: bolus of 3% saline; Reduce plasma sodium over 48-72 hours See text
Excess of water and sodium			
Water retention exceeds sodium retention	Acute (oliguric) or chronic renal failure, cardiac failure, liver failure	Poor renal function, cardiac or liver function Abnormal liver function, ascites	Tolerate values of 130 to 135 mmol/L if actively treated e.g. heart failure; fluid restrict if overload; spironolactone; avoid excess fluids
Sodium depletion			
Low intake	Inadequate supplementation of intravenous or enteral feeds	Poor weight gain Laboratory results	Add NaCl; restrict fluids if indicated
Excessive losses from the GI tract	Pyloric stenosis, high intestinal obstruction, gastric suction, gut atresia, necrotising enterocolitis, intestinal infections	According to cause: vomiting, gastric fluid aspiration, constipation or diarrhoea, abdominal distension+hypovolaemia poor peripheral perfusion	Resuscitate with isotonic saline; replace fluids, sodium chloride and potassium; See text
From the kidneys Renal immaturity	Very preterm infants	Laboratory results; self-limiting	Add NaCl to feeds
Diuretics and renal	Recovery phase of ATN congenital renal diseases, loop diuretics, osmotic diuresis, hyperglycaemia with glucosuria	Laboratory results	Stop or change diuretic, treat underlying condition
Mineralocorticoid deficiencies Congenital adrenal hyperplasia	21-hydroxylase, 3-β-hydroxysteroid dehydrogenase and StAR deficiencies	See text and Figure 4.4	Fluid and sodium replacement, glucose, hydrocortisone, fludrocortisone

Figure 4.2. Causes, presentation and management of hyponataemia (Cont...).

Aetiology	Condition	Presentation	Management
Adrenal failure	Salt-wasting crisis, hypoglycaemia		Fluid and sodium replacement, glucose hydrocortisone, fludrocortisone
Isolated aldosterone deficiency	Aldosterone synthase deficiency, salt wasting	See Figure 4.4	Fluid and sodium replacement, fludrocortisone
Mineralocorticoid receptor deficiency	Pseudohypoaldosteronism type 1 (dominant)	See text and Figure 4.4	Fluid and sodium replacement
Disorders of renal transport	Proximal renal tubular	See text and Figure 4.4	Citrate or bicarbonate to normalise plasma bicarbonate
	Bartter syndrome	See text and Figure 4.4	Fluid, sodium and potassium replacement; indomethacin (causes NEC; delay for 4-6 weeks if preterm)
	Pseudohypoaldosteronism type 1 (recessive)	See text and Figure 4.4	Fluid and sodium replacement

Figure 4.2 (Cont...). Causes, presentation and management of hyponataemia.

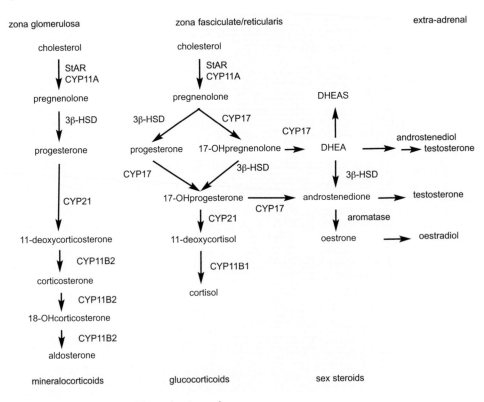

Figure 4.3. Adrenal steroid synthetic pathway.

Deficiency/defect	Presentation	Plasma K+	Plasma HCO3-	renin	Plasma aldosterone	Other diagnostic abnormalities
Congenital adrenal hyperplasia						
21-hydroxylase	salt wasting, hypovolaemia, hypoglycaemia; girls virilised; boys pigmented genitalia	↑	↓	↑	↓	*↑17-OHprogesterone, testosterone, *DHEA, androstenedione ↓cortisol
3-β-hydroxysteroid dehydrogenase	salt wasting, hypovolaemia, girls mildly virilised; boys ambiguous genitalia	↑	↓	↑	↓	*↑17-OHpregnenolone, DHEA, ↓testosterone in boys
StAR (conversion of cholesterol to pregnenolone)	salt wasting, hypovolaemia, hypoglycaemia; boys female genitalia	↑	↓	↑	↓	↓17-OHprogesterone, cortisol, testosterone, DHEA, androstenedione
Aldosterone synthase						
18-hydroxylase/ 18-oxidase activities	salt wasting: severe: hypovolaemia, crises; milder: failure to thrive	↑	↓	↑	↓	↑*DOC ; corticosterone (small) ↑18-hydroxy-corticosterone (oxidase-deficiency)
Mineralocorticoid receptor pseudo-hypoaldosteronism type 1; (dominant)	salt-wasting, hypovolaemia	↑	↓	↑	↑	
Defects of renal sodium transport						
Bartter syndrome: 3 transporter defects: Na+K+-2Cl co-transporter *ROMK channel basal chloride channel	salt-wasting, hypovolaemia, intrauterine growth retardation, polyhydramnios, polyuria, polydipsia, nephrocalcinosis	↓	↑	↑	↑	Hypercalciuria; increased prostaglandin E2 (NB: loop diuretics cause the same biochemical abnormalities)
pseudo-hypoaldosteronism type 1; (recessive) epithelial sodium channel (ENaC)	salt-wasting, hypovolaemia	↑	↓	↑	↑	Loss of ENaC, the main target for aldosterone action

Abbreviations: *17-OHprogesterone: 17-hydroxyprogesterone; DHEA: dehydroepiandrosterone; 17-OHpregnenolone: 17-hydroxypregnenolone; DOC: 11-deoxycorticosterone; ROMK: ATP sensitive K+ channel

Figure 4.4. Inherited disorders that cause hyponatraemia in neonates.

Ninety per cent of patients with CAH have a deficiency of 21-hydroxylase, an enzyme that hydroxylates progesterone and 17-hydroxyprogesterone to yield 11-deoxycorticosterone (DOC) and 11-deoxycortisol (precursors in the formation of aldosterone and cortisol respectively). The genetic defect usually results from point mutations affecting an active gene and the adjacent, inactive pseudogene. The incidence of these conditions is estimated to be about 1 in 10,000 to 15,000 in Europe and North America.

Presentation is classically with virilisation and salt wasting (75%) or virilisation alone (25%). Males without salt loss often appear normal at birth, although there may be excess genital pigmentation. They develop signs of premature sexual development during infancy or early childhood, with advanced bone age and tall stature. Females without salt loss present at birth with female pseudohermaphroditism. The clitoris is enlarged and the labia may be fused. Internal genital organs are those of a normal female. Without treatment, masculinisation progresses. In patients with a salt losing variant, there is immediate failure to thrive, then weight loss, vomiting, poor appetite, and progressive dehydration. Hypoglycaemia may be present. Clinical presentation can be at any time in the first month. Urgent investigations to make a working diagnosis are to establish the sex of the infant by chromosome analysis and to measure the plasma 17-hydroxyprogesterone concentration before starting treatment with steroids. This is markedly elevated. The sample must be taken after the age of 48 hours, as concentrations are normally somewhat elevated after birth.

Disorders of renal transporters (Channelopathies)

Ion channels are transmembrane proteins found throughout the body. Some are tissue specific. Mutations in genes encoding these proteins disturb ion transport. The number of defects recognised is increasing rapidly. Amongst them are four defects that decrease renal sodium reabsorption: three for different transporters in the thick ascending limb of the loop of Henle cause Bartter syndrome; the fourth in the collecting duct causes pseudohypoaldosteronism type 1. They present with hyponatraemia due to renal salt wasting (see Figure 4.4).

Assessment of hyponatraemic babies

Water and salt losses are often not directly measurable. They may be estimated by:

- clinical assessment of hydration status (skin turgor, peripheral perfusion, blood pressure, oedema). This is often difficult to estimate in neonates,

- taking account of any conditions leading to excessive losses (e.g. skin immaturity or damage, radiant heaters, diarrhoea and necrotising enterocolitis with hidden fluid loss into the peritoneal cavity),

- measurement of urine output,

- accurate daily weighing using electronic scales; after the first week, a weight gain of 25 to 30 g/day should be expected,

- analysis of plasma electrolytes, bicarbonate (actual or tCO_2), creatinine and urea,

- measurement of the sodium concentration of a random urine sample to differentiate between dehydration or salt depletion and a renal sodium wasting disorder,

- measurement of osmolality of a paired plasma and urine sample if excessive water retention is the suspected cause, to look for evidence of increased AVP secretion.

From these basic investigations the nature and cause of the sodium/water imbalance should be evident. Urgent specialist investigations must be initiated as well in babies where there is a strong clinical suspicion of an inherited defect such as congenital adrenal hyperplasia.

Management

Management depends upon the cause of hyponatraemia. The principles are shown in Figure 4.1. In all situations, it is recommended that the plasma sodium should not be increased at a rate faster than 8 mmol/L per day. There is a risk of brain stem demyelination if corrected faster. In hypovolaemic hyponatraemia due to sodium depletion, the sodium deficit may be calculated, assuming an expected total body water of 0.7 L/kg.

Sodium deficit (mmol) = (135-plasma [Na^+]) x 0.7 x body weight (kg)

Sodium chloride is given to correct the blood volume quickly, usually as isotonic saline (0.9%; 154 mmol/L) but as 1-2 mL/kg of hypertonic saline (3%; 513 mmol/L; 1-2 mL/kg) if the baby has seizures. The remainder of the deficit is then replaced gradually with appropriate sodium-containing fluids over 48 hours, together with replacement of fluid and electrolytes from on-going abnormal fluid losses (see Biochemical reference intervals), together with the normal obligatory fluid losses. Water overload can occur if hypotonic fluids are administered too rapidly. Signs of this include worsening of hyponatraemia, excessive weight gain and reopening of the ductus arteriosus in a preterm baby and oedema.

In acute hypervolaemic hyponatraemia, hypertonic saline (3% sodium chloride; 1-2 mL/kg) is given if there is evidence of raised intracranial pressure and/or seizures. When asymptomatic, fluid intake is restricted to two thirds of maintenance requirements and then appropriate sodium-containing fluids are given over 48-72 hours to produce a maximum fall of plasma sodium of 8 mmol/L/24h. A loop diuretic may help to remove excess water.

Hypernatraemia

Hypernatraemia (plasma sodium concentration greater than 145 mmol/L) is caused by:

- excessive sodium intake (usually iatrogenic),
- loss of body water,
- combination of the above.

The aetiology, clinical features and principles of management of hypernatraemia are summarised in Figure 4.5.

Aetiology	Condition	Presentation	Management
Low water intake	Starvation: feeding difficulties; failed breast feeding	Dehydration, hypotension	See text; 0.9% saline to restore blood pressure, then gradual rehydration with dextrose/saline, enterally or intravenously
Water loss Cutaneous	Prematurity, skin damage or disease, evaporative losses (including very preterm infant under overhead heater)	Dehydration, hypotension	Humidified environment, volume re-expansion (see above)
Gastrointestinal (loss of water in excess of sodium)	Loss of low-sodium fluids (gastric, colonic) with vomiting, diarrhoea, or sequestration in the bowel lumen (third space): NEC; colonic obstruction	Dehydration, hypovolaemia, signs of gastrointestinal malfunction	See text; 0.9% saline to restore blood pressure, then gradual rehydration with dextrose/saline.
Renal	Diabetes insipidus - central or nephrogenic (X-linked recessive) See text	Polyuria, dehydration, low urinary osmolality with high plasma osmolality, vomiting, FTT, constipation, hydronephrosis/ hydroureter, irritability, hyperthermia, seizures, death	See text; 0.9% saline to restore blood pressure, then gradual rehydration with dextrose/saline. DDAVP for cranial DI, thiazide for nephrogenic DI, adequate water intake
	Osmotic diuresis; hyperglycaemia; diabetes mellitus; excessive glucose: especially if preterm, insulin resistance, steroid treatment	Polyuria, dehydration, hyperglycaemia, glucosuria,	According to cause: intravenous fluids, reduce glucose intake; *avoid insulin or use cautiously (risk of cerebral oedema)
Sodium excess	Administration: sodium bicarbonate; hypertonic sodium chloride enterally or intra-venously (prescription errors); slow clearance of sodium-containing medications	If ≥170 mmol/L, irritability, hyperthermia, seizures, death	See text: Stop sodium supplements/medications; 5% dextrose, but add NaCl if plasma sodium fall is too rapid; loop diuretic

Figure 4.5. Causes, presentation and management of hypernatraemia.

Hypernatraemia due to sodium excess is invariably iatrogenic due to excessive sodium administration in fluids or medications, and more likely when there is also significant renal impairment. More commonly hypernatraemia results from water depletion which may be due to inadequate intake to replace water losses, or to deficiency of AVP (cranial diabetes insipidus, DI) or to a reduced or absent renal response to AVP (nephrogenic DI). In the first, there is oliguria with concentrated urine. In DI, large volumes of dilute urine are passed. In all of these disorders, without intervention, there is clinical evidence of increasing dehydration, and later of hypovolaemia which may cause circulatory collapse. The brain shrinks in severe hypernatraemia. When plasma sodium rises above around 165 mmol/L there is progressive cerebral disturbance manifest as irritability, constant crying, unexplained fever, seizures and ultimately coma. Cerebral blood vessels may be torn, causing intracranial haemorrhage. If the patient is hypotensive, normal saline (0.9%) is given to restore the blood pressure. Dehydration should then be corrected slowly to avoid the risk of cerebral oedema. It is recommended that the maximum decrease in plasma sodium should be 10-12 mmol/L/day. Hypernatraemic dehydration is corrected over 48-72 hours using 0.45% sodium chloride as appropriate to control the fall in plasma sodium. DDAVP is also commenced cautiously for cranial DI. When hypernatraemia is due to sodium overload, 5% dextrose is given, but with added sodium chloride if plasma sodium falls too quickly, sometimes with a loop diuretic.

Nephrogenic diabetes insipidus

In 90% of cases this is an X-linked disorder affecting boys in which there is a deficiency of the renal AVP receptor 2.The remaining 10% of cases have mutations of the gene encoding the vasopressin-sensitive water channel, aquaporin-2. Inheritance is autosomal. The end result is renal insensitivity to AVP. Urine is not concentrated normally in response to a test dose of the AVP analogue, DDAVP, D-deamino-(8-D-arginine) vasopressin.

Salt retention with normal plasma sodium

In renal failure, sodium chloride and water may be retained excessively with expansion of the ECF volume, but no change in plasma sodium. This also occurs in a small number of inherited disorders which cause hypertension with low plasma renin. In three disorders which may present neonatally, the cause is an increase in mineralocorticoid production. In a fourth, Liddle syndrome, production of a renal sodium transporter is increased. Figure 4.6 presents the key diagnostic abnormalities.

Deficiency/defect	Presentation	Plasma		Plasma		Other diagnostic
		K+	HCO$_3^-$	renin	aldosterone	abnormalities
Congenital adrenal hyperplasia						
11β-hydroxylase	hypertension; girls virilised (variable)	↓	↑	↓	↓	*↑17-OHprogesterone (moderate), *DOC 18-deoxy-cortisol, testosterone, *DHEA, androstendione
17α-hydroxylase	hypertension; boys female external genitalia	↓	↑	↓	↓	↑DOC; corticosterone *↓17-OHpregnenolone, cortisol, DHEA, androstenedione, testosterone, oestrogens
AMES: Apparent mineralocorticoid excess						
11β-hydroxysteroid dehydrogenase deficiency	hypertension; polyuria, polydipsia failure to thrive some nephrocalcinosis	↓	↑	↓	↓	↑cortisol:cortisone ratio; ↓ACTH
Renal sodium transport						
Liddle syndrome (pseudohyper-aldosteronism): activating mutation for the amiloride sensitive epithelial sodium channel (ENaC)	hypertension	↓	↑(some)	↓	↓	High sweat chloride Hypertension responds to amiloride

Abbreviations: *17-OHprogesterone; 17-hydroxyprogesterone; DOC: 11- deoxycorticosterone; DHEA: dehydro-epiandrosterone; 17-OHpregnenolone: 17-hydroxypregnenolone

Figure 4.6. Inherited disorders which cause sodium retention in neonates.

Potassium balance

Distribution

Potassium is the main intracellular cation, only 0.4% of total body potassium being in the plasma and interstitial fluid. The intracellular concentration of potassium (K$^+$) is about 150 mmol/L while the extracellular concentration averages 4 mmol/L. The difference is maintained by action of the cell membrane enzyme Na$^+$,K$^+$-ATPase. Insulin and β-2 adrenergic agonists, notably salbutamol, stimulate this enzyme and hence the movement of K$^+$ into cells. The distribution of K$^+$ between cells and the ECF is modulated by hydrogen ion (H$^+$) balance. In alkalosis,

K^+ enters the cells to replace lost H^+ and plasma K^+ may fall. Conversely, in acidosis, K^+ moves into the ECF as cellular H^+ increases. Plasma K^+ may increase. Because of the high potassium concentrations in blood cells, plasma concentrations are readily increased artefactually, particularly when the cells are damaged during blood sample collection, a frequent occurrence in neonates, when there is delayed separation of plasma or when there are large increases in white cell or platelet counts.

Homeostasis

The amount of potassium in the body is determined by intake and losses. The recommended potassium intake for a healthy milk-fed baby is 3-4 mmol/kg/24h (Figure 4.1). Losses from the body are regulated by adjusting renal excretion, which is normally 10 to 15% of the filtered load. Potassium is freely filtered by the renal glomeruli and reabsorbed in the proximal convoluted tubules proportionately with water. Both the distal convoluted tubules and the collecting ducts can secrete and reabsorb potassium. Secretion of potassium into the distal convoluted tubule is promoted by aldosterone which, in turn, is increased in hyperkalaemia and decreased by atrial natriuretic peptides and low plasma potassium concentration. In addition, potassium secretion is raised in alkalosis and reduced in acidosis, and potassium excretion increases in proportion to the flow rate of fluid through the distal tubules and the concentration of sodium delivered. Most diuretics increase potassium losses by increasing tubular sodium concentration and flow rate.

Hypokalaemia

Potassium deficiency is usually associated with hypokalaemia, but because the major fraction of the body's potassium is intracellular, this is not invariable. An increase in plasma bicarbonate, however, is a useful indication of potassium depletion.

Mild hypokalaemia may be asymptomatic. As plasma concentrations fall below 3.0 mmol/L, there is an increasing risk of symptoms: muscle weakness with hypotonia, apnoeas and increasing ventilator dependence, ileus with abdominal distension and vomiting, irritability, increased heart rate with conduction defects and arrhythmias with risk of cardiac arrest.

Hypokalaemia can be caused by:

- inadequate intake,
- excessive loss,
- redistribution (from extra- to intracellular fluid).

The aetiology, clinical features, management and causes are summarised in Figure 4.7 with a more detailed discussion of some of the rarer biochemical causes below.

Treatment should aim to correct the underlying cause, and replace potassium if necessary. In giving parenteral potassium, care must be taken both with regard to the concentration and rate of infusion in order to avoid hyperkalaemia.

Aetiology	Condition	Presentation	Management
Inadequate intake	Prolonged feeding problems; Intravenous fluids lacking potassium	Poor nutritional status; laboratory tests	Potassium supplement; manage feeding Potassium supplement
Intracellular shift of potassium			
Metabolic alkalosis	Administration of alkali	Reduced respiratory effort.	Stop alkali
	Loss of HCl: pyloric stenosis; high intestinal obstruction, gastric suction	Vomiting, hypovolaemia, poor peripheral perfusion; low plasma chloride	See text and Figure 4.1; Replace chloride with sodium chloride
Insulin given to control hyperglycaemia	Diabetes mellitus	Hyperglycaemia, hypovolaemia, osmotic diuresis	Give potassium
	Catabolic states: post-operative, infections, inborn errors	According to condition; insulin resistance	Treat the underlying condition Potassium supplement
Excessive losses			
Gastrointestinal	Pyloric stenosis; high intestinal obstruction, gastric suction Gut atresia Necrotising enterocolitis Intestinal infections	According to cause: vomiting, gastric fluid aspiration, constipation or diarrhoea, abdominal distension plus hypovolaemia; poor peripheral perfusion	Replace fluids and potassium See text and Figure 4.1
Renal			
1. Metabolic alkalosis: excretion of K+ in place of H+	Administration of alkali; loss of HCl: see above	See above	See above
2. Renal tubular acidosis (RTA): excretion of K+ in place of H+	Proximal RTA: isolated or with multiple proximal tubular defects	Hyperchloraemic metabolic acidosis; failure to thrive	}Citrate or bicarbonate to }normalise plasma bicarbonate
	Distal RTA	Hyperchloraemic metabolic acidosis; failure to thrive: hypercalciuria	} As above }
3. Diuretic administration	Treatment with: loop and thiazide diuretics	Laboratory test result	Potassium supplement
4. Mineralocorticoid excess aldosterone:	Secondary hyperaldosteronism: many causes	Depending on cause: water or sodium depletion, hypovolaemia, circulatory failure; plasma sodium high, normal or low	Treat underlying cause; replace potassium;

Figure 4.7. Causes and management of hypokalaemia (Cont...).

Aetiology	Condition	Presentation	Management
Other mineralocorticoids	Congenital adrenal hyperplasia: 11β-hydroxylase and 17α-hydroxylase deficiencies	See Figure 4.6	
Excessive cortisol	Therapeutic administration Apparent mineralocorticoid excess syndrome (AMES)	See Figure 4.6	Consider lower dose; give potassium Dexamethasone to suppress cortisol
5. Inherited disorders of renal transporters	Bartter Syndrome	See Figure 4.4	Replace fluid and electrolytes; indomethacin (causes NEC; delay for 4-6 weeks if preterm).
	Liddle syndrome	See Figure 4.6	Replace fluid and electrolytes;

Figure 4.7. (Cont...) Causes and management of hypokalaemia.

GASTROINTESTINAL DISORDERS

Some 'surgical' disorders such as pyloric stenosis, gut atresia, and necrotising enterocolitis can lead to large losses of fluid and electrolytes, either externally as vomitus or fluid stools, or into a 'third space' such as the gut lumen or peritoneal cavity. These may lead to dehydration, hypovolaemia with peripheral circulatory failure and secondary hyperaldosteronism. Electrolyte abnormalities are common. These must be corrected prior to surgery. Excessive losses of hydrochloric acid from the stomach from prolonged vomiting due to pyloric stenosis, high intestinal obstruction or gastric suction leads to hypochloraemic, hypokalaemic alkalosis. It may require 24 to 48 hours to correct the electrolyte imbalance with saline and potassium supplements prior to surgery. Isotonic saline (0.9%) is given first to resuscitate babies with signs of shock and/or moderate or severe hydration and the chloride deficit is estimated from the following formula:

$[Cl^-]$ deficit (mmol) = (100-measured plasma $[Cl^-]$ (mmol/L)) x body weight (kg).

Sodium chloride is replaced by infusion of 0.9% or 0.45% saline/5% dextrose with added potassium chloride. The aim is to correct plasma chloride to around 100 mmol/L, and bicarbonate to <30 mmol/L. With surgery for any neonatal gastrointestinal disorder, normal maintenance fluid and electrolyte requirements should be given in addition to replacement of losses of blood or fluids as they occur. All such losses must be recorded as accurately as possible. Immediately post-operatively, urine water and sodium output will be reduced secondary to the stress-mediated increases in AVP and renin/aldosterone secretions. Parenteral fluid intake should therefore be given cautiously, with the allowance for maintenance reduced to 40 mL/kg/24h, and guided by regular assessment of clinical hydration status, body weight, urine output and plasma and urinary sodium and potassium concentrations.

In these disorders there is a hyperchloraemic metabolic acidosis with a normal anion gap, which results from impaired renal acidification. The urinary pH or bicarbonate excretion is inappropriate for the plasma pH. These abnormalities arise either from deficient secretion of hydrogen ions or from deficient reclamation of bicarbonate by the renal tubular cells.

Proximal (type 2) renal tubular acidosis (RTA)
This can be acquired, but when it presents in the neonatal period it is usually inherited. It may be an isolated acidification defect (rare) or more commonly part of an inherited systemic disease with multiple renal tubular problems, as in the Fanconi syndrome, Lowe syndrome, cystinosis, galactosaemia or tyrosinaemia. In these conditions, in addition to hypokalaemia, associated abnormalities include salt wasting, generalised amino aciduria, glucosuria, phosphaturia, hypercitraturia and low molecular weight proteinuria.

The underlying tubular defect in isolated proximal RTA is still unknown. It could be a defect of the apical Na^+-H^+ antiporter or $H^+ATPase$ (NHE3), or of the Na^+/HCO_3^- symporter in the basolateral membrane and has been reported in rare patients with carbonic anhydrase deficiency. Babies with isolated proximal RTA present with acidosis, poor growth and failure to thrive. Nephrocalcinosis is not a feature. The diagnosis may be missed; when the babies are extremely acidotic with very low plasma bicarbonate concentrations, the combined capacity for bicarbonate reclamation of the proximal tubules with the normal capacity of the distal tubules, enables the relatively small amount of filtered bicarbonate to be reclaimed efficiently and the urine pH falls appropriately to below 5.5. However, when bicarbonate is given to achieve a normal plasma concentration (around 26 mmol/L), the tubular capacity is overwhelmed, there is a heavy urinary loss of bicarbonate (>15% of the filtered load) and urine pH is > 6.0. Treatment requires large doses of alkali (10-25 mmol/kg/24h) preferably given as a mixture of sodium and potassium citrate.

Distal RTA (type 1)
This may be acquired, sporadic, or inherited as an autosomal dominant disorder. Neonates are most likely to have an inherited defect. The cells of the distal renal tubules are unable to generate the high hydrogen ion gradient needed to excrete H^+ ions maximally in urine and, as a result, urinary pH cannot be reduced below 5.5 even when there is a metabolic acidosis. The underlying defect in the disorder is unknown. It might be due to a significant 'back-leak' of H^+ ions from the tubular lumen into the renal interstitium, or to a decreased rate of H^+ ion secretion because of defects of the apical H^+-ATPase, or H^+, K^+-ATPase, the basolateral HCO_3^-/Cl^- exchanger, or of carbonic anhydrase. In some families, distal RTA is associated with a missense mutation of the AE1 gene for the HCO_3^-/Cl^- exchanger, but it is not apparent how this could cause the acidification problem. Presentation is with metabolic acidosis, failure to thrive, muscle weakness, hypokalaemia, and hypercalciuria with nephrocalcinosis. Treatment is with bicarbonate or sodium or potassium citrate (1-3 mmol/kg/24h) to normalise plasma bicarbonate.

Hyperkalaemia

Hyperkalaemia is considered a medical emergency. The greatest concern is the risk of cardiac arrest from arrhythmias due to increased excitability of the myocardium or from conduction defects. Hypocalcaemia and hypomagnesaemia increase the risk. In addition there may be skeletal muscle weakness and even flaccid paralysis. Plasma concentrations above 10 mmol/L are generally fatal, although remarkably, some neonates even tolerate these.

Causes

Hyperkalaemia may be due to excessive intake, movement of intracellular K^+ ions into the ECF, and decreased renal excretion. The causes, clinical features and management of hyper-kalaemia are summarised in Figure 4.8. Babies at risk for hyperkalaemia should have ECG monitoring.

Hyperkalaemia in renal failure is discussed below.

In *pseudohypoaldosteronism type1* the kidneys are resistant to mineralocorticoid stimulation. The autosomal recessive form is due to a defect of the renal sodium transporter which is the main target for aldosterone action. In the dominant form, the mineralocorticoid receptor is deficient (Figure 4.4).

Acute management of hyperkalaemia

When plasma potassium is ≥ 6.0 mmol/L after excluding artefactual increases, the likely cause must be ascertained and if feasible, removed, and an electrocardiogram (ECG) examined urgently. Intervention is essential if there are ECG changes or plasma potassium is ≥ 6.5 mmol/L. Different approaches to reduce the concentration are used alone or in combination, according to circumstances: (1) with ECG monitoring, intravenous injection of calcium gluconate (10%; 0.5 mL/kg) over 5-10 minutes to reduce the excitability of the myocardium, (2) driving potassium out of the ECF and into cells by: intravenous infusion of 10% glucose (5-10 mL/kg/h) and insulin (neonates 0.1-0.6 units/kg/h; after four weeks of age 0.05-2.0 units/kg/h); sodium bicarbonate infusion 1 mmol/kg over 10-15 minutes (with close observa-tion for fluid overload); or administration of salbutamol (4 µg/kg intravenously over 5 minutes) and (3) removing excess potassium from the body, using furosemide (1 mg/kg intra-venously over 5 minutes). As a last resort, calcium resonium resin (1 g/kg/24h), may be given cautiously as a rectal suppository, but causes electrolyte imbalance and intestinal necrosis, and is contraindicated if there are bowel problems. Intragastric resonium produces abdominal distension and is not recommended. When conservative measures fail, peritoneal dialysis, haemodialysis or veno-venous haemofiltration may be required.

Aetiology	Condition	Presentation	Management*
Artefact	Haemolysed sample, delayed sample processing, very high white cell and platelet counts	Unexplained laboratory test result	Repeat sample – venous or arterial
Excessive intake 1. In intravenous fluid	Parenteral fluids, including nutrition	Laboratory test result	Reduce input
2. Blood transfusion	Administration of large volumes of stored blood	History of exchange transfusion or use of blood >5 days old	Increase fluid input
Extracellular shift of potassium 1. ATP depletion	Birth asphyxia, hypothermia, sepsis	Sick infant; laboratory test result	Treat underlying condition
2. Red cell or tissue catabolism	Intravascular haemolysis, trauma bruising, haemorrhage swallowed blood, tumour lysis	Laboratory test result	Increase fluid input
3. Severe metabolic acidosis	Birth asphyxia, acute renal failure, inherited organic acidaemias	Sick acidotic infant; laboratory test result	Treat underlying condition
Decreased renal excretion 1. Acute renal failure	Oliguria or anuria	Laboratory test results	Renal replacement treatment
2. Mineralocorticoid deficiency	Congenital adrenal hyperplasia: 21-hydroxylase, 3-β-hydroxysteroid dehydrogenase and StAR deficiencies, adrenal failure;	See text and Figure 4.4 salt-wasting crisis; hypoglycaemia	Fluid and sodium chloride, replacement, fludrocortisone, hydrocortisone, glucose
3. Aldosterone deficiency	Aldosterone synthase deficiency	Salt-wasting crisis;	Fluid and sodium chloride replacement, fludrocortisone
4. Mineralocorticoid resistance Pseudohypo-aldosteronism type 1: dominant	Deficiency of the mineralocorticoid receptor;	} } See Figure 4.4 }	} Fluid and sodium chloride } replacement }
Pseudohypo-aldosteronism type 1: recessive	Deficiency of the epithelial sodium channel (ENaC)	} } See Figure 4.4 }	} Fluid and sodium chloride } replacement }

* Hyperkalaemia may require rapid correction: see text for details.

Figure 4.8. Causes and management of hyperkalaemia.

Renal dysfunction in the neonatal period

In the fetus, most of the functions of the kidney are performed by the placenta. Presentation of renal dysfunction in the neonate is therefore different from presentation at later ages. Major abnormalities such as absent or non-functioning kidneys may present acutely in the first week after delivery in a baby whose plasma electrolyte composition is normal at birth. Additionally, there is a background of immature and changing renal function (see above: obligatory water losses). Neonates have little renal reserve capacity to cope with adverse stresses such as dehydration, water overload and metabolic acidosis. In the preterm neonate particularly, the low glomerular filtration rate together with renal tubular immaturity leads to a number of practical problems in clinical management. Many renally excreted drugs have an extremely prolonged half-life, leading to requirements for dosage interval adjustment and monitoring of plasma drug concentrations (see Chapter 15).

Renal dysfunction can be caused by a structural congenital abnormality such as posterior urethral valves, by perinatal problems such as hypoxia-ischaemia or blood loss, or by postnatal events, such as use of nephrotoxic drugs, septicaemia, shock, dehydration, renal vein thrombosis or major heart surgery.

Diagnosis

The diagnosis of renal failure depends on demonstration of a rising plasma creatinine concentration with or without oliguria. This is defined as a urinary flow rate of <0.5 mL/kg/h after the first 24 hours of life. Plasma creatinine concentration is similar to the mother's at birth. By the second week, average plasma creatinine concentration is 35 mmol/L. In acute renal failure, plasma creatinine rises consistently by more than 20 mmol/L/24h.

Urine sodium concentration is less useful than in the adult in defining the causes of renal failure, particularly because of the immaturity of renal tubular sodium handling. Proteinuria, haematuria, and red cells or granular casts on microscopy of urinary sediment are all useful pointers to renal damage or disease.

Differentiation of established renal failure from prerenal failure due to hypovolaemia is often clarified clinically rather than biochemically. Fractional excretion of sodium >3% in a term infant suggests renal disease with tubular involvement.

Management

Severe, progressive renal disease is treated by dialysis. For logistical reasons this is usually peritoneal dialysis, although there are problems with the use of standard dialysis solutions because of the large glucose load and slow metabolism of the lactate in the solutions. Another option is continuous renal replacement therapy by haemofiltration, utilising arteriovenous or venovenous access and an extracorporeal circuit with a highly permeable haemofilter.

Indications for dialysis in renal failure are:
- hyperkalaemia,
- severe acidosis,
- volume overload,
- progressively rising plasma creatinine concentration.

When there is irreversible renal pathology, dialysis may control the plasma biochemistry until the baby has grown sufficiently for renal transplantation to be feasible.

Early diagnosis of a renal problem, with meticulous attention to fluid and electrolyte balance, will frequently avert the need for dialysis in the baby with peri- or post-natally induced renal failure. Abdominal ultrasound and urinary catheterisation should be performed early. The baby's response to a fluid challenge of 10-15 mL/kg of 0.9% saline over one hour should indicate whether there is a prerenal component. Repeated intravenous frusemide, at doses of 1 mg/kg, should be given. If prerenal factors are excluded, fluid restriction to a level of 50 mL/kg/day plus urine and gastrointestinal losses is then appropriate.

Potassium-free intravenous fluids should be given on suspicion of dysfunction and in the acute phase and ECG monitoring for arrhythmias performed. Acidosis with a base deficit of more than 10 mmol/L is usually treated using sodium bicarbonate to half correct it according to the formula:

$NaHCO_3$ to be infused (mmol/L) = base deficit x 0.5 x 0.3 x body wt (kg).

The infusion is usually administered as 4.2% $NaHCO_3$ over 1-2 hours.

In persisting renal failure there is a danger of hypoglycaemia and malnutrition, and parenteral nutrition may be required. Plasma calcium and magnesium concentrations should be maintained because of the increased risk of arrhythmias when hyperkalaemia is associated with hypocalcaemia or hypomagnesaemia. Drugs that are renally excreted will require adjustment of dose and/or dose interval, and monitoring of plasma concentrations. Potentially nephrotoxic drugs should, wherever possible, be discontinued.

The prognosis reflects the underlying cause and the extent to which other body organs, particularly the brain, have been affected by an ischaemic process. This may influence the extent to which aggressive management of the renal problem is continued. Up to 40% of survivors may have persisting decreased creatinine clearance, residual concentrating defects, or renal tubular acidosis.

Further reading

Cartilidge P. The epidermal barrier. Semin Neonatol. 2000; **5:** 273-280.

Graves TD, Hanna MG. Neurological channelopathies. Postgrad Med J 2005; **81:** 20-32.

Hall MA, Noble A, Smith S (Eds). A Foundation for Neonatal Care. Oxon, UK: Radcliffe Publishing Ltd., 2009.

Masilamani K, van der Voort J. The management of acute hyperkalaemia in neonates and children. Arch Dis Child 2012; **97:** 376-380.

Modi N. Hyponatraemia in the newborn. Arch Dis Child Fetal Neonatal Ed 1998; **78:** F81-F84.

Polin RA, Fox WW, Abman SH (Eds). Fetal and Neonatal Physiology, 4th edn. Philadelphia: Saunders, 2011.

Rolim ALR, Lindsey SC, Kunii IS, Fujikawa AM, Soares FA, Chiamolera MI *et al.* Ion channelopathies in endocrinology: recent genetic findings and pathophysiological insights. Arq Bras Endocrinol Metab. 2010; **54:** 673-681.

Soriano JR. Renal tubular acidosis: the clinical entity. J Am Soc Nephrol 2002; **13:** 2160-2170.

Vellaichamy M. Pediatric hyponatraemia. T.E. Cordon Chief Editor. Medscape; 22 April 2013 emedicine.medscape.com/article/907841-treatment.

Chapter 5
Acid-base disorders

Summary

- Neonates are particularly vulnerable to disturbance of acid-base balance because of the relative immaturity of their organ systems. This vulnerability is exacerbated in premature infants.

- Causes of acid-base disturbance in the neonate may be of respiratory or metabolic origin.

- Blood gas analysis should be available on site. Care should be taken with collection and transport of blood prior to analysis.

- Pulse oximetry (non-invasive monitoring) offers an alternative method for determining oxygen saturation and correlates closely with validated arterial saturation measurements.

Adaptation to extra-uterine life

The perinatal period is one of major change for a baby. Before the onset of labour, the fetal environment, compared with that outside the womb, is relatively hypoxic. During labour some tissue hypoxia and placental insufficiency occur resulting in a mixed respiratory and metabolic acidosis. With the first breath the lungs become inflated and the respiratory system rapidly adapts to take on gas exchange. The cardiovascular system also undergoes a dramatic change with the rapid transition from fetal to adult circulation. Difficulties in cardiorespiratory adaptation are frequent and can have serious consequences. Perinatal asphyxia occurs when there is inadequate gas exchange to meet the needs for oxygen consumption and carbon dioxide removal. Lactic acid, the product of anaerobic metabolism, and carbon dioxide accumulate resulting in acidosis. pH can be assessed in labour by fetal blood sampling and delivery expedited if necessary.

Neonatal acid-base homeostasis

Normal extracellular hydrogen ion (H^+) concentration in healthy newborn infants ranges from 38 to 48 nmol/L (pH 7.32 to 7.43). Metabolism and growth are dependent on maintaining a normal acid-base status. Severe acidosis can cause reduced peripheral perfusion and may produce or prolong pulmonary hypertension and right-to-left intracardiac shunting of blood through the patent foraman ovale and the ductus arteriosus. Maintenance of acid-base homeostasis in neonates is dependent upon maintaining appropriate respiration and perfusion and adequate renal and hepatic function.

Neonates are particularly vulnerable to disturbance of acid-base balance because of the relative immaturity of their organ systems. This vulnerability is exacerbated in premature infants and/or if there is superimposed organ dysfunction e.g. intrinsic renal disease or systemic dysfunction secondary to poor perfusion or infection.

The maintenance of normal hydrogen iron concentration depends on a balance between acid production, consumption by metabolism, and excretion. Short-term imbalances are absorbed through buffering.

The major buffer system in extracellular fluid is carbonic acid (H_2CO_3)/bicarbonate (HCO_3^-).

$$H^+ + HCO_3^- \leftrightarrow H_2CO_3 \leftrightarrow H_2O + CO_2$$

The efficiency of this buffer system is increased because carbonic acid can be formed by the hydration of carbon dioxide or disposed of by the reverse process, and by carbon dioxide excretion in the expired breath. Buffering also occurs in the intracellular environment, with hydrogen ions crossing cell membranes in exchange for potassium, and HCO_3^- in exchange for chloride; acute acidosis may therefore result in hyperkalaemia, whereas alkalosis can lower extracellular potassium concentration.

Long-term maintenance of hydrogen ion concentration depends on the balance between production and excretion. The kidney has a key role in acid-base homeostasis through the reabsorption of filtered bicarbonate in the proximal convoluted tube and the excretion of acid in the distal convoluted tubule. The balance between carbon dioxide production and its excretion by the respiratory system and bicarbonate utilisation in buffering and its reabsorption and regeneration in acid excretion determines the extracellular fluid (ECF) hydrogen ion concentration or pH (Figure 5.1).

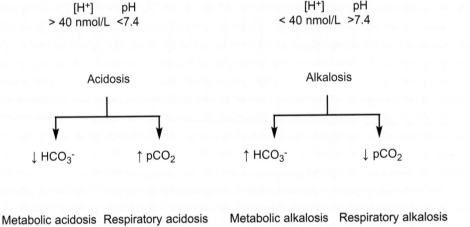

Figure 5.1. Acid-base balance.

Respiratory causes of acid-base disturbance

Respiratory depression at birth

Urgent management of respiratory failure in newborn infants is of paramount importance. Hypoxaemia (and its consequences) is the commonest cause of perinatally acquired brain injury in term babies, although only a minority of cases of hypoxia-induced ischaemic damage arise during labour. In the majority of otherwise normal newborns who require resuscitation, the cause is due to complications arising during labour. In the remainder however, there is an apparently normal labour with no evidence of fetal compromise. The baby may fail to establish adequate respiration or more rarely may breathe regularly, but fail to become centrally pink.

Drugs used as maternal analgesics or sedatives, or general anaesthetics given during labour will cross the placenta and can depress the fetal respiratory centre. This may be particularly important in premature infants or those whose respiratory drive is already compromised.

Premature infants

Premature infants often require active resuscitation. The mechanism of respiratory failure in this group is multifactorial and includes difficulty of establishing lung inflation and respiration with non-compliant, surfactant-deficient lungs. Avoidance of perinatal hypoxia is particularly important because of the association of hypoxia with more severe surfactant deficiency, persistent pulmonary hypertension and with intraventricular haemorrhage and periventricular leukomalacia. Infants with established surfactant deficiency usually have a respiratory acidosis initially because of carbon dioxide retention. Underventilation may be due to inadequate respiratory effort, irregular respiration or muscle weakness. When hypoxia ensues, and if respiratory management is inadequate, the acidosis is compounded by a metabolic component due to increased lactic acid production from anaerobic metabolism. It is important that these disturbances are minimised by providing appropriate ventilatory support for the baby and maintaining adequate oxygenation. The use of antenatal corticosteroids given to women with threatened preterm delivery and postnatal exogenous surfactant administration to preterm babies with respiratory distress has significantly reduced the incidence of respiratory distress syndrome (RDS) or surfactant-deficient lung disease. Early respiratory support including additional oxygen, continuous positive airway pressure (CPAP) and endotracheal intubation and positive pressure ventilation (PPV) reduces the likelihood of respiratory compromise.

Apnoea

Apnoeas, or pauses in respiration, are common in neonates. The duration and severity are less in mature than in premature infants. Neonates, especially if preterm, often exhibit periodic breathing with increasing and decreasing amplitude of breath; an apnoea represents a pause during the 'shallow breathing' phase. Maturation of the respiratory centre leads to the abolition of this pattern. Prolonged apnoea leads to hypoxaemia, carbon dioxide retention, acidosis and bradycardia. These episodes are usually self-limiting, but sometimes the hypoxaemia itself can lead to hypoventilation or there is a mechanical obstructive element to the apnoea which then becomes prolonged.

Monitoring on NNUs includes continuous oxygen saturation (SaO$_2$) and heart rate monitoring in at-risk babies, or in the more stable baby, the use of a pressure sensitive external thoracic 'apnoea alarm' set to 20 second time delay. Apnoeas usually respond to external stimulation or can be reduced in frequency by administration of a respiratory stimulant (caffeine) to preterm babies.

Metabolic causes of acid-base disturbances

Hypoperfusion

The commonest reason for acidosis in newborn babies is lactic acidosis secondary to poor perfusion. There are numerous causes including sepsis, necrotising enterocolitis, blood loss and structural abnormalities e.g. hypoplastic left heart.

Overproduction of acid

Severe metabolic acidosis, usually with a compensatory respiratory alkalosis, can occur in babies with a range of inherited defects of organic acid metabolism (see Chapter 10). In these situations acidosis is not present at birth, but will usually occur within 24 to 72 hours, often presenting as tachypnoea (respiratory rate > 60/minute) in a previously well baby. Blood hydrogen ion concentration may be normal owing to the presence of a compensatory respiratory alkalosis.

Renal dysfunction

Primary renal dysfunction e.g. renal tubular acidosis (see Chapter 4) may lead to an inability to excrete an acid load and hence the development of a metabolic acidosis. If there is significant acidosis, the baby will attempt to compensate by hyperventilation and pCO$_2$ will fall. Secondary, or transient renal dysfunction, for instance following perinatal asphyxia, may also lead to metabolic acidosis, but this does not usually cause a problem in clinical management. Preterm babies may develop a mild chronic metabolic acidosis due to renal immaturity and an inability to excrete the physiologically generated acid load.

Measurement of blood gases and acid-base assessment

All sick babies, particularly if there is clinical evidence of poor perfusion, respiratory insufficiency, dehydration or infection should have their acid-base status assessed. A combination of blood gas measurements and complementary non-invasive monitoring allows the clinician to assess the patient and make therapeutic decisions. Monitoring includes a combination of oxygen saturation monitoring and invasive arterial monitoring (umbilical artery or peripheral arterial line) and is indicated if the baby is unstable, or requiring significant intensive care. Particular challenges in assessment are the rapidly changing physiology of neonates, difficult access to arterial sampling and small blood volume.

Collection and transport of blood

It is extremely important to pay attention to the quality of specimen obtained for acid-base monitoring. Capillary blood is not suitable in seriously ill patients e.g. those with shock, hypotension or poor perfusion. The best specimens for measuring pO_2 are those collected with minimal disturbance through an indwelling catheter sited in the umbilical artery or a peripheral artery (see above). Haemodilution can be a potential problem associated with peripheral arterial catheters if care is not taken to flush out the heparinised saline. Repeated sampling may itself change the pO_2 as the infant responds to pain by crying, leading to misleadingly low results. When capillary blood is used, it is essential that the person collecting the blood must have been properly trained to collect these specimens (see Appendix A). The blood must be free-flowing from a well perfused limb (almost always the heel) and collected into the special heparinised capillary tubes designed for blood gas analysis and 'mixed' to avoid clot formation. Great care must be taken to ensure that the tube and specimen do not contain air bubbles or clots, and if the blood gas analyser is at a remote site that the blood is maintained at 4°C during transit. Capillary values for hydrogen ion concentration and pCO_2 are usually close to arterial values ([H^+] +/- 5 nmol/L, pCO_2 + 1 kPa). However, capillary pO_2 under-estimates the arterial value and this result is of no clinical significance. Pulse oximetry and to a lesser extent, transcutaneous pO_2 have now replaced capillary pO_2 measurement and capil-lary blood is not considered suitable for this analysis.

Blood gas analysis

When choosing a blood gas analyser for a neonatal unit, small sample size and ease of use with capillary tubes or syringes are obviously key factors. In the units that have their own blood gas analyser and where clinical staff are trained to use the instruments, there should be an appro-priate quality assurance programme, maintenance programme, support for training and trou-bleshooting all provided from the laboratory. This must include provision of a designated 'back up' instrument which can be easily accessed.

Non-invasive blood gas monitoring.

Pulse oximetry (or oxygen saturation monitoring) is a useful non-invasive technique to esti-mate oxygenation and complements blood gas analysis. However it cannot replace blood gas monitoring in critically ill infants.

Oxygen saturation monitoring (pulse oximetry)

Oxygen is present in the blood in two physical forms:
- freely dissolved in plasma water,
- bound reversibly to haemoglobin within red cells.

The first of these is directly related to the partial pressure of oxygen in blood (pO_2). This accounts for about 2% of total blood oxygen content. The other 98% is the oxygen bound to haemoglobin. This is also related to pO_2, although it cannot be increased by increasing the pO_2 above normal, as haemoglobin is fully saturated with oxygen at normal pO_2. This relationship is defined by the oxygen haemoglobin affinity curve. This can be graphically represented as a comparison between the percentage of haemoglobin fully saturated with oxygen ([HbO_2] x 100 /[Hb] + [HbO_2]) and blood pO_2. In neonates, this curve will tend to be shifted to the left because of the characteristics of neonatal red cells (Figure 5.2).

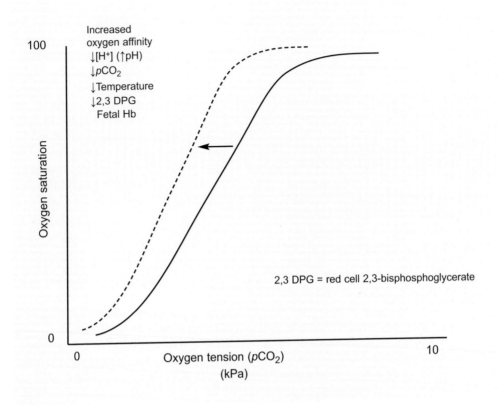

Increased
oxygen affinity
$\downarrow$[H$^+$] ($\uparrow$pH)
$\downarrow$pCO$_2$
$\downarrow$Temperature
$\downarrow$2,3 DPG
Fetal Hb

100

0

Oxygen saturation

0   10

Oxygen tension (pCO$_2$)
(kPa)

2,3 DPG = red cell 2,3-bisphosphoglycerate

Figure 5.2. Factors affecting oxygen-haemoglobin affinity in neonates.

Total oxygen carrying capacity thus depends on the haemoglobin concentration, which falls in the first weeks of postnatal life. During this period however the proportion of fetal haemoglobin also falls, and the oxygen released to tissues increases.

Direct measurement of the percentage of haemoglobin saturated with oxygen may be of theoretical as well as practical value. It provides an indication of the adequacy of tissue oxygen supply. This will be compromised if oxygen saturation (SaO$_2$) is less than 80%.

Pulse oximetry uses a light-emitting probe attached to a hand or foot and computes oxygen saturation from the light absorption characteristics of the pulsatile flow (containing both oxygenated and deoxygenated haemoglobin) as it passes beneath the probe. The results correlate closely with validated arterial saturation measurements. Rapidly responding saturation results can be obtained without initial calibration and provided for poorly perfused babies and older babies with chronic oxygen dependency. No recalibration of probes is required during use. However since the normal values of SaO$_2$ in the neonate are 95-100%, hyperoxaemia may go undetected in babies receiving additional oxygen unless the pO$_2$ is also known. This is because only small changes in SaO$_2$ occur, even with the large alterations in partial pressure of oxygen at this upper end of the dissociation curve. A false estimate can occur if the probe is applied incorrectly or if there is excessive movement of the patient or probe. In preterm babies the aim is to keep SaO_2 in the 92-95% range (because of the potential risk of retinopathy of prematurity with hyperoxaemia), whereas term infants should have saturations >94%.

Pulmonary circulation, ductus arteriosus diameter and cellular and tissue injury from oxygen free radical production all relate to pO_2 to rather than oxygen content. Knowledge of pO_2 is therefore vital when oxygen saturation monitoring is being used in acutely ill neonates.

ARTERIAL pCO_2

Arterial pCO_2 provides an assessment of adequacy of alveolar ventilation. The pCO_2 reflects the balance between the metabolic production of carbon dioxide and its excretion by ventilation. Reduction in pCO_2 can be achieved by reducing the metabolic rate or by increasing ventilation. Transcutaneous pCO_2 monitoring correlates well with directly measured pCO_2 and provides a good means of following trends. Unlike transcutaneous pO_2 monitors, pCO_2 monitors do not cause skin burns. *In vivo* calibration against arterial or capillary gases is required.

Interpretation of acid-base status

Normal values for arterial blood [H⁺], pCO_2 and pO_2, are dependent on postnatal age. After birth, as pulmonary gas exchange is established [H+], pCO_2 and pO_2 move towards adults values. There are dramatic changes in the first 30 minutes after birth (pO_2 ↑, [H⁺] ↓, pCO_2 ↓and pH↑). The changes continue over the first two hours (see Figure 5.3).

Interpretation of acid-base measurements must take into account the type of specimen (capillary/arterial), the clinical state of the baby and the results of other relevant investigations. A base deficit of lower than -4 mmol/L is potentially significant although in practice, further investigations is not usually undertaken until it falls to below -8 mmol/L.

	[H⁺] nmol/L	pH	pCO_2 kPa	pO_2 kPa
1-6 hours	46-49	7.31-7.34	4.7-6.0	8.0-10.6
6-24 hours	37-43	7.37-7.43	4.4-4.8	9.3-10.0
2-7 days	42-44	7.36-7.38	4.4-4.8	9.3-11.3

Figure 5.3. Arterial [H⁺], pH and blood gas values in normal full-term infants.

Differential diagnosis of acid-base disturbance (see Figures 5.4 and 5.5)

Acid-base disturbances may be simple. i.e. having an isolated respiratory or metabolic cause. Physiological compensation of the primary disorder, i.e. by changes in the renal acid excretion in respiratory disorders and in ventilation, and hence carbon dioxide excretion in metabolic disorders, usually occurs. Absence of adequate compensation will result in persistent acidosis or alkalosis until the underlying cause is corrected. It should be noted that effective renal compensation is a slower process than respiratory mechanisms and there may be a time lag of several days before compensation is complete. A simple approach to interpretation is to ask these questions:

1. Is the baby acidotic or alkalotic?

   i.e. $[H^+]$ <38 nmol/L (pH >7.42) – alkalotic

   $[H^+]$ >48 nmol/L (pH <7.32) – acidotic

2. If acidotic:

   If pCO_2 is high – respiratory cause

   If pCO_2 is low – metabolic cause

   If alkalotic

   If pCO_2 is low – respiratory cause

   If pCO_2 is high – metabolic cause

3. Is the expected compensation present?

   e.g. in metabolic acidosis, a compensatory fall in pCO_2.

Acidosis

The commonest causes of acidosis in neonates are hypoxia and poor tissue perfusion which may derive from perinatal asphyxia or later illness. Infants with infections are particularly likely to be acidotic due to poor perfusion and overproduction of hydrogen ions.

METABOLIC ACIDOSIS

The commonest cause of metabolic acidosis is lactic acidosis as a consequence of poor perfusion. If hypovolaemia is present, the primary management of such a baby would be administration of fluid (e.g. 0.9% saline). The metabolic component of acid-base disturbances can be assessed from calculation of the bicarbonate and base excess in freely flowing blood. Base excess is a calculated parameter and provides an assessment of the metabolic component of an acid-base disturbance. It requires calculation of 'standard' bicarbonate which is defined as the concentration of bicarbonate at a pCO_2 of 5.3 kPa (i.e removal of any respiratory component). A negative base excess is referred to as a base deficit. A commonly used formula to assess the amount of base required for correction is as follows:

Base required = 0.3 x body weight (kg) x base deficit (mmol) = mmol bicarbonate required.

In practice, half this amount is given as sodium bicarbonate solution (maximum strength 4.2%) into a large vein and acid-base status reassessed. Major changes in perfusion and cardiac output may follow such therapy. It should therefore only be used in situations where the acidosis is severe and likely to persist without treatment. The bicarbonate infusion should be given over at least one hour except in an acute emergency.

Metabolic acidosis in neonates caused by renal failure or renal tubular acidosis (RTA) (see Chapter 4). The commonest cause of renal failure is poor renal perfusion secondary to asphyxia; it is usually reversible and only conservative management is required. If plasma crea-tinine concentration is normal and there is hyperchloraemia with metabolic acidosis then RTA is probable. There are many inherited disorders (see Chapter 10) that may cause metabolic acidosis such as the organic acid disorders of methylmalonic acidaemia and propionic acidaemia. Differential diagnosis of metabolic acidosis may be aided by calculation of the plasma anion gap i.e. $([Na^+]+[K^+])-([HCO_3^-]+[Cl^-])$. A gap of greater than 20 mmol/L is sugges-tive of an organic acid disorder or lactic acidosis due to hypoxia. Biochemical investigations that may help with the differential diagnosis include urinary ketones, plasma glucose, ammonia and lactate concentrations, urine and plasma amino acids and urinary organic acids. If plasma chloride is increased with normal concentrations of amino acids and organic acids, renal tubular disease should be considered (see Chapter 4).

	$[H^+]$	pH	pCO_2	$[HCO_3^-]$	Causes
Respiratory acidosis	↑	↓	↑	N/↑*	Hypoventilation CNS depression Lung disease Neuromuscular disease Airway obstruction Inadequate ventilation
Respiratory alkalosis	↓	↑	↓	N/↓*	Overventilation Hyperammonaemia
Metabolic acidosis	↑	↓	N/↓**	↓	Renal impairment Hypoxia Poor perfusion Loss of fluid from GI tract Metabolic disorders
Metabolic alkalosis	↓	↑	N/↑**	↑	HCO_3 administration Vomiting Pyloric stenosis Hypokalaemia Diuretics Chloride deficiency

*A small change in $[HCO_3]$ accompanies an acute respiratory disturbance; compensation causes a greater change in the same direction; **Compensatory change

Figure 5.4. Causes of acid-base disturbance in neonates.

Cause	Supporting evidence
Circulatory	↑ plasma lactate, ↑anion gap, ↓ blood pressure
Renal	N/↑ creatinine, ↑ [Cl⁻]. N/↑ urine pH, normal anion gap
Respiratory	Clinical signs, ↑pCO$_2$
Metabolic	↑ anion gap, +ve urinary ketones, N/↓ urine pH

Figure 5.5. Differential diagnosis of acidosis.

Alkalosis

The commonest cause of alkalosis is iatrogenic respiratory alkalosis due to overventilation in ventilated babies. Excess administration of bicarbonate can also produce alkalosis when acidosis has been overestimated clinically. Metabolic alkalosis in a vomiting baby is suggestive of pyloric stenosis with loss of gastric acid.

Hypoxia

The normal arterial pO$_2$ for term babies breathing air is 8-11 kPa. A pO$_2$ below 2-3 kPa will cause metabolic acidosis secondary to anaerobic metabolism and demands urgent attention.

A low pO$_2$ may be due to pulmonary disease, failure of circulatory adaptation at birth (persistent pulmonary hypertension), or an anatomical bypass of the pulmonary circulation (e.g. cyanotic congenital heart disease). It is important to diagnose an anatomical cause so that urgent corrective surgery can be undertaken if appropriate. Most pulmonary causes of hypoxia can be differentiated by a combination of history, examination, chest x-ray and bacteriological investigation. Even with a normal pO$_2$, insufficient oxygen delivery to the tissues can be caused by cardiac failure, severe anaemia or low oxygen concentration (Figure 5.6). This leads to metabolic acidosis.

Low cardiac output
    Hypovolaemia
    Sepsis
    Cardiac defect

Low pO$_2$ (hypoxaemia)
    Lung disease (e.g. RDS, pneumonia)
    Congenital heart defect with right to left shunt
    Anaemia (feto-maternal transfusion, haemolysis, blood sampling)

Figure 5.6. Causes of tissue hypoxia in newborn infants.

In severely hypoxaemic babies, the 'nitrogen washout' test can be used to separate the pulmonary causes from failure of adaptation or 'bypass' causes. The procedure involves determining the oxygen saturation in the right arm (i.e. preductal part of the circulation) using a pulse oximeter. The baby is then given as near to 100% oxygen as is practical using a headbox. In hypoxia of pulmonary origin, this manoeuvre will cause an increase in pO_2 and SaO_2. In pulmonary bypass the saturation increase is modest and the baby will remain significantly hypoxic. Cardiac ultrasound examination will define any structural abnormality. If the heart is structurally normal and the lungs clear on chest x-ray this makes persistent pulmonary hypertension more likely. This represents a failure of pulmonary vasodilation of birth and can arise de novo or after asphyxia and can be diagnosed by echocardiography. Pulmonary vasodilators usually lead to steady improvement within the first week. Nitric oxide is given by inhalation together with attention to maintaining mean arterial blood pressure and H^+ <40 nmol/L (pH > 7.40) if possible, until the pulmonary hypertension has resolved.

The aim of oxygen therapy is to maintain adequate oxygenation and thereby minimise cardiac work and respiratory effort. Premature infants should have SaO_2 values of 92-95% to optimise tissue oxygenation, but minimise the risk of blindness caused by retinopathy of prematurity (see below). By contrast, full-term infants with diaphragmatic hernia for example may require pO_2 values of 11-13 kPa as relative hypoxaemia may worsen pulmonary hypertension.

Hyperoxaemia

Excess oxygen carries significant hazards, particularly in immature infants. The major hazards are lung toxicity and retinopathy of prematurity.

PULMONARY TOXICITY

This is related to the concentration of inspired oxygen and is a significant risk if a baby receives oxygen concentrations of 80% or more over a period of more than a few hours. Chronic lung disease of prematurity, recognised as a complication particularly in extremely preterm infants who have received mechanical ventilation, has many histopathological features in common with those produced by oxygen toxicity in animals. The earliest changes resemble exaggerated normal repair processes in the bronchiolar walls. The lungs become solid and oedema develops around the bronchioles followed by fibroblastic proliferation if the high inspired oxygen is maintained. Foci of distorted proliferated capillaries are seen in some areas, while in others there is a relative lack of a capillary bed. Organised secretions occlude bronchiolar lumina and there is hyperplasia and squamous metaplasia of the bronchial epithelium. These latter features are probably associated with the positive pressures used in ventilation and are difficult to disentangle from those related to oxygen administration.

These abnormalities develop most readily in very immature lungs particularly in association with air leaks. Preventative measures include the use of adequate ventilation to reduce the ambient oxygen requirements while avoiding high ventilatory pressures if possible. Avoidance of air leaks by appropriate ventilation including patient trigger ventilation is equally important.

RETINOPATHY OF PREMATURITY (ROP)

This condition, previously known as retrolental fibroplasia was first recognised in 1940 in the USA. It came to public notice in the 1940s and 1950s when its occurrence and the major consequence – blindness – reached almost epidemic proportions in surviving premature infants particularly in the USA. At that time, the condition was thought to be caused purely by oxygen toxicity. Since the 1970s the frequency of the disease has increased again in the 'new' population of surviving very premature babies (i.e. < 28 weeks gestation or < 1000 g birthweight). It remains the commonest cause of blindness in the neonatal period although it is now very unusual in infants more than 32 weeks gestation.

The disease is recognised in the perinatal period by indirect ophthalmoscopy and this is now performed on at-risk babies in neonatal units. Milder grades of severity are common and 80-90% regress spontaneously. They are probably of little importance. Occasionally, however they progress to severe disease (cicatrical ROP) leading eventually to distortion and detachment of the retina. Treatment by laser therapy may arrest progressive disease.

The relationship with oxygen appears to be a complex one. Retinal blood vessels also grow out to the periphery during gestation but do not reach the temporal margin until after term. High levels of local tissue oxygenation cause spasm of these vessels and ischaemia of the retinal periphery. Subsequently new, poorly organised, blood vessels proliferate from remaining central vessels and attempt to vascularise the periphery. Bleeding and retinal detachment can follow, the time interval between initiation of disease and damage averaging four to six weeks. The damaging effects of oxygen in preterm infants are probably exaggerated because of the poor function of oxygen-generated free radical scavengers in this population. Thus, the level of pO_2 causing retinal damage may vary. It is widely recommended that oxygen saturation is kept below 96% and some previously accepted treatments e.g. use of 100% oxygen instead of air is now no longer routine practice.

Factors other than oxygen are associated with ROP, possibly through direct effect on the retinal vasculature: they include intraventricular haemorrhage, hypoxia, apnoeas and hypercapnia (producing cerebral vasoconstriction).

Hypo- and hypercapnia

The normal pCO_2 in neonates after the first week of life is 4.0-5.5 kPa. A low pCO_2 is uncommon in a spontaneously breathing newborn baby. The commonest cause is over-ventilation secondary to metabolic acidosis. Over-ventilation can also occur in spontaneously breathing babies with cerebral irritability due to birth trauma or perinatal asphyxia. An increased pCO_2 is usually caused by hypoventilation either primary or secondary to metabolic alkalosis

Other abnormalities

Carboxyhaemoglobin is of relevance in mothers who smoke. Carbon monoxide crosses the placenta and binds strongly to fetal haemoglobin making it unavailable for oxygen transport, causing a functional anaemia. Inhaled nitric oxide is used to treat pulmonary hypertension in the newborn. The nitric oxide-haemoglobin complex is converted to methaemoglobin. High concentrations of nitric oxide can lead to methaemoglobinaemia. Patients receiving inhaled nitric oxide should be monitored to keep the methaemoglobin concentration below 5% of the total haemoglobin.

Further reading

Armstrong L, Stenson BJ. Use of umbilical cord blood gas analysis in the assessment of the newborn. Arch Dis Child Fetal Neonatal Ed. 2007; **92:** F430-F434.

Bourchier D, Weston PJ. Metabolic acidosis in the first 14 days of life in infants of gestation less than 26 weeks. European Journal of Pediatrics 2015; **174:** 49-54.

Brouillette RT, Waxman DH. Evaluation of the newborn's blood gas status. Clin Chem 1997; **43:** 215-221.

Chen J, Smith LEH. Retinopathy of prematurity. Angiogenesis 2007; **10:** 133-140.

Ewer A *et al.* Pulse oximetry as a screening test for congenital heart defects in newborn infants: a test accuracy study with evaluation of acceptability and cost-effectiveness. Health Technol Assess 2012; 16(2).

Goel N, Calvert J. Understanding blood gases/acid-base balance. Paediatrics & Child Health 2012; **22:** 142-148.

Guideline for the Screening and Treatment of Retinopathy of Prematurity. Royal College of Paediatrics and Child Health 2008 http://www.bapm.org/publications/documents/guide-lines/ROP_Guideline

Tan S, Campbell M. Acid-base physiology and blood gas interpretation in the neonate Paediatrics & Child Health 2008; **18:** 172-177.

Chapter 6
Jaundice

Summary

• Physiological jaundice is common and can be exacerbated by other factors.

• Bilirubin exists in four fractions in plasma, however laboratory methodologies measure different fractions of unconjugated and conjugated bilirubin.

• Chronic bilirubin encephalopathy is a condition that can be avoided with timely identification of hyperbilirubinaemia and utilisation of phototherapy, exchange transfusion or intravenous immunoglobulin.

• Early jaundice suggests haemolysis and requires investigation to identify the underlying cause.

• Prolonged jaundice requires investigation to identify whether unconjugated or conjugated in origin and hence investigation of the underlying pathology.

Physiological Jaundice

Thirty to seventy percent of healthy babies develop 'physiological' jaundice after 48h of age. Total bilirubin does not usually increase above 200 µmol/L, with a peak at 3-4 days, and usually falls to normal by 7-10 days. Almost all the bilirubin is unconjugated. These babies with physiological jaundice are well and thriving and require no investigation or treatment. A variety of factors may exacerbate the bilirubin concentration (Figure 6.1).

Prematurity	Infections	Inadequate calorie intake
Dehydration	Hypoxia	Meconium retention
Haemolysis	Hypoglycaemia	Intestinal obstruction
Polycythaemia	Hypothyroidism	Breast feeding
Bruising/cephalohaematoma*		Oxytocin during delivery

* 1g of haemoglobin yields 600 µmol bilirubin on breakdown.

Figure 6.1. Factors exacerbating physiological jaundice.

Although physiological jaundice is the commonest cause of jaundice in the neonate, there are numerous potential underlying conditions that require diagnosis so that appropriate treatment can be given. Features suggesting a pathological cause are:
- early jaundice (< 24 hours),
- jaundice in a sick neonate,
- total bilirubin high (> 300 µmol/L),
- rapid increase in bilirubin concentration (> 8.5 µmol/L/hour),
- jaundice prolonged beyond 14 days,
- conjugated bilirubin > 25 µmol/L.

How is bilirubin measured?

There are four bilirubin fractions in plasma:
- unconjugated bilirubin (alpha),
- monoglucuronide conjugated bilirubin (beta),
- diglucuronide conjugated bilirubin (gamma),
- bilirubin that is covalently bound to albumin (delta).

Measurement of bilirubin fractions is fraught with confusion as there are numerous methods which can give different results. Reference ranges are lower for methods that allow more specific measurement of the conjugated and unconjugated bilirubin fractions.

1. Direct methods: bilirubin is reacted with a dye (diazo reagent) and the resulting coloured compound is measured spectrophotometrically. Conjugated bilirubin reacts rapidly with the dye and is referred to as 'direct reacting'. Measurement of the direct reacting fraction is dependent on the exact conditions in the assay and different methods may give different results. Routinely used methods for 'direct reacting' bilirubin overestimate the true conjugated fractions because other components also react, with the result that reference ranges are higher than with the more specific methods that measure 'true' conjugated bilirubin. For example in healthy neonates with physiological jaundice there is very little true conjugated bilirubin (< 20 µmol/L) but for 'direct reacting' bilirubin methods this should be < 40 µmol/L. In a baby with prolonged jaundice, a concentration of 'direct reacting' bilirubin greater than 15% of the total bilirubin is abnormal.

2. Indirect method: measurement of the unconjugated fraction requires the addition of a chemical 'accelerator'; and is therefore termed 'indirect reacting'.

3. Chemical or enzymatic methods using bilirubin oxidase in which the bilirubin is oxidised to biliverdin will provide a more specific measurement of conjugated bilirubin due to less cross-reactivity with delta bilirubin.

4. Dual wavelength dry slide method to directly measure unconjugated and conjugated bilirubin fractions. This methodology is prone to interference from bilirubin photoisomers generated by phototherapy (in the treatment of hyperbilirubinaemia) when used to measure the conjugated bilirubin fraction.

5. Blood gas analysers equipped with bilirubin module. Multiwavelength absorbance meas-

urements used to calculate bilirubin concentration in whole blood samples.

6. Transcutaneous bilirubinometry – These hand held meters work by transmitting light into the skin. The light is reflected and the multiple readings made are converted via a mathematical algorithm to calculate a transcutaneous bilirubin concentration. The algorithms adjust reflected light for dermal thickness, melanin and haemoglobin concentration. They may be used in babies >35 weeks gestation and >24 hours of age to identify those at risk of severe hyperbilirubinaemia. Results >250 μmol/L must be checked with a laboratory serum bilirubin measurement. The meters should not be used for monitoring patients at or above treatment thresholds, or during treatment.

It is very important to be aware of these analytical differences, especially if a baby transfers between hospitals with different laboratory services.

Neonatal hyperbilirubinaemia

Severe, unconjugated hyperbilirubinaemia incurs a risk of kernicterus (chronic bilirubin encephalopathy) in which circulating free, unconjugated bilirubin crosses the blood brain barrier. The risk of kernicterus is increased in babies >37 week gestational age (GA) when plasma bilirubin concentration exceeds 340 μmol/L or if bilirubin concentration is rapidly increasing (>8.5 μmol/L/hr).
Features of kernicterus include:
- fits,
- lethargy,
- opisthotonic posturing.

Late consequences of untreated hyperbilirubinaemia without the classic features of kernicterus include:
- progressive nerve deafness,
- athetoid cerebral palsy (rarely),
- visual and dental problems.

Preterm babies are thought to be at greater risk of bilirubin toxicity because of reduced albumin binding of bilirubin due to relative hypoproteinaemia; acidosis or hypoxia may reduce the effectiveness of the physiological blood-brain barrier, and the immature brain may be more vulnerable to bilirubin toxicity. The potential for severe jaundice in the pre-term population is compounded by the greater liver immaturity and tendency to more frequent bruising and the delayed establishment of enteral feeding in this group. Polycythaemia caused by delayed clamping of the umbilical cord or associated with intrauterine growth retardation may also be seen.

Management

Adequate hydration, which may involve tube feeding or an intravenous infusion, together with phototherapy, will usually avert the need for exchange transfusion in non-haemolytic jaundice. Single 'blue light' or fibre optic phototherapy generates unconjugated photo-isomers products when bilirubin absorbs blue-green light. These harmless photo-oxidation products are then excreted in bile or urine. Bilirubin will need to be monitored frequently (4-6 hourly initially, but 6-12 hourly if stable or falling). Treatment should be instituted according to guidelines (NICE CG98) and if the bilirubin rises above a predetermined concentration an exchange transfusion must be performed.

Because preterm infants are at greater risk of severe hyperbilirubinaemia, phototherapy and exchange transfusion are instituted at lower bilirubin concentrations according to the formula below. In the UK, consensus plasma bilirubin thresholds (µmol/L) for phototherapy and exchange transfusion in babies >72 hours of age:
- for phototherapy: (gestational age [weeks] x 10) - 100
- for exchange transfusion: (gestational age [weeks]) x 10.
NB. In babies <72 hours of age thresholds should be lower.

All babies who have had a bilirubin concentration exceeding the threshold for exchange transfusion must have a neonatal hearing screening test.

Early versus prolonged jaundice

The aetiology of early jaundice as compared with late presenting or prolonged jaundice reflects whether the disorder is primarily a haemolytic or a hepatitic jaundice and thus dictates the different approach to treatment and management.

Early jaundice

Jaundice that appears unusually early (i.e. within the first 24 h) suggests haemolysis (Figure 6.2). The hyperbilirubinaemia will be predominantly unconjugated and due to a number of conditions in which there is excessive breakdown of red cells in the fetus and neonate (Chapter 11). These may present as early neonatal jaundice. If more severe, such that the rate of haemolysis is greater than the rate of red cell production, they will present as anaemia from birth. Early jaundice should always be investigated (Figure 6.3) and as advised by the National Metabolic Biochemistry Network (MetBionet) guideline.

- Haemolysis
            - blood group incompatibility
            - red cell membrane defects
            - spherocytosis
            - bruising/haemorrhage
            - G6PD deficiency
            - PK deficiency

- Infection (intrauterine and perinatal)

- Genetic defects of bilirubin metabolism e.g. Crigler-Najjar syndrome

Figure 6.2. Causes of early jaundice.

• Unconjugated and conjugated bilirubin

• Haematology
    - Hb, blood group, packed cell volume, FBC (including reticulocytes), film
    - direct antiglobulin test

• G6PD deficiency screen
    - consider other red cell enzyme deficiencies

• Microbiology
    - blood, urine and/or CSF culture (if infection is suspected)

Figure 6.3. Laboratory investigation of early onset jaundice.

BLOOD GROUP INCOMPATIBILITY (CHAPTER 11)

The commonest causes of haemolytic disease of the newborn are blood group incompatibilities between mother and fetus. The principal blood group incompatibilities are those involving the ABO system, the Kell system and the Rhesus system. This last group can present with very severe disease (hydrops fetalis) or even produce fetal death.

ERYTHROCYTE DEFECTS

Intrinsic red cell abnormalities that cause anaemia and that can present at this time include spherocytosis, an autosomal dominant condition with excessive red cell fragility, and red cell enzyme abnormalities, the common ones being glucose 6-phosphate dehydrogenase (G6PD) deficiency and pyruvate kinase (PK) deficiency. Haemoglobinopathies do not usually present as neonatal jaundice. Acquired defects producing haemolysis include both intrauterine and postnatal infection

GLUCOSE 6-PHOSPHATE DEHYDROGENASE DEFICIENCY

A significant number (20-30%) of G6PD deficient infants develop neonatal jaundice. The jaundice occurs spontaneously without drug contact and can occur in the full term as well as the pre-term infant. It usually occurs by the second to third day of life and subsides by the end of the first week. However the timing of the jaundice may be later or extended if there is additional drug contact. Affected neonates may also become jaundiced after contact with one of the offending drugs through the placenta, in breast milk or after contact with clothes impregnated with naphthalene (mothballs). A large number of drugs, including antimalarials, antibiotics and analgesics, can precipitate haemolysis. The possibility of G6PD deficiency should be considered in jaundiced newborns of either sex with immigrant parents. Affected persons should carry a card listing drugs to be avoided.

INFECTION

Both intra-uterine and post-natally acquired infections can cause both early haemolytic jaundice and prolonged jaundice (Figure 6.6).

GENETIC DEFECTS IN BILIRUBIN METABOLISM IN THE NEONATE

These are all rare inherited defects and, in the absence of a family history, should only be considered after exclusion of the above more common causes.

This is caused by the absence of hepatic bilirubin UDP-glucuronyl transferase. It manifests as severe unconjugated non-haemolytic hyperbilirubinaemia (> 340 µmol/L) in the first few days of life. The jaundice is persistent, and lifelong phototherapy is required to prevent kernicterus, but the only effective treatment is liver transplantation.

A definitive diagnosis can be made by the measurement of glucuronyl transferase activity in liver tissue after 3-4 months of age, and by demonstrating the absence of bilirubin glucuronides in the bile. DNA-based prenatal diagnosis can be undertaken where the mutation in the index case is known.

Prolonged jaundice

Jaundice presenting or persisting after fourteen days in the term baby, or 21 days in the preterm infant is abnormal. It is important to perform some measurement of bilirubin conjugation, and consider the possible causes (Figure 6.4). In the majority of instances, prolonged conjugated hyperbilirubinaemia reflects underlying liver disease and will be reflected in derangements of liver function tests. A significant delay in diagnosis or treatment of an infant with cholestasis can be devastating if the erroneous assumption is made that the jaundice is 'physiological' or due to breast feeding. Therefore, unexplained conjugated hyperbilirubinaemia in the newborn must always be investigated.

- Breast feeding
- Prematurity
- Congenital infection/immune disorders
- Parenteral nutrition (see Chapter 14)
- Biliary atresia (and other structural defects)
- Endocrine disorders
    - hypothyroidism (see Chapter 9)
    - hypopituitarism
    - adrenal disorders
- Genetic disorders
    - alpha1-antitrypsin deficiency
    - cystic fibrosis (see Chapter 9)
    - galactosaemia
    - disorders of bilirubin metabolism
    - other inherited metabolic disorders

Figure 6.4. Causes of prolonged jaundice.

It is particularly important to be alert to the signs of liver dysfunction. These are:

- conjugated bilirubin > 25 µmol/L
- pale/chalky stools

- bilirubinuria (dark urine)
- bleeding/prolonged clotting
- failure to thrive
- hypoglycaemia
- abnormal liver function tests (including γGT).

Liver function tests

These biochemical tests are frequently used to detect and assess liver damage and function, in addition to monitoring disease progression. They are of limited use in making a diagnosis of a specific type of liver disease, but guide the need for further investigations. Abnormalities in each of them can occur in non-hepatic disease: they are not specific for the liver. The normal values differ from those in infants/older children (see Biochemical reference ranges). Liver dysfunction also affects clotting factors (see Chapter 11) and clotting tests are included as part of liver function assessment. The liver function tests commonly comprise measurements of plasma aminotransferase (transaminase), alkaline phosphatase and γ–glutamyl transferase activities, and the plasma concentration of albumin in addition to that of bilirubin.

Aminotransferases

Both aspartate aminotransferase (AST) and alanine aminotransferase (ALT) are usually increased to a similar degree in liver disease. AST can be elevated in other conditions, e.g. muscle disease and cardiac damage, whereas ALT is raised to a lesser degree, if at all, in other conditions. ALT is, therefore, a more specific marker of liver disease. Plasma activities are increased (approximately 2-fold) in the early months of life compared with later infancy. Gross increases (more than 20-fold) of activity occur if there is liver cell necrosis as the enzyme leaks out into the extracellular fluid, e.g. in acute hepatitis, significant trauma and tissue hypoxia (for example with asphyxia). In chronic liver disease and with cholestasis, transaminase activities are increased (2 to 10-fold).

Alkaline phosphatase (ALP)

ALP is present in the liver, bone, intestine, placenta and the kidneys. Plasma total activity is therefore of poor specificity in detecting liver disease. Plasma ALP is high at birth (placental ALP) but falls rapidly (half life 3-4 days) within the first week (see Biochemical reference ranges). Whilst increased activity is particularly associated with cholestatic as opposed to hepatitic liver disease, it is also increased in osteopenia of prematurity (see Chapter 8) and other bone disease. Although ALP has tissue specific isoenzymes, and measurement can help determine the origin of an increased activity, in practice specific isoenzyme measurement is not routinely available.

Albumin

Low plasma concentration can occur as a result of reduced synthesis in chronic liver disease but there are many other potential causes. It is both a non-specific and insensitive indicator of hepatic function.

γ-Glutamyl transferase (γGT)

This enzyme is widely distributed in human tissue. Most of the activity in the blood appears to originate primarily from the hepatobiliary system, specifically the biliary tract. Increased activity may arise from enzyme induction by drugs (e.g. some anticonvulsants) or from damage to, or disease of, the bile ducts. Plasma activities of the enzyme are much higher in neonates than in older children (see Biochemical reference ranges). Activity declines after the first 1-3 months, reaching adult levels by 5-7 months. Increased activities (e.g. 10-fold) occur in biliary atresia and other causes of cholestatic disease. In hepatitis, values are usually normal or only slightly elevated. γGT can also be elevated in cholestatic liver disease caused by prolonged parenteral nutrition (see Chapter 14). In the inherited disorders of bile acid metabolism, plasma levels of γGT are normal or low.

Specific causes of prolonged jaundice

Prematurity

Physiological jaundice is frequently prolonged beyond ten days in the preterm infant. This would not normally merit investigation in a well, preterm baby prior to 21 days of age when the total and conjugated bilirubin fractions would be checked.

Breast feeding and jaundice (see Chapter 14)

Plasma bilirubin concentration tends to be higher in breast-fed than in bottle-fed infants, but usually the difference is minimal. In an estimated 2.5% of breast-fed infants, unconjugated hyperbilirubinaemia persists beyond the second week up until 16 weeks. Affected infants are well and thriving and the conjugated bilirubin is not increased. This condition is benign; if breast feeding is discontinued for 24 to 48h, the bilirubin falls. A similar degree of jaundice occurs in 25% of siblings of affected infants; the exact cause of the jaundice is probably multifactorial although in some infants polymorphisms in the gene encoding glucuronyl transferase have been detected. These polymorphisms result in reduced activity of the conjugating enzyme and a predisposition to Gilbert's Syndrome in later life.

Perinatal infections (see Chapter 12)

Neonatal hepatitis may be caused by a variety of infections (see Figure 6.6) that can be acquired *in utero*, during delivery or early in the newborn period from the mother or from blood transfusions. The baby with an intrauterine infection is more likely to be small for dates, to have failed to thrive and have splenomegaly in addition to hepatomegaly. Infective liver disease presents with conjugated hyperbilirubinaemia, bilirubinuria, pale stools, and increased plasma activities of liver enzymes. However, although a common problem worldwide, infective hepatitis accounts for only a small proportion of cases of conjugated hyperbilirubinaemia in developed countries.

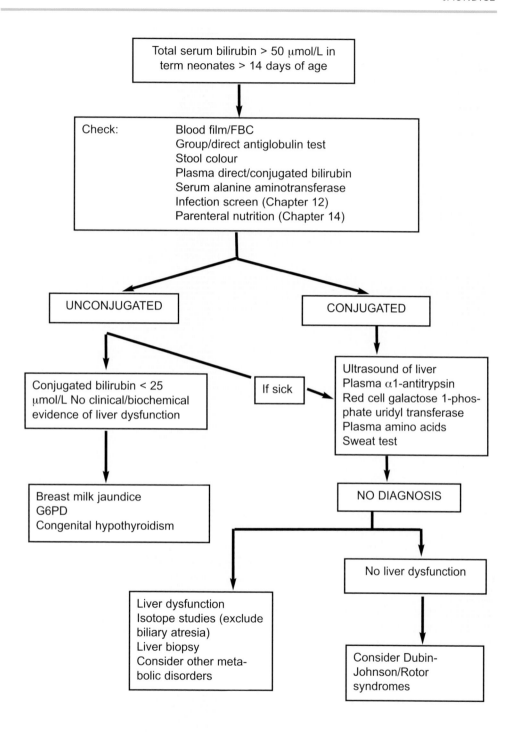

Figure 6.5. Investigation of prolonged jaundice.

	Time of presentation	Diagnostic test(s)
Transplacental		
Rubella	Day 1	Serology, culture
Cytomegalovirus	Day 1	PCR, serology, culture
Toxoplasmosis	Day 1 Day 1 - 12 weeks	PCR, serology Serology
Perinatally or post-natally acquired		
Herpes simplex virus	1-2 weeks	Isolation from vesicles or swabs PCR antigen detection
Cytomegalovirus	4-8 weeks	PCR, serology, culture
Hepatitis A	Any	Serology
Hepatitis B	6-12 weeks	Serology
Enteroviruses, e.g. Coxsackie	Any	Culture (stool and throat swabs) PCR

Figure 6.6. Infections causing neonatal hepatitis.

Biliary atresia

Approximately 1 in 10-20,000 babies born in the UK has biliary atresia – the principal cause of extrahepatic biliary disease in neonates. Babies with biliary atresia are usually of normal birth weight and have hepatomegaly without splenomegaly. Suspicion of the diagnosis should however be raised by prolonged jaundice due predominantly to conjugated bilirubin and pale stools. Liver enzymes are usually elevated and it may be difficult to distinguish this condition from neonatal hepatitis. Diagnosis is made by visualisation of the biliary tree by ultrasound, liver biopsy and radioisotope scan or endoscopic retrograde cholangiopancreatography (ERCP), and liver biopsy. It is very important to make the diagnosis promptly as surgery (hepato-portoenterostomy procedure) gives the best results if performed before eight weeks of age. As a result of increased publicity and professional awareness, late referral is less common, but sadly still occurs with consequent poorer outcome.

The other major cause of extrahepatic biliary disease in the neonate is a choledochal cyst, which can be diagnosed by ultrasound.

α1-Antitrypsin deficiency

α1-Antitrypsin deficiency with either the ZZ or SZ phenotypes can present as prolonged neonatal cholestatic jaundice, although liver disease is by no means an invariable consequence. The incidence is approximately 1 in 2000 births. The presentation is variable: some infants have evidence of only mild liver disease that resolves completely, while others progress rapidly to liver failure and, without liver transplantation, will die. The clinical picture can be indistinguishable from that of biliary atresia. Interpretation of plasma α1-antitrypsin concentration is difficult in the newborn because of changing concentrations (see Biochemical reference ranges); plasma concentrations *per se* do not allow a definitive diagnosis to be made, although a concentration of <1.1 g/L during the first four weeks of life is suggestive of a possible deficiency. Phenotyping is required to establish the diagnosis.

Byler disease (Progressive familial intrahepatic cholestasis I)

Byler disease is one of several, clinically similar, congenital disorders characterised by progressive familial intrahepatic cholestasis (PFIC), and caused by a group of bile duct transport defects.

In PFIC 1, presentation is with cholestatic jaundice and hepatomegaly. A prominent finding is a low γGT. Pancreatitis and diarrhoea are common and plasma cholesterol concentration is normal or low, i.e. atypical of cholestasis. Patients with PFIC 2 have a different mutation but also a low γGT. A further variant (PFIC3) has been identified with an elevated γGT.

Alagille syndrome

This syndrome is characterised by cholestasis caused by a decreased number of intrahepatic bile ducts and various congenital malformations. Hepatomegaly is usually present together with facial dysmorphism and congenital cardiac anomalies. It is very rare with an incidence of approximately 1 in 100,000 births, and with equal sex incidence. The genetic defect has been identified to mutations of a transmembrane protein coded on chromosome 20.

Genetic defects of bilirubin metabolism in the neonate

As for Crigler-Najjar Syndrome Type I which presents with early and severe neonatal jaundice, these are all rare inherited defects and, in the absence of a family history, should only be considered after exclusion of the above more common causes.

Crigler-Najjar syndrome type II

This is a milder form of the disease with serum unconjugated bilirubin usually below 340 μmol/L. Although UDP-glucuronyl transferase activity is reduced, it is not completely deficient as in Crigler-Najjar Type I, and jaundice can be significantly reduced by phenobarbital treatment. The family, i.e. parents and siblings, should be investigated for jaundice. Some parents have a mild unconjugated hyperbilirubinaemia with no liver dysfunction; this may represent a heterozygous form of the disease.

Dubin-Johnson and Rotor syndromes

Presentation of both syndromes is with a benign conjugated hyperbilirubinaemia with normal liver size, normal plasma liver enzyme activities and abnormalities of coproporphyrin metabolism. The extent of jaundice is enhanced by stress, intercurrent illness or fasting. Both these disorders are benign with an excellent prognosis. Although the two disorders are phenotypically similar, they differ with respect to urinary coproporphyrin excretion. Analysis of the

ABCC2 gene allows definitive diagnosis of Dubin-Johnson syndrome.

Neonatal haemochromatosis (Gestational alloimmune liver disease)

Although rare, this condition is an important cause of acute liver failure in neonates. The major cause is gestational alloimmune liver disease, where it is hypothesized that activation of the complement cascade and membrane attack complexes results in fetal hepatocyte damage. Excess storage of hepatic and extra-hepatic iron begins prenatally and may be secondary to a deficiency of fetal hepcidin as a result of fetal hepatocyte injury. The phenotypic spectrum of the disorder is wide as it is now apparent that hepatic iron overload is not always present. There is an increased risk of recurrence in subsequent pregnancies of > 90%, but maternal treatment from the second trimester onwards with high dose IV immunoglobulin has been shown to improve neonatal outcome in such cases.

Presentation is with jaundice, hypoglycaemia and coagulopathy. Plasma ferritin concentration is greatly elevated. Exchange transfusion and treatment with high dose intravenous immunoglobulin has recently been shown to improve the poor outcome above previously seen with chelation and antioxidant therapy.

Endocrine disorders

Congenital hypothyroidism, adrenal disorders and congenital hypopituitarism are recognised causes of prolonged neonatal jaundice and should always be considered. Endocrine investigations should include measurement of plasma free thyroxine, TSH (check neonatal screening results) and cortisol concentrations. Liver disease usually resolves within six weeks following appropriate treatment.

Inherited metabolic disease and prolonged jaundice

Whilst individually rare, collectively inherited metabolic disorders account for a significant percentage of causes of neonatal liver disease (Chapter 10). The jaundiced baby with an inborn error of metabolism (IEM) may be acutely unwell with associated signs and symptoms eg dysmorphism. The diagnosis of a metabolic disorder requires further biochemical investigation (Figure 6.7). Principal amongst disorders of carbohydrate metabolism, galactosaemia is known to present with severe liver disease. Conversely fructosaemia is unlikely to present in the neonate unless a sucrose-containing milk formula or medicines have been given. Within some ethic groups, tyrosinaemia is known to be an important cause of neonatal liver disease. Although cystic fibrosis rarely causes cholestasis, in a few cases biliary obstruction can be severe enough to resemble biliary atresia. G6PD deficiency (see Chapter 11) should be considered in any jaundiced infant of Mediterranean descent. Amongst the lysosomal storage disorders, Niemann-Pick type C is a rare cause of neonatal hepatitis caused by a defect of cholesterol esterification. Some infants have fetal ascites and 60-70% present with prolonged cholestasis, hepatomegaly and splenomegaly. The liver has a characteristic histological appearance. In most infants, the jaundice and liver disease resolve. Neurological symptoms usually develop after five years of age.

Other rarer causes of cholestatic jaundice include disorders of bile acid synthesis, Zellweger syndrome, and bile salt transport defects. In addition LCHAD deficiency, mevalonic kinase deficiency, carbohydrate deficient glycoprotein syndrome and Smith-Lemli-Opitz syndrome, ARC syndrome, citrin deficiency and mitochondrial DNA deletion syndromes can all present with cholestatic jaundice.

BLOOD
- Acylcarnitines (plasma/dried blood spot)

- Very long chain fatty acids (plasma)

- Amino acids (urine and plasma)

- Galactose 1-phosphate uridyltransferase (qualitative screen) (erythrocytes)

- Glucose 6-phosphate dehydrogenase – if high risk group, check that screening has been performed (erythrocytes)

- DNA testing

URINE
- Amino acids

- Bile acids

- Organic acids

Figure 6.7. Specific biochemical investigation for metabolic disease in patients with persistent neonatal jaundice.

A comprehensive investigative strategy for prolonged jaundice is presented in Figure 6.8. Highly specialist tests should be considered in the context of history, clinical presentation and the results of other investigations eg radiology, virology, bacteriology, haematology and histology.

Disorder	Type of jaundice	Supporting information	Further investigations
Breast feeding	U	Jaundice spontaneously resolves if breast feeding withdrawn. No clinical or biochemical evidence of liver dysfunction	Genotyping for Gilbert polymorphism.
Infection	C/U	Improves with treatment	Infection screen (see Figure 6.6) Urine culture
Rhesus/ABO isoimmunisation	C	History of early haemolytic jaundice	
Total parenteral nutrition (TPN)	C	History of TPN	Nil if resolves after TPN has been discontinued
Biliary atresia	C	Pale stools	Liver ultrasound/Tc-DISIDA scan
α1-antitrypsin deficiency	C	Reduced concentration of α1-antitrypsin	Plasma phenotyping
Hypothyroidism	U	Clinical signs	TSH, free T4
Intrahepatic biliary disease: Alagille syndrome	C	Characteristic facies Congenital abnormalities:- Pulmonary artery hypoplasia	Hypoplasia or reduced intra-hepatic bile ducts on liver biopsy
Galactosaemia	C	Hepatomegaly, hypoglycaemia Urinary reducing substances +ve	Red cell galactose 1-phosphate uridyltransferase
Tyrosinaemia type I	C	Hypoglycaemia, abnormal clotting. Alkaline phosphatase increased	Plasma amino acids (tyrosine and methionine). Plasma AFP and urine succinylacetone.
Zellweger syndrome	C	Hypotonia Dysmorphic features Neurological dysfunction	Plasma very long chain fatty acids
Glucose 6-phosphate dehydrogenase deficiency	U	Usually present early Drug induced family history Asian or African race	Erythrocyte glucose 6-phosphate dehydrogenase

Figure 6.8. Investigation of prolonged or late presenting jaundice (Cont.).

Disorder	Type of jaundice	Supporting information	Further investigations
Crigler-Najjar types I & II	U	No liver dysfunction Type II responds to phenobarbitone	Glucuronides in bile Glucuronyl transferase in liver
Cystic fibrosis	C	Meconium ileus Family history	Neonatal screening blood spot immunoreactive trypsin Sweat chloride DNA testing
Hypopituitarism	C	Hypoglycaemia Dysmorphism Optic nerve hypoplasia Low free T4	Plasma free T4 and TSH Plasma cortisol
Citrin deficiency	C	Hepatic steatosis, mild hepatomegaly,	DNA testing, plasma amino acids, sugar chromatography hypoglycaemia
Mitochondrial DNA deletion syndrome		Hepatomegaly, acute/ progressive hepatic failure, hypoglycaemia, lactic acidosis, neurological dysfunction	DNA testing
Progressive familial intrahepatic cholestasis	C	Hepatomegaly, pruritis, pancreatitis	GGT, Total bile acids, DNA testing

C = conjugated   U = unconjugated

Figure 6.8 (Cont.). Investigation of prolonged or late presenting jaundice.

Notes

If plasma amino acids show an increased tyrosine or methionine, further investigation for suspected tyrosinaemia should include α-fetoprotein. Because this is increased post-natally, age related neonatal reference ranges are required for interpretation. Depending on the result further investigation includes erythrocyte porphobilinogen synthetase and urinary succinylacetone/urinary d-ALA. If the baby is acutely ill, consider investigating for urea cycle defects, fatty acid oxidation defects and glycogen storage disorders.

Further reading

Ahlfors CE, Wennberg RP, Ostrow JD, Tiribelli C. Unbound (free) bilirubin: Improving the paradigm for evaluating neonatal jaundice. Clin Chem 2009; **55**: 1288-1299.

Cabrera-Abreu JC, Green A. γ-Glutamyltransferase: value of its measurement in paediatrics. Ann Clin Biochem 2002; **39**: 22-25.

Debray F-G, de Halleux V, Guidi O, Detrembleur N, Gaillez S, Rausin L *et al*. Neonatal liver cirrhosis without iron overload caused by gestational alloimmune liver disease. Pediatrics 2012; **129**: e1076-e1079.

Hartley JL, Davenport M, Kelly DA. Biliary atresia. Lancet 2009; **374**: 1704-1713.

Heap S, Holder G. National Metabolic Biochemistry Network Best Practice Guidelines Neonatal & Infant Jaundice in Inherited Metabolic Disorders.v3 July 2012 www.metbio.net downloaded June 2013.

Investigation of Neonatal Conjugated Hyperbilirbinaemia. Liver Steering Group BSPGHAN, Revised Feb 2012. Accessed October 2013.

Jaundice in newborn babies under 28 days.https://www.nice.org.uk/Guidance/CG98 NICE Clinical Guideline 98 May 2010.

Kirk JM. Neonatal jaundice: a critical review of the role and practice of bilirubin analysis. Ann Clin Biochem 2008; **45**: 452-462.

Lopriore E, Mearin ML, Oepkes D, Devlieger R, Whitington PF. Neonatal hemochromotosis: management, outcome and prevention. Prenatal Diagnosis 2013; **33**: 1221-1225.

O'Connor MC, Lease MA, Whalen BL. How to use: transcutaneous bilirubinometry. Arch Dis Child Educ Pract Ed. 2013; **98**: 154-159.

Preer GL, Philipp BL. Understanding and managing breast milk jaundice. Arch Dis Child Fetal Neonatol Ed. 2011; **96**: F461-466.

Diseases of the Liver and Biliary System in Children. Edited by Deirdre A. Kelly. Chapters 2, 3. Blackwell 1999.

Shapiro SM. Chronic bilirubin encephalopathy: diagnosis and outcome. Seminars in Fetal & Neonatal Medicine 2010; **15**: 157-163.

Chapter 7
Glucose

Summary

- Blood glucose falls rapidly after birth but normalises by 12 hours of life.

- Prolonged severe hypoglycaemia can result in death and brain damage.

- Babies at risk of hypoglycaemia should be identified at birth and blood glucose monitored.

- The commonest cause of severe prolonged hypoglycaemia is hyperinsulinism.

- Diagnostic samples should be collected during a hypoglycaemic episode before giving glucose.

- Transient hyperglycaemia is common in very low birth weight neonates receiving intravenous glucose.

- POCT is invaluable for glucose monitoring.

- Abnormal POCT results must be confirmed by laboratory measurements.

Blood glucose in the neonate

In utero the fetus receives a continuous glucose supply via the placenta, and fetal blood sugar concentrations reflect those of the mother. Glucose is the major source of energy for the fetal brain. Post-delivery, with the sudden discontinuation of nutrient supply, the blood glucose concentration falls abruptly, often to as low as 1.7 mmol/L at 1-2 hours after birth in healthy neonates. Normally hypoglycaemia is corrected rapidly and with normal feeding, blood glucose is usually ≥ 2.5 mmol/L by 12 hours of life. Fatty acid oxidation contributes significantly to energy production and also generates ketone bodies which are used effectively by the brain as an alternative fuel to glucose. The metabolic adaptation to extrauterine life is highly integrated and dependent on a normal endocrine response, substrate availability (glycogen and fat stores), and enzyme pathways. If these are inadequate or defective, postnatal hypoglycaemia may be prolonged and persistent without intervention.

Definition of hypoglycaemia

Neonatal hypoglycaemia in both term and preterm babies is widely defined as a plasma glucose concentration of < 2.5 mmol/L. Although this lacks rigorous scientific justification it is useful practically for identifying babies who may be at risk of symptomatic hypoglycaemia. These risks are influenced by the availability of other metabolic fuels, particularly ketone bodies, and by co-morbid conditions such as circulatory compromise and sepsis. The risk is also increased significantly in endocrine and metabolic disorders in which the supply of ketone bodies is also reduced, as in hyperinsulinaemic disorders and fatty acid oxidation defects. *Symptomatic* hypoglycaemia usually occurs when plasma glucose falls to ≤ 1.1-1.5 mmol/L.

Clinical sequelae of hypoglycaemia

The clinical manifestations of acute hypoglycaemia in the neonate are neurological. They range from irritability (often described as 'jitteriness'), sweating, lethargy, poor feeding, hypothermia and hypotonia to severe disturbances with cyanotic spells and apnoea, stupor, coma and seizures. Clinical signs caused by hypoglycaemia should be alleviated by correction of the blood glucose. The transient, self-limiting, fall in glucose during adaptation to extra-uterine life does not cause symptoms in the vast majority of healthy neonates. Prolonged or recurrent profound hypoglycaemia may cause brain damage.

Measurement of blood glucose

Glucose can be measured in plasma or whole blood. Whole blood glucose concentration is 13-18% lower than plasma glucose depending on the haematocrit. Further, glucose concentrations are 10-15% higher in arterial than venous blood, with intermediate values in capillary blood.

Point of care testing

Neonatal units use Point of Care Testing (POCT) with reagent strips and glucose meters as a rapid means of estimating glucose concentration in whole blood. Glucose meters can also measure haematocrit to give a better approximation of plasma glucose concentration. Most systems can be interfaced with laboratory and hospital information systems. The advantages of POCT are that ≤ 10 µL of blood can be collected by capillary heel prick, repeated sampling is feasible, and results are available within one to two minutes. The disadvantages are lack of precision and accuracy at the decision levels of 2.5 mmol/L and 10 mmol/L.

Confirmatory analysis

It is essential that abnormal results from POCT are confirmed quickly either via a blood gas analyser equipped with a glucose module or in the laboratory. This must not delay treatment of a symptomatic baby, which should be started promptly after taking the confirmatory sample. Continuous monitoring of glucose with subcutaneous electrodes might, in future, have a role for monitoring glucose in selected neonates.

Quality assurance and recording results

Responsibility and accountability for POCT glucose measurements must be clear, with written protocols for operation, audits, internal and external quality assurance schemes, training and review of performance. It is essential that there is a permanent record of all POCT glucose results, whether normal or abnormal.

Screening neonates for hypoglycaemia

Hypoglycaemia is a common metabolic problem in neonatal medicine particularly in premature infants. In the majority of healthy, full-term neonates, the frequently observed low blood glucose concentration is a reflection of normal metabolic adaptation to extra uterine life. However in order to protect babies from hypoglycaemic brain damage, it is essential that those at risk at birth are identified, their blood glucose monitored and their glucose intake supplemented, if necessary, to avoid hypoglycaemia. Figure 7.1 lists pre- and perinatal risk factors.

Disturbances in maternal metabolism before and during labour
Diabetes: gestational or pre-gestational
Treatment with β sympathomimetic drugs
Treatment with oral hypoglycaemic agents
Intrapartum dextrose infusion

Known fetal abnormalities
Erythroblastosis fetalis, fetal hydrops

Abnormalities in the baby at birth
Prematurity
Intrauterine growth restriction (IUGR) - wasted appearance
Small or large for gestational age
Polycythaemia
Presence of syndromic features: hypopituitarism, Beckwith-Wiedemann syndrome

Poor condition perinatally
Hypoxia-ischaemia
Hypothermia
Cyanosis/heart failure

Figure 7.1. Pre and perinatal risk factors for hypoglycaemia.

Management of hypoglycaemia

Whilst there is no indication for measuring blood glucose in term neonates who are well, babies at risk should be screened from birth. Prematurity is the most common risk factor. Prevention is the most appropriate management in high risk infants. Early, frequent enteral feeding and close monitoring of blood glucose should minimise the risk of hypoglycaemia occurring. Any baby with clinical signs consistent with hypoglycaemia must have blood or plasma glucose measured immediately. 'Operational thresholds' for blood glucose concentrations have been proposed for continued monitoring and/or intervention. Management should follow a schedule similar to that shown in Figure 7.2.

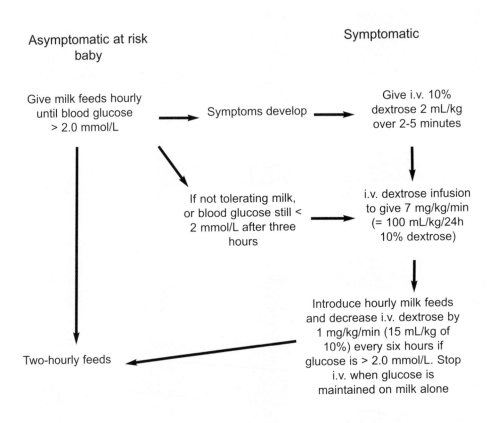

Figure 7.2. Initial management of babies at risk of hypoglycaemia – both asymptomatic and symptomatic.

Causes of hypoglycaemia

Hypoglycaemia can occur as a consequence of an inadequate supply of glucose, an excessive glucose requirement, or conditions associated with hyperinsulinism. It is often multifactorial. Figure 7.3 summarises the main causes. After the first 24 hours of life, hyperinsulinism is the most common cause of resistant hypoglycaemia.

Preterm or small for gestational age (SGA) infants

Prematurity is the most common risk factor. Usually hypoglycaemia is transient and resolves quickly. However it may persist for several days, notably in babies who are small or large for gestational age. The risk of hypoglycaemia is due to inadequate glycogen reserves at birth and little adipose tissue. This is exacerbated by high energy demands and a blunted hepatic response to the glucose-raising counter-regulatory hormones. If glucose infusion is needed initially, weaning onto milk feeds can usually be achieved after 2-3 days. Occasionally, high glucose administration rates are necessary to maintain plasma glucose ≥ 2.5 mmol/L.

Cause	Aetiology
Antenatal/perinatal treatments of the mother	β-sympathomimetics, oral hypoglycaemic agents, intrapartum dextrose infusion
Low glycogen and fat stores	Prematurity; intrauterine growth restriction
Excessive demands for glucose	Perinatal hypoxia/ischaemia; sepsis; respiratory distress; cyanotic heart disease; hypothermia (low environmental temperature); polycythaemia
Poor glucose intake	Delayed feeding; feeding difficulties; inadequate supply of milk or intravenous dextrose (parenteral nutrition)
Defects of glycogenolysis, gluconeogenesis or ketogenesis	
Acquired	Liver failure
Inherited enzyme defects	Glycogen storage disease
	Gluconeogenic defects
	Defects in fatty acid catabolism, ketogenesis and ketone body utilisation
	Galactosaemia
	Organic acid disorders
Hormone deficiencies	Hypopituitarism; growth hormone (GH) deficiency; ACTH deficiency; cortisol deficiency; congenital adrenal hypoplasia; adrenal hypoplasia/ insufficiency
Hyperinsulinism	
Transient	Infant of a diabetic mother (gestational or pre-gestational)
	Rhesus haemolytic disease
	Birth hypoxia/ischaemia
	Small for gestational age (SGA) infants
	Beckwith-Wiedemann syndrome
	Insulin administration: iatrogenic; malicious
Persistent	Congenital hyperinsulinism of infancy (CHI)
	Congenital disorders of glycosylation (CDG)
	Tyrosinaemia type 1

Figure 7.3. Causes of hypoglycaemia.

Hypoxia and/or ischaemia

Babies who become hypoxic during labour or suffer perinatal hypoxia/ischaemia often have extremely low blood glucose concentrations within minutes of delivery, particularly those with low birth weight. Babies with cyanotic heart disease and/or poor peripheral perfusion are also at risk of hypoglycaemia. This is due to rapid consumption of glycogen reserves. Hyperinsulinism may also occur in these babies and contribute to hypoglycaemia.

Hormone deficiencies

Hypoglycaemia can result from defects of the glucose counter-regulatory hormones:
- Hypopituitarism.
- Isolated ACTH (hence cortisol) deficiency.
- Cortisol deficiency due to primary adrenal insufficiency: congenital adrenal hyperplasia/ hypoplasia.

Hyperinsulinism

Hyperinsulinaemic hypoglycaemia results from continued and inappropriate insulin secretion when the plasma glucose is low. It may be a transient or persisting disturbance (Figure 7.3). Excessive insulin suppresses glycogenolysis, gluconeogenesis, lipolysis and ketogenesis. Reduction of both of the main fuels for the brain – glucose and the ketone bodies – makes this a particularly dangerous situation. Hyperinsulinaemic babies are at high risk for acute symptomatic hypoglycaemia and irreversible brain damage. Newborns who were hyperinsulinaemic *in utero* are often macrosomic. The requirement for glucose infusion rates of greater than 10 mg/kg/min to maintain the plasma glucose above 3.0 mmol/L is an alerting clue to inappropriate insulin secretion.

TRANSIENT HYPERINSULINISM

Hyperinsulinism occurs transiently in a variety of disorders or circumstances (see Figure 7.3) and generally resolves within a few days. It is most common in infants of poorly controlled diabetic mothers. Hyperinsulinism following perinatal hypoxia/ischaemia and in babies with intrauterine growth restriction and Beckwith-Wiedemann syndrome may persist for several weeks and require treatment. Generally the cause of hyperinsulinism is evident in these situations and does not require further investigation.

Maternal or gestational diabetes mellitus

Most infants of mothers with well-controlled diabetes mellitus are of normal size, healthy and not hyperinsulinaemic. However, they fall into the 'at risk' category for hypoglycaemia and should all have blood glucose screening as outlined above (Figure 7.2) for at least 12 hours after birth. The fetus of a poorly controlled diabetic mother has episodic hyperglycaemia and increased insulin secretion. Hyperinsulinism is the primary cause of the hypoglycaemia which may develop as early as one hour of age and usually by 12 hours. It is transient and generally resolves within the first 24-72 hours of life. The fetus can be as severely affected in gestational diabetes as in established maternal diabetes. An unexpectedly large infant with early hypoglycaemia may result when the mother has hitherto unrecognised glucose intolerance.

Beckwith-Wiedemann syndrome

This condition is an overgrowth disorder with a prevalence of around 1 in 15,000 live births, with mutation or deletion of genes within the short arm of chromosome 11 which are imprinted (expressed differently) depending on whether they are of maternal or paternal origin. Hypoglycaemia is reported in 30% to 50% of cases and is associated with islet cell hypertrophy. It is usually transient and resolves in a few days. These babies must be monitored for hypoglycaemia from birth following guidelines for 'at risk' babies.

Exogenous hyperinsulinism

Insulin may be administered accidentally, surreptitiously (factitious hypoglycaemia) or maliciously. This can be confirmed by demonstrating a high insulin concentration, without an increase in C-peptide, in the presence of hypoglycaemia.

Persistent hyperinsulinism

Persistent hyperinsulinism is likely when the plasma glucose can only be maintained at ≥ 3.0 mmol/L by continuous intravenous infusion of glucose at a high rate. Figure 7.4 presents the criteria for establishing this diagnosis, in the absence of an obvious cause (see above). This must be done quickly to avert the risk of a prolonged hypoglycaemic episode and, if confirmed, prompt consultation with an endocrinologist/metabolic specialist is essential.

Clinical clues
Macrosomia (not invariable)
Severe symptomatic hypoglycaemia (glucose often < 1.0 mmol/L)
Glucose infusion > 10mg/kg/min to maintain plasma glucose > 3.0 mmol/L

Biochemical criteria when hypoglycaemic
Laboratory or blood gas analyser glucose ≤ 2.5 mmol/L
Insulin and C-peptide raised inappropriately
No ketonuria
Increase in plasma glucose following i.v. glucagon

Associated biochemical abnormalities
Raised ammonia: Hyperinsulinaemia and hyperammonaemia (HIHA) syndrome

Genetic testing
Available for genetic defects causing congenital hyperinsulinism with diffuse pancreatic hyperplasia

Figure 7.4. Diagnosis of neonatal hyperinsulinism.

The commonest cause is congenital hyperinsulinism of infancy (CHI), formerly termed persistent hyperinsulinaemic hypoglycaemia of infancy (PHI).

Congenital hyperinsulinism of infancy (CHI)

The incidence is around 1 in 35,000 to 40,000 in the general population. The disorder may be familial or sporadic. There is unregulated insulin secretion by the pancreatic β islet cells because the pathway which links glucose uptake to insulin secretion is defective (see Figure 7.5).

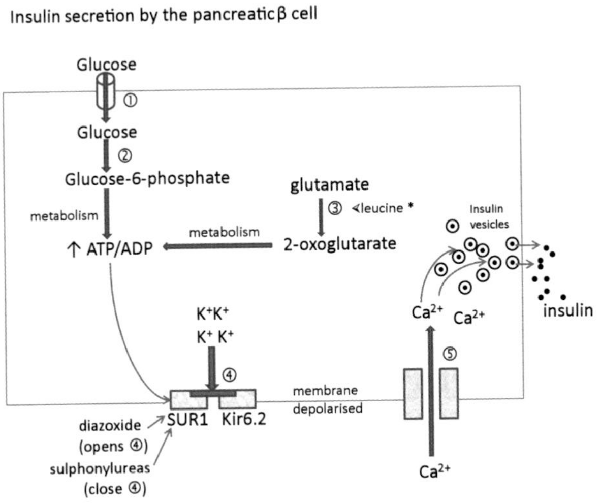

Insulin secretion by the pancreatic β cell

Figure 7.5. Mechanism of insulin secretion by the pancreatic β cell.

Normally, glucose is transported from the blood into the β cells (1), phosphorylated by gluco-kinase (2), and oxidised. This increases the ATP/ADP ratio which, in turn, closes ATP-gated potassium (K_{ATP}) channels (4) in the cell membrane. The resulting increase in intracellular K^+ depolarises the membrane, opening voltage-gated calcium channels and cellular influx of Ca^{2+} triggers (5) release of insulin from storage granules. Mutations of eight genes involved in this pathway have been identified to date. Some present neonatally.

POTASSIUM K_{ATP} CHANNEL MUTATIONS.

Loss of function mutations of the genes encoding the potassium channel are the commonest defects. Mutations cause persistent closure of the potassium channels, membrane depolari-sation and uncontrolled insulin release. There is diffuse islet cell hyperplasia throughout the pancreas. The priority in management is to maintain the blood glucose between 3.5-6.0 mmol/L. Feeds are supplemented with glucose polymers and dextrose is given intravenously, and glucagon for short-term management. Insulin-lowering drugs such as diazoxide and octreotide are also employed. When medical treatment fails, babies require a near-total pancreatectomy. This has a high risk for diabetes mellitus and exocrine pancreatic insuffi-ciency.

HYPERINSULINAEMIA AND HYPERAMMONAEMIA (HIHA) SYNDROME.

This is the second commonest cause of CHI. It is due to an activating mutation of glutamate dehydrogenase (GDH). GDH(3) is activated by leucine (Figure 7.5), and affected babies may become hypoglycaemic both before and after feeds. They also have persistently raised ammonia concentrations, which has been attributed to an increased release of ammonia by GDH in the liver. Although the presentation is usually later in infancy, HIHA must be excluded in hyperinsulinaemic neonates since it responds to diazoxide treatment.

Inherited metabolic disorders

Inherited deficiencies of enzymes needed for glycogenolysis, gluconeogenesis, fatty acid oxidation and ketogenesis may present neonatally (Chapter 10).

Glycogen storage diseases (GSDs)

Defects of the glucose-6-phosphatase system are the most severe GSDs presenting neonatally, since they block glucose release from both glycogenolysis and gluconeogenesis. Affected babies are very intolerant of fasting and have severe recurrent hypoglycaemia and lactic acidosis, sometimes within only two hours of feeding.

Gluconeogenic defects

Although rare, deficiencies of phosphoenolpyruvate carboxykinase (PEPCK) and fructose 1,6 bisphosphatase may present with severe neonatal hypoglycaemia.

Fatty acid oxidation defects

These may be caused by a deficiency of one of the enzymes of the fatty acid β-oxidation cycle, by a defect in the carnitine cycle which transports fatty acid into the mitochondria, or by a defect in the transfer of electrons from β-oxidation to the respiratory chain (glutaric aciduria type II). Impaired fatty acid oxidation reduces the availability of ketone bodies as an ancillary source of energy with a greater dependency on glucose metabolism and glycogen stores. Hypoglycaemia is hypoketotic, and insulin secretion is suppressed. In most disorders plasma carnitine is low with an abnormal acylcarnitine profile, and the urinary organic acid profile is abnormal and frequently diagnostic.

Galactosaemia

Galactosaemia usually presents neonatally with liver dysfunction and encephalopathy, but hypoglycaemia also occurs infrequently.

Organic acidaemias

Babies presenting neonatally with organic acidaemias are very sick, acidotic and have a rapidly progressing encephalopathy. Hypoglycaemia may occur in those disorders of branched chain amino acid metabolism. Plasma amino acid and acylcarnitine profiles and urinary organic acids are diagnostic.

Disorders of ketone body synthesis and utilisation

Deficiency of 3-hydroxy-3-methylglutaryl-CoA (HMG-CoA) lyase prevents ketone body production from fatty acid and leucine catabolism. At presentation neonates have severe acidosis, hypoglycaemia without ketosis, and hyperammonaemia, abnormal plasma amino acids, acylcarnitines and urine organic acids. With deficiencies of mitochondrial acetoacetyl-CoA thiolase (β-ketothiolase) and succinyl-CoA 3-oxoacid CoA transferase (SCOT), ketone bodies are produced but cannot be used. Neonates presenting with these disorders are acidotic with tremendous ketosis and may be hypoglycaemic.

Investigation of hypoglycaemia

In many cases there is a clear explanation for hypoglycaemia, blood glucose concentration is restored and maintained as predicted by appropriate intervention, and the disturbance is transient and does not recur. However, if hypoglycaemia recurs, is prolonged, is symptomatic, or is asymptomatic but severe (blood glucose ≤ 1.5 mmol/L), urgent investigation is imperative. The differential diagnosis is between hyperinsulinism and a hypoglycaemic disorder with appropriately suppressed insulin secretion. This can only be established on blood collected at the time of hypoglycaemia *before* giving glucose, since this will stimulate insulin secretion and make the results uninterpretable. Because of the other endocrine and metabolic abnormalities that can cause hypoglycaemia, it is also important to obtain as much additional information as possible at the time of hypoglycaemia in order to classify the cause. Figure 7.6 lists a core of tests which will facilitate classification. It is common practice to have 'Hypoglycaemia packs' or 'Hypo Kits' with all the appropriate sample tubes for the individual analytes, details of the minimum specimen volumes required and their corresponding request forms See http://www.metbio.net/docs/MetBio-Guideline.

Glucose*†
Insulin *and C peptide
Ammonia
Lactate†
3-Hydroxybutyrate
Free fatty acids
Cortisol
Growth hormone
Amino acids
Acylcarnitines
Bicarbonate†

The first urine passed: ketones (stick test), reducing substances, organic acids and amino acids.

*priority requests; †glucose, lactate and bicarbonate are often analysed together with pH and blood gases on a blood gas analyser in the neonatal unit.

Figure 7.6. Biochemistry tests for a baby with symptomatic hypoglycaemia.

The blood sample may be taken without delaying the start of glucose infusion if an intravenous cannula is already *in situ* and the dextrose ready to connect. Laboratories may require at least 3 mL of blood for the full range of tests but, for small samples, the first priority must be insulin and an accurate plasma glucose concentration, followed by ammonia, 3-hydroxybutyrate (3-OHB) and lactate. The first urine is passed into a sterile container, ideally 3-5 mL for analysis of ketones (stick test), reducing substances, organic acids and amino acids.

Interpretation of biochemistry results when hypoglycaemic

Figure 7.7 summarises the diagnostic features of the biochemistry profiles obtained from the above investigation protocol. The concentrations of 3-OHB and FFA and their ratio can aid in the differential diagnosis of hypoglycaemia. In hyperinsulinism both concentrations will be reduced because insulin suppresses lipolysis. In defects of fatty acid oxidation, lipolysis occurs but there is failure to metabolise fatty acids to ketones so the ratio of FFA to 3-OHB is increased.

Cause of hypoglycaemia	Insulin	3-OHB	FFAs	Lactate	Additional clues
Hyperinsulinism	↑	↓	↓	↓	low branched chain amino acids
Inherited gluconeogenic defects	↓	↑	↑	↑	metabolic acidosis
Glycogen storage disorders (GSDs)	↓	↓		↑	
Inherited fatty acid oxidation disorders (defects of β-oxidation; carnitine cycle defects; glutaric aciduria type II)	↓	↓	↑	often ↑	high FFA:3-OHB ratio (>2.0) abnormal acylcarnitine profile abnormal urine organic acids raised ammonia raised ALT and AST
Inherited disorders of ketone body synthesis (HMGCoA lyase deficiency)	↓	↓	↑	↑	high FFA:3-OHB ratio (>2.0) raised ammonia, abnormal urine organic acids & blood acylcarnitines
Inherited disorders of ketone body utilisation (β-ketothiolase deficiency SCOT deficiency)	↓	↑	↑	variable	gross ketonuria urine organic acids: methylacetoacetate (β-ketothiolase deficiency)
Organic acidaemias	↓	↑		often ↑	metabolic acidosis abnormal acylcarnitines abnormal plasma amino acids often raised ammonia abnormal urine organic acids
Hypopituitarism; growth hormone deficiency/resistance	↓	↓	↓	N	
ACTH/cortisol deficiency	↓	↓	↓	N	low sodium/high potassium (congenital adrenal hyperplasia/hypoplasia); raised conjugated bilirubin
Acute liver failure	variable	variable		↑	high ALT and AST high ammonia; raised conjugated bilirubin

N = normal; FFA:3-OHB ratio = free fatty acid: 3-hydroxybutyrate ratio; ALT = alanine aminotransferase; AST= aspartate aminotransferase; HMG-CoA lyase = 3-hydroxymethylglutaryl-CoA lyase; GSD1a = glucose-6-phosphatase deficiency; GSD1b = glucose-6-phosphate transporter deficiency; β-ketothiolase = mitochondrial acetoacetyl-CoA thiolase deficiency; SCOT = succinyl-CoA 3-oxoacid CoA transferase deficiency.

Figure 7.7. Insulin and metabolite profiles of hypoglycaemic disorders.

Hyperglycaemia

Neonatal hyperglycaemia is generally defined as a plasma glucose concentration > 8.0 mmol/L. As with hypoglycaemia, accurate laboratory measurement of blood glucose is essential to confirm the diagnosis. It occurs frequently during the first week of life in very low birth weight babies in whom the mechanisms to control glucose homeostasis are still at an early stage of development. The immature endocrine and metabolic glucose-raising system is commonly stressed by severe illness including sepsis and treatment with glucocorticoids for lung disease. The problems are further compounded by excessive administration of intravenous glucose as dextrose alone or parenteral feeding. Figure 7.8 lists the risk factors.

Low birth weight for gestational age

Preterm birth

Stress from disease, medical procedures, surgery

Sepsis

Glucose infusion in excess of 6 mg/kg/min

Intralipid infusion associated with lipaemia

Medications: cortisol, dexamethasone, theophylline, aminophylline, metanephrine

Figure 7.8. Risk factors for hyperglycaemia.

Clinical sequelae of transient neonatal hyperglycaemia

Normally hyperglycaemia is transient and resolves without sequelae. Without an associated clinical disorder such as an underlying organic acidaemia, hyperglycaemia alone does not cause acidosis or ketosis. Hyperglycaemia with glycosuria may cause an osmotic diuresis, leading to dehydration with weight loss and hypotension if prolonged.

MANAGEMENT

Hyperglycaemia must be confirmed with an accurate plasma glucose measurement and a spurious result from dextrose contamination of the sample excluded. The suspected cause should be identified quickly and corrected if possible, by reducing the glucose infusion rate to the normal requirement and correction of fluid balance. Sepsis should be treated and the frequency and dose of steroids adjusted as applicable. If hyperglycaemia persists despite these measures, insulin may be given cautiously by continuous intravenous infusion. There is no consistency about the threshold for starting this treatment, but plasma glucose concentrations > 14.0 mmol/L or > 16.7 mmol/L have been proposed arbitrarily.

Neonatal diabetes

Neonatal diabetes mellitus is very rare (1 in 300,000 to 500,000 live births). It presents with failure to thrive, and in some cases dehydration and ketoacidosis which may be severe and lead to coma. Plasma insulin concentrations are low and insulin is needed to control hyperglycaemia. It is not an autoimmune disease, but results from a heterogeneous assortment of genetic defects that lead to abnormal development of the pancreatic islets, increased pancreatic β-cell apoptosis, or islet cell dysfunction with low insulin secretion. There are two distinct sub-types:

Permanent neonatal diabetes (PNDM)

PNDM accounts for around 40-50% of cases and persists throughout life. Defects of at least 10 genes are implicated, the commonest causes being activating mutations of the gene encoding the potassium channels of the β-islet cells (Figure 7.5). The mutated channels remain permanently open (as compared with the molecular defect in hyperinsulinism where the potassium channels are permanently closed). As a result, the cells do not secrete insulin in response to glucose. The next commonest causes are mutations of the insulin gene which lead to abnormal folding of proinsulin and to its intracellular destruction.

Transient neonatal diabetes (TNDM)

TNDM accounts for 50-60% of neonatal diabetes. Affected babies usually have intrauterine growth restriction (IUGR), and most present in the first week of life. Around one third have a family history of diabetes. The neonates have severe hyperglycaemia but are not usually ketonuric. Insulin concentrations are low or undetectable, and they require insulin treatment for around 3 to 18 months. The diabetes then resolves spontaneously, but in around 50% of cases recurs during childhood and adolescence. The majority of the other babies with TNDM are heterozygous for mutations of the genes coding the potassium channels.

Management of neonatal diabetes requires continuous intravenous infusion of insulin initially. There is limited experience of the best means of managing these babies safely long-term and they should be under the care of paediatric diabetic specialists.

Further reading

Aynsley-Green A, Hawden JM. Hypoglycaemia in the neonate: current controversies. Acta Paediatr Japonica 1997; **39 (suppl 1):** 512-516.

Beardsall K. Measurement of glucose levels in the newborn. Early Human Development 2010; **86:** 263-267.

Beardsall K, Vanhaesebrouck S, Ogilvey-Stuart AL, *et al.* Early insulin therapy in very-low-birth-weight infants. N Engl J Med. 2008; **359:** 1873-1884.

Cornblath M, Hawdon JM, Williams AF, Aynsley-Green A, Ward-Platt MP, Schwartz R, *et al.* Controversies regarding definition of neonatal hypoglycaemia: Suggested operational thresholds. Pediatrics 2000; **105:** 1141-1145.

Cowett RM, Farrag HM. Neonatal glucose metabolism. Cowett RM editor: Principles of Perinatal-Neonatal Metabolism. New York: Springer, 2nd edition, 1998. p. 683.

Flanagan SE, Patch A-M, Mackay DJG. Mutations in ATP-sensitive K$^+$ channel genes cause transient neonatal diabetes and permanent diabetes in childhood or adulthood. Diabetes 2007; **56:** 1930-1936.

Glaser B, Thornton P, Otonkoski T, Junien C. Genetics of neonatal hyperinsulinism. Arch Dis Child Neonatal Ed 2000; **82:** F79-F86.

Güemes M, Rahman SA, Hussain K What is a normal blood glucose? Arch Dis Child 2016; **101:** 569-574.

Hawdon JM, Aynsley-Green A. Disorders of blood glucose homoeostasis in the neonate. In Textbook of Neonatology, 3rd edition, Rennie JM, Robertson NRC (eds), London: Churchill Livingstone, 1999.

Hawdon J. Disorders of metabolic homeostasis. Rennie JM, Ed., Rennie and Roberton's Textbook of Neonatology 5th Edn., Churchill Livingstone, Elsevier, London UK 2012; Chapter 34 Part 1: pp 850-867.

Hemachandra AH, Cowett RM. Neonatal hyperglycemia. Pediatrics in Review. 1999; 20: e16. http://pedsinreview.aappublications.org/content/20/7/e16

Henderson M. Neonatal Hypoglycaemia. CPD Bulletin Clinical Biochemistry. 1999; **1:** 45-48.

Jain V, Chen M, Menon RK. Disorders of carbohydrate metabolism. C.A. Gleason, S.U. Devaskar, Eds., Avery's Diseases of the Newborn 9th Edn. Elsevier Saunders, Philadelphia PA, 2012; Chapter 94: pp 1320-1329.

James C, Kapoor RR, Ismail D, Hussain K. The genetic basis of congenital hyperinsulinism. J Med Genet 2009; **46:** 289-299.

Le HT, Harris NS, Estilong AJ, Olson A, Rice MJ. Blood glucose measurement in the intensive care unit: what is the best method? J Diabetes Sci Technol 2013; **7:** 489-499.

Palladino AA, Stanley CA. The hyperinsulinism/hyperammonemia syndrome. Rev Endocr Metab Disord 2010; **11:** 171-178.

Polak M, Cave H. Neonatal diabetes mellitus: a disease linked to multiple mechanisms. Orphanet Journal of Rare Diseases 2007; **2:** 12. http://www.OJRD.com/content/2/1/12.

Saudubray J-M, de Lonlay P, Touati G, Martin D, Nassogne MC *et al.* Genetic hypoglycaemia in infancy and childhood: Pathophysiology and diagnosis. J Inherit Metab Dis. 2000; **23:** 197-214.

Senniappan S, Shanti B, James C, Hussain K. Hyperinsulinaemic hypoglycaemia: genetic mechanisms, diagnosis and management. J Inherit Metab Dis 2012; **35:** 589-601.

Stanley CA, Baker L. The causes of neonatal hypoglycaemia. New Engl J Med 1999; **340:** 1200-1201.

Williams AF. Hypoglycaemia of the newborn – a review. Bull World Health Org 1997; **75:** 261-290.

Chapter 8
Calcium, magnesium and phosphate

Summary

- There is a transient, and self-correcting, physiological drop in calcium concentration in the first 24-48 hours of life.

- Disturbances in calcium homeostasis outwith this immediate postnatal period require investigation to determine the underlying cause.

- Disturbances in magnesium homeostasis are relatively uncommon in neonates.

- Very premature infants can be at particular risk of metabolic bone disease secondary to inadequate enteral phosphate intake.

Introduction

Disturbances in mineral metabolism, notably calcium, are common in premature infants and those requiring intensive care. In many cases the disturbances in calcium metabolism are thought to be an exaggerated response to the normal physiological transition from the intrauterine environment to neonatal independence. Disturbances in mineral metabolism may also result from pathological intrauterine conditions, birth trauma, maternal vitamin D deficiency and rarely hereditary disorders in hormone synthesis and function.

Calcium metabolism

There is active placental transport of calcium to the fetus from the maternal bloodstream, particularly in the third trimester such that fetal concentrations exceed those of the mother. This is to mineralise the fetal skeleton and is now thought to be controlled by fetal PTHrp. The principal calciotrophic hormones – parathyroid hormone (PTH) and vitamin D (1, 25-dihydroxy-vitamin D) – do not cross the placenta and together with calcitonin are thought to have a limited role in fetal calcium homeostasis. In addition circulating calcium is in metabolic flux with that in the developing skeleton.

At birth, the placental supply of calcium is abruptly lost and the neonate becomes dependent on intestinal calcium intake and the skeletal calcium stores to maintain a normal calcium at a time of accelerated skeletal growth. Plasma calcium concentration falls physiologically after birth to a nadir at 24-48 hours. In term neonates this may be to around 2.0 mmol/L but in premature infants, in whom the incidence of hypocalcaemia is between 30-90%, calcium can fall to below 1.75 mmol/L. Thereafter, there is a slow rise to a constant level with plasma calcium concentration maintained at 2.2-2.6 mmol/L. This is due to a compensatory increase in PTH synthesis in response to the falling calcium. PTH also stimulates the production of the active form of vitamin D which increases the intestinal absorption of calcium from the intestine. In addition renal control of plasma calcium through reabsorption and excretion becomes an important regulatory mechanism.

Calcium circulates in two forms – 60% is ultrafiltrable and 40% is protein bound. Of the bound calcium, 80-90% is bound to albumin, so that a decrease of plasma albumin concentration results in a decreased total calcium concentration. In hypoalbuminaemia, it can be assumed that each 1 g/L decrease in plasma albumin concentration decreases total plasma calcium concentration by approximately 0.025 mmol/L although this relationship is not maintained in preterm infants who are profoundly hypoalbuminaemic. Of ultrafiltrable calcium, 25% is complexed with phosphate and citrate and the remainder is free calcium ions. Ionised calcium in term neonates is normally 1.2 mmol/L. It is changes in this free, ionised fraction that produce clinical effects. Acidosis increases, and alkalosis decreases, the proportion of ionised calcium. Ionised calcium can be measured directly.

Regulation

Calcium homeostasis is under complex hormonal control. Total body calcium is mainly determined by gut absorption and renal excretion of calcium and is in dynamic exchange between bone and extracellular fluid as illustrated by Figures 8.1 and 8.2.

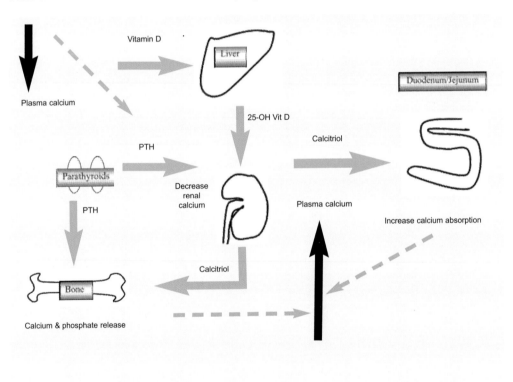

Figure 8.1. Hormonal maintenance of calcium concentration through bone resorption, reduced calcium excretion and increased intestinal absorption.

Factor	Action	Renal action	Effect
1,25-hydroxy cholecalciferol (calcitriol – active vitamin D)	Increased calcium absorption from duodenum/jejunum Releases calcium from bone	Decrease calcium excretion	Increase plasma calcium
PTH	Increased renal calcium reabsorption Releases calcium from bone Increased renal production of calcitriol	Decrease calcium excretion	Increase plasma calcium
Calcitonin NB. The physiological relevance of these effects is not well understood	Inhibits bone resorption	Increase calcium excretion	Decrease plasma calcium
Other: Hyperphosphataemia Loop diuretics		Increase calcium excretion	Decrease plasma calcium

Figure 8.2. Factors regulating calcium concentration.

Hypocalcaemia

In the neonate, small decreases in plasma calcium concentration below normal are usually asymptomatic. Hypocalcaemia, as defined as a total plasma calcium concentration below 1.8 mmol/L or ionised calcium concentration of less than 0.7 mmol/L, can cause clinical effects. Hypocalcaemia is classified as early – occurring in the first three days of life or late as in presenting from day four onwards. Late hypocalcaemia is less common.

Early hypocalcaemia is very often asymptomatic though infants can be jittery, have muscle twitching and if severe, seizures. The symptoms of late hypocalcaemia are more evident clinically and include:
• Twitching,
• Apnoeas,
• Fits,
• Prolonged QT interval on ECG,
• Chvostek's sign (of hypocalcaemia).

Note: Chvostek's sign can be demonstrated easily in a baby (tapping the facial nerve over the parotid gland in front of the ear causes a unilateral facial twitch).

Causes

Symptomatic early hypocalcaemia occurs more commonly in preterm infants, infants of diabetic mothers, and following perinatal hypoxia-ischaemia.

Pathogenesis	Cause
Exaggerated postnatal physiological fall	Prematurity Perinatal hypoxia-ischaemia Infants of diabetic mothers
Low intake	Inadequate oral/enteral intake Inadequate parenteral nutrition
Inadequate fetal accretion of calcium	Maternal vitamin D deficiency due to diet or treatment with anticonvulsants

Figure 8.3. Conditions associated with early neonatal hypocalcaemia.

In contrast the commonest cause of late neonatal hypocalcaemia is either PTH deficiency – either transient or sustained – or inadequate response to PTH

Pathogenesis	Cause
Transient hypoparathyroidism	Magnesium deficiency Cyanotic congenital heart disease Maternal hyperparathyroidism
Permanent hypoparathyroidism	Di George syndrome
Pseudohypoparathyroidism	End-organ resistance
Vitamin D deficiency	Fat malabsorption Maternal vitamin D deficiency 1α-hydroxylase deficiency
Chronic or metabolic disease in which metabolism of fat soluble vitamins is compromised	Liver or renal disease Organic acid disorders
Increased renal losses	Loop diuretics
Complex formation	High phosphate intake
Defective osteoclastic activity	Osteopetrosis

Figure 8.4. Conditions associated with late neonatal hypocalcaemia.

Investigation

Initial investigations in unexplained, persistent hypocalcaemia in a term baby should include measurement of plasma phosphate, magnesium, alkaline phosphatase, albumin and creatinine, and assessment of acid-base status. The mother should be investigated for vitamin D deficiency by measurement of plasma 25-hydroxycholecalciferol. Further investigation, including measurement of PTH and calcitriol, may be required (see Figures 8.5 and 8.6)

Cause	Presenting age	Plasma phosphate	Plasma alkaline phosphatase	Other plasma investigations
Physiological	24h-48h	N	N	
Vitamin D deficiency (maternal)	24h-48h	N/↓	↑	PTH↑/N
1α-hydroxylase deficiency	Infancy (rarely neonatal)	N/↓	↑	PTH↑/N
Malabsorption	Any	N/↓	↑	PTH↑/N
Hypoparathyroidism	Any (rarely neonatal)	N ↑		PTH ↓↓
Pseudohypo-parathyroidism	Any (rarely neonatal)	↑	N	PTH↑/N
Hypomagnesaemia	> 5 days	N	N	Mg++ <0.4 mmol/L
Iatrogenic	> 5 days	N/↑	N	

Figure 8.5. Typical biochemical findings in neonatal hypocalcaemia.

Management

Asymptomatic hypocalcaemia requires no treatment. Seizures respond to slow IV injection of 2 mL/kg 10% calcium gluconate under ECG control followed by oral supplements of calcium gluconate 200-500 mg/kg/24h and appropriate management of the underlying cause.

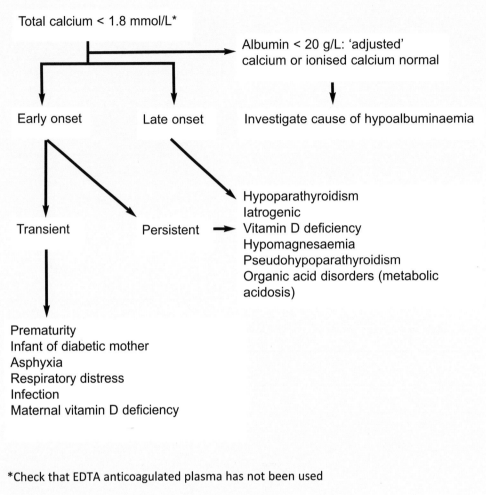

Total calcium < 1.8 mmol/L*

Albumin < 20 g/L: 'adjusted'
calcium or ionised calcium normal

Investigate cause of hypoalbuminaemia

Early onset

Late onset

Transient

Persistent

Hypoparathyroidism
Iatrogenic
Vitamin D deficiency
Hypomagnesaemia
Pseudohypoparathyroidism
Organic acid disorders (metabolic
acidosis)

Prematurity
Infant of diabetic mother
Asphyxia
Respiratory distress
Infection
Maternal vitamin D deficiency

*Check that EDTA anticoagulated plasma has not been used

Figure 8.6. Investigation of neonatal hypocalcaemia.

Hypercalcaemia

Hypercalcaemia is less common than hypocalcaemia in the neonatal period. It is defined as a calcium concentration greater than 2.60 mmol/L or an ionised calcium of greater than 1.33 mmol/L in a sample derived from free-flowing venous blood. The clinical features and causes of hypercalcaemia are shown in Figure 8.7.

Clinical features	Causes
Irritability	Transient or persistent hyperparathyroidism
Constipation	
Failure to thrive	Thyroid aplasia – absence of calcitonin producing cells
Polydipsia	Adrenal Insufficiency
Polyuria (caused by reduced renal concentrating ability)	Vitamin D intoxication
	Phosphate depletion
Nephrocalcinosis with renal failure	Subcutaneous fat necrosis
	Familial hypocalciuric hypercalcaemia
	William syndrome*

*William syndrome is a serious, sporadic disorder in which hypercalcaemia, thought to be caused by hypersensitivity to vitamin D, is associated with typical 'elfin' facies, developmental delay and supravalvular aortic stenosis. Treatment of the hypercalcaemia does not appear to affect the other features of this condition.

Figure 8.7. Clinical features and conditions associated with hypercalcaemia.

Iatrogenic causes of hypercalcaemia include phosphate depletion due to feeding with inadequately supplemented feeds and the use of thiazide diuretics. In phosphate-depleted preterm infants, hypercalcaemia can occur with hypercalciuria. Hypercalciuria without hypercalcaemia can also occur in preterm infants with poorly acidified urine, particularly when there is a low urine flow rate. Over 20% of babies who are less than 32 weeks gestation are affected. This condition can also complicate long-term administration of frusemide. To prevent the development of temporary nephrocalcinosis in this situation, frusemide should be replaced by a thiazide.

Investigation

The investigative strategy is identical to that for hypocalcaemia but may also include a paired random urine for measurement of calcium:creatinine ratio to confirm or refute hypercalciuria.

Magnesium

Hypomagnesaemia

This is defined as a plasma magnesium less than 0.6 mmol/L, but because so little of the total body magnesium circulates in plasma, this is a very poor indicator of tissue stores. Clinical signs similar to those observed in hypocalcaemia may appear at concentrations below 0.5 mmol/L. Hypomagnesaemia can lead to hypocalcaemia by reducing parathyroid hormone secretion or diminishing the responsiveness of the parathyroids to calcium; thus the parathyroid hormone concentration may be low or normal. The hypocalcaemia is typically refractory to calcium replacement. Hypomagnesaemia is particularly common in infants of mothers with diabetes. Intramuscular 50% magnesium sulphate 0.2 mL/kg, should be given to babies who develop hypocalcaemia and whose plasma magnesium concentration falls to 0.4 mmol/L or below. The causes of hypomagnasaemia are shown in Figure 8.8.

Pathogenesis	Cause
Maternal magnesium deficiency	Poorly controlled diabetes Malnutrition GI disease
Excessive intestinal losses	GI pathology
Excessive renal losses	Diuretics Antibiotics Gitelman syndrome

Figure 8.8. Causes of hypomagnesaemia.

A number of rare renal tubular disorders have been described where the presenting feature is hypomagnesaemia:
- Familial hypomagnesemia with hypercalciuria and nephrocalcinosis.
- Familial hypomagnesemia/neonatal severe hyperparathyroidism.
- Hypomagnesemia with secondary hypocalcemia.
- Gitelman syndrome.
- Isolated dominant hypomagnesemia.

Whilst description of these disorders is beyond the scope of this text the reader should be aware of their existence.

Hypermagnesaemia

Hypermagnesaemia rarely occurs in neonates, but has been reported where mothers have received high dose intravenous magnesium sulphate for treatment of eclampsia. Clinical signs include impaired respiratory function, hypotonia and gastrointestinal hypomobility. Hypermagnesaemia can also arise from excessive intake due to accidental infusion errors. Severe renal failure is another cause of hypermagnesaemia due to an inability to excrete magnesium.

Phosphate

Like calcium, fetal plasma phosphate concentrations are higher than those of the mother with the highest rates of accretion of phosphorus occurring in the third trimester during the period of accelerated skeletal mineralisation.

At birth the infant becomes dependent on intestinal absorption of dietary sources of phosphate either from human breast milk or standard formula milks. Both provide less phosphorus than is acquired *in utero* and this deficit is exacerbated for formula milk by the lower rate of intestinal absorption compared to human breast milk.

More than 80% of body phosphorus in the neonate is extracellular, mainly in bone, the rest being distributed throughout all soft tissues and body fluids. When dietary phosphate is restricted, as in enterally fed preterm infants receiving breast milk or unsupplemented formula, fractional intestinal absorption increases. This is largely independent of 1,25-dihydroxy vitamin D. The daily requirement is 1-2 mmol/kg at term, and 2-3 mmol/kg for preterm infants.

Phosphorus in body fluids is either inorganic – the commonly measured component – or organic, mainly in phospholipids and phosphoesters. Regulation of plasma inorganic phosphate is mainly through the PTH-mediated control of renal tubular reabsorption and is limited by the reabsorptive capacity of the tubules. Parathyroid hormone decreases tubular reabsorption, and therefore leads to an increase in urinary phosphate excretion.

Plasma concentrations of inorganic phosphate in neonates are higher than those in adults. Plasma inorganic phosphate values are a little lower in breast-fed than in bottle-fed babies. Mean plasma phosphate concentration at seven days is around 2.0 mmol/L, (range 1.7 to 2.3 mmol/L). Whilst there are instances of hypo- and hyperphosphataemia in neonates primarily related to dietary phosphate intake or very rarely disorders of the parathyroid gland, the main pathology of neonates in which phosphate deficiency is implicated is in the development of metabolic bone disease of prematurity.

Metabolic bone disease of prematurity

This is a disorder of growing bones which occurs in preterm infants particularly those fed exclusively on breast milk. Chronic deficiency of calcium or phosphorus intake results in poor mineralisation of new bone or demineralisation of existing bone, leading to osteopenia. In severe cases, this can produce radiological changes and a risk of fracture on minimal trauma of ribs or long bones. In such babies, whilst plasma calcium concentration is normal, plasma phosphate is less than 1.8 mmol/L (sometimes less than 1.0 mmol/L). In some very small infants, plasma phosphate concentrations below 1 mmol/L can co-exist with active demineralisation of bone, hypercalciuria, and development of nephrocalcinosis. Alkaline phosphatase activity is often grossly elevated but no single value of ALP is predictive of bone changes and data suggests that ALP does not correlate with bone mineral density. Tubular reabsorption of phosphate (TRP) is typically greater than 90%, giving a low urinary phosphate:creatinine ratio. This situation of prolonged insufficient mineral intake is particularly likely to affect preterm babies. This condition is referred to as metabolic bone disease of prematurity (previously known as 'osteopenia of prematurity', 'rickets of prematurity') as vitamin D deficiency is not thought to have a primary role.

Affected babies are:
- usually less than 30 weeks gestation at birth,
- have been in receipt of long-term diuretics or steroids,
- on parenteral nutrition for > four weeks.

They are clinically and radiologically normal at birth, but bony changes develop over the first 6 to 12 weeks, and there is a fall off of longitudinal growth. In more severe disease, radiological changes of loss of bone density are seen first, followed, if the condition continues, by flaring and cupping of the bone ends, and fractures of ribs or long bones. Fractures can be mis-attributed to non-accidental injury.

Management

The management of metabolic bone disease of prematurity includes adequate provision of vitamin D (800 IU daily) and dietary phosphate supplementation. Typically phosphate supplements are prescribed for all babies of less than 30 weeks gestation and/or < 1500g who are receiving unfortified breast milk. In other infants, surveillance, in the first instance, requires monitoring of plasma phosphate.

Preventive measures such as increased mineral provision in parenteral nutrition solutions, and the widespread use of preterm milk formulae supplemented with calcium and phosphate and also commercially available additives for breast milk have made this condition less common. Because of the interactions between calcium and phosphate, molar ratios of 1.3-1.4:1 Ca:P are recommended in milks and parenteral nutrition solutions.

Further reading

Enteral Nutrient Supply for Preterm Infants: Commentary from European Society for Paediatric Gastroenterology, Hepatology and Nutrition Committee on Nutrition. JPGN 2010; **50:** 1-9.

Harrison CM, Gibson AT. Osteopenia in preterm infants. Arch Dis Child Fetal Neonatal Ed. 2013; **98:** F272-F275.

Rustico SE, Calabria AC, Garber SJ. Metabolic bone disease of prematurity. Journal of Clinical & Translational Endocrinology 2014; **1:** 85-91.

Tinnion RJ, Embleton ND. How to use: Alkaline phosphatase in neonatology. Arch Dis Child Educ Pract Ed. 2012; **97:** 157-63.

Chapter 9
Neonatal laboratory screening

Summary

- Newborn screening aims to identify infants who may be at high risk for treatable disorders before symptoms develop.

- An initial positive screening result is confirmed with more specific 'second tier' diagnostic tests.

- Rapid high throughput tandem mass spectrometry, immunoassays and DNA analysis offers the potential to screen for numerous disorders.

- Expansion of newborn screening raises ethical dilemmas and treatment issues.

- In the UK, nine disorders are now included in the neonatal screen.

Introduction

The aim of neonatal screening is to detect and diagnose disorders before symptoms appear so that treatment or management can be instituted early and outcome improved. In 1963, Guthrie introduced neonatal screening for phenylketonuria (PKU) using dried blood spots. Blood spots could also be used to detect other disorders which included congenital hypothyroidism (CHT), sickle cell disease (SCD) and cystic fibrosis (CF). With the application of tandem mass spectrometry (MS/MS) to neonatal screening in the 1990s it became feasible to analyse a large number of intermediary metabolites simultaneously on a single blood spot sample providing the opportunity to screen for many other conditions. Advances and automation in immunochemical and molecular diagnostics have extended the potential screening repertoire still further. Consequently there has been a large expansion globally in the range of neonatal screening programmes. Figure 9.1 lists important factors to consider when selecting tests for neonatal screening.

In the UK, all newborns are screened for PKU, CHT, CF, SCD and MCADD and since 2015, the screen for babies in England has also included homocystinuria (HCU), maple syrup urine disease (MSUD), glutaric aciduria type 1 (GA1) and isovaleric acidaemia (IVA). There are excellent publications on all aspects of the screening process provided by the UK NHS Newborn Blood Spot Screening Programme centre which readers are referred to for a more detailed discussion. (https://www.gov.uk/topic/population-screening-programmes/newborn-blood-spot).

Definition of the abnormality	**Is the abnormality adequately defined?**
Population to be screened	What is considered to be the appropriate population to screen?
Incidence	Are there data on the incidence of the condition in the population?
Screening methods	Is a suitable, efficient and cost-effective method available?
Follow-up procedures	Are confirmatory diagnostic tests available and is there an acceptable treatment/management protocol?
Monitoring the effects	Is the natural history of the disease favourably affected by the screening procedure? Are there any adverse effects?
Costs	What are the resource implications: education, operating costs, follow-up?
Equivocal results	What is to be done about 'borderline' results?

Figure 9.1. Factors guiding selection of disorders for neonatal screening.

Expansion of newborn screening raises ethical dilemmas and treatment issues. Screening has identified a much larger number of affected babies than was predicted from clinical presentation indicating that they may have mild or asymptomatic forms of the disease. This may result in excessive medical attention in the neonatal period which causes needless family stress where the outcome is good without any therapy. Severe *untreatable* disorders, not in the primary screening protocol, may unintentionally be identified by multi-metabolite profiling. Because of the rarity of the disorders, there may not be treatments or management protocols of proven value from controlled trials. Where there are treatments, the cost of life-long treatment may be prohibitive, for example enzyme replacement therapy for lysosomal disorders.

Overview of the neonatal screening process

Informing parents and consent

Antenatally, mothers are told about screening and given information sheets (https://www.gov.uk/topic/population-screening-programmes/newborn-blood-spot). Community midwives collect the blood spot samples when the infants have been discharged home after birth. When parents wish to opt out of one or more of the screening tests, these tests must be indicated on the blood spot card.

Timing

The optimal time for discriminating between normal and affected babies differs for each of the disorders, necessitating compromise. Increases in analytical sensitivity have enabled earlier testing. In Europe and Australia, this is mostly between 48h and 72h, in the USA 24h-72h and in the UK at 5-8 days when most infants are at home. Because immaturity may influence screening results, it is advised that preterm babies are re-tested prior to discharge or at four weeks of age if still hospitalised.

Samples must be collected before a planned blood transfusion, and if this was before the normal screening time, repeated 48h post-transfusion and at two months for SCD when most of the transfused red cells will have been destroyed.

Blood spots

These are generally obtained from the medial or lateral side of the heel. Four spots are required. Generally the analyses are done on 3 mm diameter punched discs.

Screening laboratories

Screening is usually undertaken on a large scale in laboratories serving a newborn population in excess of 50,000. Not only is this cost-effective, but it concentrates experience and information, facilitates audit and promotes development of expertise for these relatively rare disorders. A laboratory screening programme not only involves specimen collection and analytical procedures, but also an advisory service. A specification for a screening service should include standards against which the performance of the programme can be monitored; some countries, including the UK (NHS Newborn Blood Spot Screening Programme Centre), have national standards covering process, systems and outcome measures. Data on age at testing, the number of cases diagnosed, age at diagnosis and start of treatment and the number of false positives and negative are all important measures of performance. It is vital to be able to identify babies who have not been screened in order to prevent missed cases or delayed diagnoses.

The screen

The aim is to identify all babies with high probability of having a defect (high sensitivity for the test with a low false positive rate) without missing affected babies (no false negatives), and with a minimal number of requests for repeat blood sampling, which cause parental anxiety. Screening is undertaken in two stages: the first separates the vast majority of normal samples from those indicating possible risk for an abnormality. In those samples with values outside the analytical cut-offs, the analysis is repeated on the same day and if the result is confirmed, second tier analyses are undertaken to define the abnormality. These may provide a definitive diagnosis (for example two pathological mutations identified for cystic fibrosis) or, if not diagnostic, indicate a strong risk and need for clinical referral and further investigation.

The analyses

For the disorders of intermediary metabolism, the preliminary MS/MS screen measures phenylalanine, tyrosine, other amino acids, acylcarnitines and other intermediary metabolites. CHT and CF screening employ immunometric methodology for the measurement of TSH and immunoreactive trypsinogen.

Sickle cell screening employs either MS/MS, ion-exchange chromatography or capillary electrophoresis for haemoglobin analysis.

For second tier testing, MS/MS analyses may be repeated on derivatised (butylated) metabolites. DNA analyses for pre-selected groups of mutations with DNA micro-array technology enables high throughput follow-up for confirmation of CF.

Newborns identified by screening as positive or presumptive positive for a disorder

Referral mechanisms for confirmatory testing, clinical examination and, above all, communication of accurate and detailed information to anxious parents, are essential. The finding of a positive case, although of great interest to health care professionals, is devastating news to the family of a newborn baby. There are clearly documented protocols for this with names and contact details for responsible individuals. In addition, because these are rare disorders, fact sheets must be available for parents and professionals about the disorder and the meaning of a positive screen result
https://www.gov.uk/topic/population-screening-programmes/newborn-blood-spot.

There are many causes for repeat specimens being requested (e.g. equivocal results, insufficient blood, specimen being lost in the post, unsatisfactory analysis) and the reason for a repeat specimen request requires good communication with community services and, where appropriate, hospital paediatricians.

Screened disorders in the UK

The reader should refer to https://www.gov.uk/topic/population-screening-programmes/newborn-blood-spot for more detailed information regarding the screening process, and to reference texts for detailed descriptions of the disorders and their management. This section provides an overview of the nine disorders now included in the UK screening programme, with greater detail for the five longest-running programmes.

Phenylketonuria (PKU)

PREVALENCE
Between 1 in 5000 and 1 in 20,000 live births. In the United Kingdom the average is 1 in 10,000 with a carrier frequency of 1 in 50.

INHERITANCE
Autosomal recessive.

THE DEFECT
Mutations of the gene for the liver enzyme phenylalanine hydroxylase. More than 400 mutations causing this enzyme deficiency have been described. The extent of the enzyme deficiency varies from complete absence to residual activity as high as 25%, depending on the particular mutation. Phenylalanine hydroxylase normally converts the amino acid phenylalanine to tyrosine. A cofactor, tetrahydrobiopterin, is essential for this reaction (Figure 9.2.)

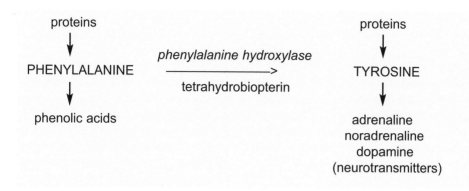

Figure 9.2. The enzyme defect in PKU.

Phenylalanine hydroxylase deficiency results in accumulation of phenylalanine and phenolic metabolites in blood and tissues. Blood tyrosine is low or low normal. High concentrations of phenylalanine and a reduced supply of tyrosine cause severe brain damage. The exact mechanisms are still disputed. The very high phenylalanine concentrations may prevent the transport into the brain of precursors of neurotransmitters (for example tryptophan, the precursor of 5-hydroxytryptamine, serotonin). A further problem is that myelin, which forms the insulating nerve sheaths, is abnormal in untreated PKU and may break down, causing nerve damage.

CLINICAL PRESENTATION

PKU is a heterogeneous disorder. The clinical consequences depend on the magnitude of the phenylalanine increase which, in turn, depends on the residual enzyme activity.

The classical presentation: Untreated babies with very little enzyme activity, whose phenylalanine concentrations are persistently very high, suffer irreversible brain damage. Their blood phenylalanine concentrations rise rapidly with commencement of normal milk feeding. Brain damage starts very quickly, is progressive and causes severe developmental delay (mean IQ in classically-presenting PKU is around 50). Untreated most, eventually, require permanent institutional care. Girls have normal fertility but high concentrations of phenylalanine are teratogenic and, without treatment, their pregnancies have a poor outcome. Their babies are of low birth weight and may have heart defects and mild congenital malformations. Most (95%) will have severe learning difficulties.

The diagnosis is confirmed by the finding of a plasma phenylalanine concentration above 240 µmol/L and usually in excess of 1000 µmol/L (normal <100 µmol/L), with other amino acids not increased, normal liver enzymes and normal biopterin investigations (see below).

Mild hyperphenylalaninaemia: Babies with relatively high residual enzyme activity may have only modest, persistent, increases in phenylalanine concentrations (≤ 500 µmol/L) and develop normally as far as we can tell. They should be classed as having mild hyperphenylalaninaemia and not PKU.

Babies with confirmed phenylalanine concentrations > 600 µmol/L should be commenced on a phenylalanine-restricted diet within two weeks of birth without waiting for biopterin results. Several milk products provide a phenylalanine-free amino acid mixture as a substitute for natural protein, with vitamin and trace element supplements. Very small amounts of breast milk or a formula feed are given as well to supply phenylalanine which is essential for normal growth and development. The amount given has to be titrated very carefully against blood phenylalanine concentration to avoid both phenylalanine deficiency and toxicity. The aim is to keep concentrations within the range 120-360 µmol/L. This requires frequent monitoring of blood spot phenylalanine until concentrations have stabilised. The strict diet and regular monitoring are continued throughout childhood. Adolescents are advised to continue on a moderately restricted phenylalanine diet, with monitoring, throughout life. Girls must return to a strict diet before becoming pregnant, and their phenylalanine concentrations monitored closely throughout pregnancy. Neonates with *mild hyperphenylalaninaemia* may maintain phenylalanine concentrations <360 µmol/L on breast milk or a standard formula without dietary intervention, or require only mild protein restriction to achieve this target.

OUTCOME WITH EARLY TREATMENT

With early treatment and good dietary management, the outcome for patients with phenylketonuria is good, with normal growth and development. Although most children probably come close to their full intellectual potential, there is some evidence that a few children suffer a mild degree of neurological impairment. Girls managed carefully during pregnancy have normal babies. Because of the good outcome from dietary treatment, prenatal diagnosis for PKU is rarely undertaken.

THE SCREEN

All samples with an initial phenylalanine concentration greater than 200 µmol/L are subjected to second tier testing. More details of the diagnostic algorithm can be found in the Laboratory Guide to Newborn Screening in the UK for Phenylketonuria. https://www.gov.uk/topic/population-screening-programmes/newborn-blood-spot. New siblings of a child with PKU should be tested at 48-72h and also at 5-8 days as part of the routine newborn blood spot screen.

NEWBORNS WITH SUSPECTED PKU

Other explanations for an isolated increase in phenylalanine must be considered at the first referral. It is ESSENTIAL to exclude a deficiency of the tetrahydrobiopterin cofactor of phenylalanine hydroxylase due to inherited defects of biopterin synthesis or dihydropteridine reductase. This accounts for 1-3% of inherited hyperphenylalaninaemia. Tetrahydrobiopterin is not only an essential cofactor for the phenylalanine to tyrosine conversion, but also for conversion of tyrosine to L-DOPA, the dopamine precursor, and tryptophan to 5-hydroxytryptophan, the precursor of serotonin (5HT) (Figure 9.3). Untreated, these children have extreme deficiencies of several neurotransmitters – adrenaline, noradrenaline, dopamine, and 5-hydroxytryptamine (serotonin) which are not corrected by a low phenylalanine diet. Without early institution of treatment with tetrahydrobiopterin and neurotransmitters they develop a progressive neurological disorder and die in early childhood. It is essential that every baby found to have hyperphenylalaninaemia is tested for these defects so that appropriate therapy can be initiated if necessary. The tests involve measurement of erythrocyte or whole blood dihydropteridine reductase activity and whole blood spot pterin quantification.

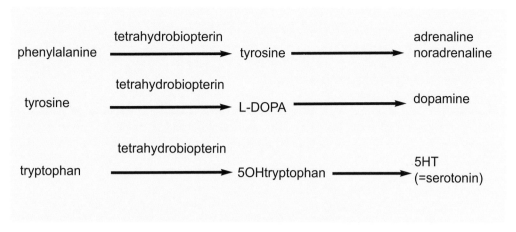

Figure 9.3. Tetrahydrobiopterin in neurotransmitter synthesis.

OTHER CAUSES

False positives may be due to overlaying of blood on the card or sample contamination; prematurity, feed or parenteral nutrition. These increases are frequently transient and phenylalanine is normal on follow-up.

NEWBORNS WITH RAISED TYROSINE

An increased tyrosine with or without raised phenylalanine may indicate liver dysfunction and babies must be examined and investigated urgently. Galactosaemia may present with acute liver failure and encephalopathy within the first week of life, and requires urgent diagnosis and treatment. The incidence is approximately 1 in 40,000 births in the UK. A raised tyrosine should prompt urgent analysis of galactose-1-phosphate uridyl transferase in the initial blood spot sample, preferably by the screening laboratory. Whilst tyrosine may be increased transiently in preterm babies on high protein intakes it is also important to exclude Tyrosinaemia type 1 – an inherited but treatable disorder causing liver disease.

Congenital hypothyroidism (CHT)

PREVALENCE

1 in 3,000 in Europe and the USA.

DEFECT AND INHERITANCE

CHT arises most commonly from an abnormality of the thyroid gland (*primary CHT*). This leads to decreased thyroxine production or release and stimulation of the hypothalamic/pituitary axis with a compensatory increase in thyroid stimulating hormone (TSH). The cause in around 85% of cases is maldevelopment of the thyroid gland (thyroid dysgenesis). The other 15% of cases with primary CHT have inherited disorders of hormone biosynthesis. CHT may also be caused by an inadequate supply of TSH because of dysfunction of hypothalamic/pituitary axis (*secondary CHT*), which in some cases is genetic. The reported incidence ranges from 1 in 16,000 to 1 in 100,000 and in the UK it is estimated to account for up to 5% of cases of CHT.

CLINICAL PRESENTATION

Many affected babies are asymptomatic at birth and only a few have the full range of the classical clinical features which include: jaundice, constipation, feeding difficulties and lethargic behaviour. Without treatment the main symptoms are growth retardation and delayed cognitive development leading to mental retardation.

TREATMENT

Treatment with L-thyroxine should be commenced by 14 days of age, aiming to normalise TSH within the first month. Except for transient hypothyroidism (see below) treatment will be life-long.

OUTCOME WITH EARLY TREATMENT

From long-term studies, the outcome of screened children treated early and appropriately is generally excellent, with normal IQ.

THE SCREEN

Whole blood TSH concentrations are high (20-50 mU/L) in the first 24h of life. Concentrations fall to the normal level for infants (1-8 mU/L) by 5-7 days. Blood should not be collected before five days of age. Some babies have mild but significant elevation of TSH in the newborn period, which returns to normal within a few weeks. In the UK and most screening laboratories in Europe, the USA and Australia, TSH is the primary screen for CHT. Other centres measure fT4 as the primary screen, with TSH as the second test. Whilst this detects both primary and secondary CHT, it has a high recall rate because of transiently low fT4 concentrations, particularly in premature and sick newborn. Following a positive screening test of a TSH greater than 10 mU/L in whole blood spot, the diagnosis is confirmed by the finding of a grossly elevated plasma TSH (typically >200 mU/L) (Figure 9.4). A more detailed discussion of the diagnostic algorithm is available.
https://www.gov.uk/topic/population-screening-programmes/newborn-blood-spot.
Babies with suspected CHT must have an urgent referral (within one working day) to the paediatric endocrine team.

BABIES BORN AT LESS THAN 32 WEEKS GESTATION

Premature babies with CHT, particularly those of < 28 weeks of gestation, have a delayed rise in TSH because of immaturity of the hypothalamic/pituitary axis and may not be picked up on screening at five days (hence false negative), but should be detected when re-tested at 28 days.

TRANSFUSION

Blood should not be collected for at least 72 hours after transfusion.

	TSH	free T4
Positive results		
True positive		
Primary CHT	↑ (≈140 mU/L)	↓
Transient primary CHT	↑	↓
Subclinical (mild compensated) primary CHT	↑ (10-25 mU/L)	N
False positive		
Prematurity	↑	N/↓
Maternal medication (iodine; antithyroid drugs)	↑	↓
Iodine excess (e.g. topical iodine)	↑	N/↓
Iodine deficiency	↑	↓
Poor samples: collection before 5 days;	↑	N/↓
multilayered blood spots	↑	N/↓
False negative		
Secondary CHT	↓	↓
pathological disorders of hypothalamic/pituitary axis		
Primary CHT with delayed rise in TSH	N	↓
(prematurity, especially < 28 weeks; acute illness)		
Poor samples: insufficient blood; compressed spots	N/↓	↓
Transfusion	N/↓	N/↓

Figure 9.4. Causes of positive and negative screening results.

Some babies with biochemical hypothyroidism on the screen subsequently develop normal thyroid function. Others have mild primary 'subclinical' CHT on screening, with a slightly or moderately raised TSH, normal free T4, but an exaggerated TRH response. Follow-up at 3-5 years found that around 25% of these cases had normal thyroid function and hence a transient abnormality, and 50% had mild hypothyroidism. When the cause or persistence of hypothyroidism is uncertain, thyroid function should be reassessed after withdrawal of treatment at 2-3 years of age.

Cystic fibrosis (CF)

PREVALENCE

This is the commonest disorder identified by newborn screening with a prevalence of 1 in 2,000-3,000; UK overall, 1 in 2,500 live births.

DEFECT AND INHERITANCE

Autosomal recessive. Mutations of the cystic fibrosis transmembrane regulator (CFTR) gene, causing deficiency of CFTR which is part of the chloride transporter of cell membranes. Over 800 different mutations have been found. In the UK a single mutation (phe508del; ΔF508) accounts for about 75% of defective genes.

CLINICAL PRESENTATION

There is wide heterogeneity reflecting the severity of the mutations. *With severe defects*, around 10% of affected infants present within 48h of birth with intestinal obstruction due to meconium ileus. Around 70% have some symptoms in the first six weeks of life, sometimes with persistent conjugated hyperbilirubinaemia and abnormal liver function which may resolve. The clinical effects of untreated CF are due to progressive lung disease and severe malabsorption secondary to pancreatic insufficiency. Without active intervention, death occurs during the first and second decades of life. Without screening, diagnosis was often considerably delayed. At the other extreme are individuals with *'mild' genetic defects* who present as adults with milder pulmonary disease or male infertility due to absent vas deferens.

TREATMENT

The mainstays are diet, pancreatic supplements, physiotherapy, and continuous or intermittent antibiotics instituted from the time of diagnosis. These have a significant impact on quality of life. The median life-expectancy is now > 30 years.

BENEFITS OF NEWBORN SCREENING

Early diagnosis reduces diagnostic delay and early treatment decreases hospital admissions in the first year of life and prevents early vitamin deficiencies. There is some evidence that it improves growth and may benefit pulmonary status in childhood. Early diagnosis of CF in a baby, however, will allow the parents the opportunity of prenatal diagnosis for the next pregnancy. A problem from screening is detection of CF mutations that are believed to be 'mild' or of uncertain pathogenicity. These may not cause problems until adult life, but knowing about them may lead to significant parental anxiety and over-protection.

THE SCREEN

Blood concentrations of immunoreactive trypsinogen (IRT) are increased during the first few weeks of life in babies with CF, but then fall to subnormal concentrations. After 40 days they discriminate poorly between affected and normal babies. Following a positive screening test of an IRT greater than the 99.5th centile in a whole blood spot, the sample is referred for second tier testing for CFTR mutations. A more detailed discussion of the diagnostic algorithm, in which the outcome can be classified as CF suspected or probable carrier, can be found at https://www.gov.uk/government/collections/newborn-blood-spot-screening-programme-supporting-publications#cystic-fibrosis-cf.
When the definitive result is available, babies classed as suspected CF should be referred to a designated CF clinician within one working day.

CONFIRMATORY TESTS

Sweat test with quantitative pilocarpine iontophoresis is undertaken at the baby's first visit to clinic to obtain a phenotypic evidence of CF and if necessary complete DNA sequencing to confirm the diagnosis. The significance of a probable carrier result should be discussed with the parents within one working day of the results becoming available.

FALSE POSITIVE SCREEN RESULTS

IRT has a low discriminating power in the first 1-2 days of age since transient increases are common in neonates comparable to those seen in neonates with CF.

FALSE NEGATIVE SCREEN RESULTS

Babies with CF who have meconium ileus may give a false negative result. It should be remembered that if there are clinical concerns that the baby has signs of CF, for example, poor weight gain, nasal polyps, rectal prolapse despite a screening result of 'CF Not Suspected' referral to an appropriate CF specialist should be made.

Sickle cell disease (SCD)

PREVALENCE

SCDs are particularly common in the Black Caribbean and Black African ethnic groups with an incidence of approximately 1 in 100-300 births and 1 in 600 of African Americans.

DEFECT AND INHERITANCE

SCDs are haemoglobinopathies due to the S mutation of the gene for β-globin of haemoglobin. Inheritance is autosomal recessive. They include the homozygous SS state (sickle cell anaemia) and compound heterozygosity for the S mutation and another β-globin mutation, namely HbSC disease, HbSD^{Punjab}, Hb sickle β-thalassaemia (both Sβ^0 and Sβ$^+$ variants expressing no, or some β-globin, respectively) and HbS HPFH (hereditary persistent fetal Hb). Aggregation of HbS in low oxygen tensions leads to sickling of the red cells with consequent vaso-occlusion and red cell destruction. In normal term newborns, 70-90% of total haemoglobin is fetal haemoglobin with 10-30% adult haemoglobin (HbA). The proportion falls progressively to <2% by one year. HbF protects against sickling and hence SCD rarely presents in the first two months of life.

CLINICAL PRESENTATION

SCD causes life-long haemolytic anaemia with acute crises. Infants with SCD are at risk of pneumoccocal septicaemia and there is a high risk of mortality from this infection. Other life-threatening crises include stroke, aplastic crises and acute lung damage. Even with good care, around 90% of individuals with all types of SCD die before 20 years of age. Individuals with the sickle cell trait (carriers for HbS) are usually asymptomatic and have a normal life span.

TREATMENT

Prophylaxis against pneumococcal infection should be started as soon as the diagnosis is confirmed with pneumoccocal vaccination and folate. Complications are treated with analgaesia, intravenous fluids, transfusion and iron chelation. Hydroxyurea stimulates γ-chain (and hence HbF) synthesis and may be useful.

BENEFITS OF SCREENING

Early diagnosis improves morbidity and mortality The use of prophylactic penicillin is very effective in preventing pneumococcal sepsis. Early referral to a sickle cell centre, close monitoring, education and genetic counselling of the parents, and open access to appropriate inpatient care are added benefits. The diagnosis of carrier status allows couples to be counselled about the risks for future pregnancies.

THE SCREEN

Transfused cells may invalidate the result. Pre-transfusion blood for sickle cell screen must be collected. The diagnosis can be made by DNA analysis of white blood cells from a transfused baby. If this test is not available, screening must be deferred until at least four months after transfusion.

Primary screen: Lysates eluted from the blood spots are analysed by MS/MS, HPLC, or capillary electrophoresis to separate haemoglobins. The analytical procedure used must be able to detect all the common clinically significant Hb variants. Great care must be taken in interpretation due to the large percentage of fetal haemoglobin present at the time of screening. Unaffected babies have HbF and HbA, with HbA accounting for 5-30% of Hb in term babies.

Second tier tests: Confirmation of a suspected abnormality must be undertaken using the same blood spot by an alternate procedure.
For a more detailed discussion of screening diagnostics consult:
https://www.gov.uk/topic/population-screening-programmes/sickle-cell-thalassaemia

Presumptive positives should be confirmed by repeat analysis on a further specimen at a later age (e.g. 3-6 months), together with family studies.

Other pathological haemoglobinopathies detected

The screen may identify infants who are homozygotes or compound heterozygotes for conditions other than SCD. Only HbF and the Hb variants will be present and no HbA. These are reported. In addition, the majority of babies with β-thalassaemia major will be detected since they will have only HbF and no, or very low HbA. However, other thalassaemias will not be detected.

Medium-chain acyl-CoA dehydrogenase deficiency (MCADD)

PREVALENCE
1 in 10,000 to 27,000 babies of northern European descent; 1 in 10,000 live births in the UK.

DEFECT AND INHERITANCE
An autosomal recessively inherited deficiency of medium chain acyl-CoA dehydrogenase which is required to metabolise medium chain (C6-C12) fatty acids. This disorder of fatty acid oxidation severely limits the ability to produce ketones and maintain blood glucose during periods of metabolic stress and/or prolonged fasting. Around 80% of clinically diagnosed MCADD cases in the UK are homozygous for the 985A>G mutation. However, only 53% of babies with MCADD detected by neonatal screening in the UK are homozygous for this mutation. This is due to the ethnic diversity of screened babies, and also to lower pathogenicity of some mutations compared with 985A>G.

CLINICAL PRESENTATION
Typically MCADD presents with encephalopathy in a previously well child during an intercurrent illness associated with fasting and/or vomiting. This may progress rapidly to coma and death in those presenting too late for effective intervention. However, with early diagnosis and intervention, children recover completely and can lead a full and normal life. Most cases present before two years of age (mean 13 months), but there is a broad spectrum, and the

first presentation may occur neonatally or in adult life. Around one third of affected individuals never have symptoms, but they are at risk of encephalopathy during hypocaloric stress. The biochemical hallmarks during acute decompensation are hypoketotic hypoglycaemia with a gross derangement of medium chain fatty acid metabolism. This is evident in the blood acylcarnitine profile and an abnormal urinary organic acid profile which includes hexanoylglycine, which is only found when MCAD is deficient (in MCADD, and multiple acyl-CoA dehydrogenase deficiency, MADD). The blood acylcarnitines are persistently abnormal even when asymptomatic and hexanoylglycine is usually detectable, albeit at very low concentration, and is often the only urinary organic acid abnormality.

TREATMENT

Acute episodes are treated by giving glucose intravenously or enterally as indicated clinically and with vigorous resuscitation following National BIMDG guidelines:
http://www.bimdg.org.uk/store/guidelines/MCADD.
Long-term management involves avoidance of prolonged fasting and the use of an emergency regimen during intercurrent illness in order to prevent metabolic decompensation.

BENEFITS OF SCREENING

Using episodes of acute decompensation as an end-point, outcome data worldwide have shown great benefit from screening for MCADD. With early detection and monitoring and avoidance of fasts, children can lead normal lives.

THE SCREEN

Primary screening: Octanoyl (C8) carnitine and its ratio to decanoyl (C10) carnitine are measured by MS/MS. If MCADD is suspected (C8>0.5 µmol/L and C8:C10 >1.0) the patient is referred to a paediatric metabolic specialist. A full acylcarnitine scan is undertaken to support the provisional diagnosis as octanoylcarnitine can also be non-specifically raised in premature and hypoxic infants as well as in other disorders of intermediary metabolism.

Second tier tests: Confirmatory tests include organic acid analysis for the presence of hexanoyl glycine and genetic testing for the common 985A>G mutation and, if necessary, extended mutation testing. The interested reader is directed towards the more detailed MCADD newborn screening protocol at https://www.gov.uk/government/collections/newborn-blood-spot-screening-programme-supporting-publications#medium-chain-acyl-coa-dehydrogenase-deficiency-mcadd.

Sibling testing: Collect samples for blood spot C8 and C10 carnitines and urine for organic acids.

Maple syrup urine disease (MSUD)

PREVALENCE

Estimated to be 1 in 120,000 live births in Europe.

DEFECT AND INHERITANCE

An autosomal recessively inherited deficiency of branched chain 2-oxoacid dehydrogenase which is a key enzyme in the catabolism of leucine, isoleucine and valine. These branched chain amino acids and their oxo-acids accumulate, resulting in severe metabolic ketoacidosis and encephalopathy.

CLINICAL PRESENTATION

There are four sub-types: A severe classical form with < 2% residual enzyme activity which presents neonatally (the commonest), intermediate and intermittent forms with higher enzyme activity in which symptoms are generally delayed, and a very rare thiamine-responsive form. The classical neonatal presentation is of feeding difficulties, lethargy, failure to thrive and progressive CNS dysfunction. Urine and sweat have a characteristic sweet odour of maple syrup. Biochemical abnormalities include metabolic acidosis and hypoglycaemia. The disorder is severe with a progressive downhill course which, if untreated, leads to early death. The disorder is characterised by grossly increased concentrations of the branched chain amino acids leucine, isoleucine and valine. Treatment involves a special diet low in the branched chain amino acids. In patients with the severe form of MSUD the initiation of correct dietary therapy may be life-saving but the longer term outlook is poor. Patients with the milder/atypical form of the disorder may have a good outcome if these bouts of episodic illness can be avoided by good dietary management.

TREATMENT

Is with a low branched chain amino acid diet, and aggressive early intervention of acute decompensation.

BENEFITS OF SCREENING

With meticulous care started within the first week of life, some children may achieve normal growth and psychomotor development. They are at continued risk of decompensation during inter-current illness.

THE SCREEN

Primary screening: Leucine is measured by MS/MS. If raised, the baby must be referred immediately to a designated paediatrician.

Second tier tests: Quantitative plasma amino acids including alloisoleucine and urine organic acids are measured within 24h. If alloisoleucine is present, the diagnosis is MSUD. If alloisoleucine is not detectable, but the branched chain amino acids are increased, further investigation should be undertaken.
https://www.gov.uk/government/collections/newborn-blood-spot-screening-programme-supporting-publications#maple-syrup-urine-disease-msud

False negative results: milder intermediate and intermittent forms may be missed.

Glutaric aciduria type 1 (GA1)

PREVALENCE

Estimated to be around 1 in 100,000 live births in Europe, but GA1 is probably significantly underdiagnosed.

An autosomal recessive disorder with deficiency of glutaryl-CoA dehydrogenase, a key enzyme involved in lysine and tryptophan metabolism. Glutaric acid accumulates in the tissues and body fluids, but plasma and urine glutaric acid may not be persistently raised.

CLINICAL PRESENTATION

70% of affected babies have macrocephaly at birth or have a progressive increase in head circumference, but are otherwise asymptomatic in early infancy. The majority present with an acute encephalopathic episode between three months and three years of age (most at around 9-12 months) which is triggered by an infection. This causes irreversible brain damage with a severe movement disorder. Further attacks may lead to death in early adult life. However, asymptomatic adults have been reported.

TREATMENT

Is with dietary restriction of lysine and tryptophan, with carnitine and riboflavin supplements and possibly vigabatrin, started in the pre-symptomatic phase and vigorous antibiotic treatment when sick. *Early treatment* can usually prevent brain damage. Treatment does not reverse brain damage once it has occurred.

THE SCREEN

Primary screening test: Underivatised glutarylcarnitine by MS/MS.

Second tier tests: If glutarylcarnitine > 0.7 µmol/L analysis of a full acylcarnitine profile is undertaken.

Confirmatory tests: Urine organic acids for glutarate and 3-hydroxyglutarate. If the biochemistry is normal or equivocal, it may be necessary to conduct full gene sequencing. More information is provided on the screening and diagnostic/confirmatory protocols at: https://www.gov.uk/government/collections/newborn-blood-spot-screening-programme-supporting-publications#glutaric-aciduria-type-1-ga1

Homocystinuria (HCU)

PREVALENCE

Estimated to be 1 in 100,000 live births in Europe, but this underestimates those with pyridoxine-responsive defects.

DEFECT AND INHERITANCE

An autosomal recessive disorder with deficiency of cystathionine β-synthase, which is essential for conversion of methionine to cysteine and inorganic sulphate. Pyridoxal phosphate is a co-factor for the enzyme. Deficiency leads to increased concentrations of methionine and homocysteine in the blood. In around 50% of patients, the defect is responsive to pyridoxine.

CLINICAL PRESENTATION

Affected babies are normal at birth. The diagnosis is not usually made until 2-3 years of age, but there may be evidence of developmental delay before this. The main features of untreated classical HCU are lens dislocation (ectopia lentis), learning difficulties and behavioural problems, lengthening of the long bones with a Marfanoid appearance, osteoporosis and thromboembolism with serious complications which may be fatal in early adult life. The disease is usually milder in pyridoxine-responsive defects.

TREATMENT

Pyridoxine-responsive patients are treated with large doses of pyridoxine often with folate and vitamin B12, and non-responsive patients with a low methionine diet and cystine supplement. Betaine is given to both groups to re-methylate homocysteine.

OUTCOME WITH EARLY TREATMENT

This varies with the severity of the defect and, particularly, whether it is pyridoxine-responsive. If started within six weeks of life, it may reduce complications substantially.

THE SCREEN

Primary screening test: measurement of blood spot methionine by MS/MS.

Confirmatory tests: If methionine is greater than 50 µmol/L, analyse plasma amino acids and total plasma homocysteine.
https://www.gov.uk/government/collections/newborn-blood-spot-screening-programme-supporting-publications#homocystinuria-hcu.

False positive screen results: Methionine may be very high in liver disease and may be increased transiently due to immaturity.

False negative screen results: Blood methionine concentrations may not be increased by the time of sampling, as happens in a significant proportion of pyridoxine-responsive defects.

Isovaleric acidaemia (IVA)

PREVALENCE

Estimated to be 1 in 100,000 live births in Europe.

DEFECT AND INHERITANCE

An autosomal recessive disorder due to deficiency of isovaleryl-CoA dehydrogenase, a key enzyme in the catabolic pathway for leucine. The defect results in accumulation of isovaleric acid and its metabolites, notably isovalerylglycine which is readily excreted in urine along with other organic acid metabolites, and isovalerylcarnitine, a C5 carnitine which is a useful diagnostic marker in blood. There are many mutations and generally no genotype/ phenotype correlation. An exception is the 932C>T mutation identified by newborn screening which may represent a mild or clinically insignificant phenotype.

CLINICAL PRESENTATION

There are two clinically different presentations (1) a severe acute neonatal illness generally at three to six days in babies who are well at birth. They develop a rapidly progressive encephalopathy with ketoacidosis, hyperammonaemia, often hyperglycaemia and pancytopaenia and with an odour of sweaty feet. Without prompt intervention, they lapse into coma and die. With aggressive early treatment, babies survive and may develop normally, but are at risk for further acute episodes; (2) a chronic illness with similar, but intermittent, acute episodes generally starting in the first year of life and triggered by inter-current infections or high protein intakes. Most have normal psychomotor development, but some have developmental delay and learning problems.

TREATMENT

Acute episodes are managed intensively with intravenous glucose to suppress catabolism, carnitine and glycine to enhance excretion of isovalerate. Long-term management is with a low protein diet, and oral carnitine and glycine, with an emergency regimen for inter-current illnesses.

BENEFITS OF SCREENING

Early institution of treatment and awareness of the condition will reduce the risk for acute decompensation.

THE SCREEN

Primary screening test: Measurement of C5 carnitine by MS/MS. Babies with C5 > 2.0 µmol/L are referred immediately for clinical assessment and confirmatory tests.

Confirmatory tests: Repeat blood spot C5 carnitine with analysis of a full acylcarnitine profile if still raised; urine organic acids; rapid analysis of DNA for the 932C>T variant.
https://www.gov.uk/government/collections/newborn-blood-spot-screening-programme-supporting-publications#isovaleric-acidaemia-iva

Further reading

Clarke GM, Higgins TN. Laboratory investigation of hemoglobinopathies and thalassemias: Review and update. Clin Chem 2000; **46:** 1284-1290.

Davies SC, Cronin E, Gill M, *et al.* Screening for sickle cell disease and thalassaemia: a systematic review with supplementary research. Health Technology Assessment 2000; Vol. 4 No.3.

Dodge JA. Why screen for cystic fibrosis? A clinician's view. Acta Paediatr Suppl. 1999; **432:** 28-32.

Dhondt J-L. Expanded newborn screening: social and ethical issues. J Inherit Metab Dis 2010; **33 (suppl 2):** S211-217.

Inborn Metabolic Diseases 5th Edn., J-M Saudubray, G van den Berghe, Eds. Springer-Verlag Berlin Heidelberg 2012.

LaFranchi SH. Newborn screening strategies for congenital hypothyroidism: an update. J Inherit Metab Dis. 2010; **33 (suppl 2):** S225-233.

National Institute for Health Research. Expanded Newborn Screening Study July 2012 to July 2013. Report to National Screening Committee 21st November 2013.

National Society for Phenylketonuria (UK) Ltd. Management of PKU. A consensus document for the diagnosis and management of children, adolescents and adults with phenylketonuria. 2nd Edn 1999. http://web.ukonline.co.uk/nspku.

Oerton J, Khalid JM, Besley G, *et al.* Newborn screening for medium chain acyl-CoA dehydrogenase deficiency in England: prevalence, predictive value and test validity based on 1.5 million screened babies. J Med Screen 2011; **18:** 173-181.

Sahai I, Levy HL. Newborn Screening. CA Gleason, SU Devaskar, Eds., Avery's Diseases of the Newborn 9th Edn. Elsevier Saunders, Philadelphia PA, 2012: pp316-327.

UK National Screening Committee useful web site.
https://www.gov.uk/topic/population-screening-programmes/newborn-blood-spot (blood spots; screening programmes; protocols , and laboratory guidelines)

Zeuner D, Ades EA, Karnon J, Brown J, Dezateux C, Anionwu EN. Antenatal and neonatal haemoglobinopathy screening in the UK: review and economic analysis. Health Technology Assessment 1999; Vol. 3: No. 11.

Chapter 10
Inherited metabolic diseases

Summary

- Most babies with inherited metabolic disorders are born after an uneventful pregnancy and develop symptoms within the first week of life.

- The presentation is often with a range of non-specific clinical features.

- Early discussion with a specialist laboratory can guide appropriate investigation and facilitate prompt diagnosis and treatment of an inherited metabolic disorder.

- In neonates suffering acute life-threatening illness or sudden unexpected death a range of samples should be collected as soon as possible, ideally pre-mortem, in order to enable investigation for metabolic disease.

- Following the diagnosis of an inherited metabolic disorder, siblings should be investigated.

Introduction

There are many individually rare inherited metabolic disorders (IMDs) that present clinically in the neonatal period. The incidence of individual disorders ranges between 1 in 10,000 and 1 in 500,000. In spite of their relative rarity, collectively IMD present a significant disease burden. It is important to consider IMD in certain patients, particularly in very sick neonates, for whom there is no obvious diagnosis.

The IMDs most likely to present acutely in the neonate are those due to defects in energy production and intermediary metabolism. In addition, there are a few specific disorders of other metabolic processes e.g. cholesterol metabolism and defects of glycosylation. The disorders listed in Figure 10.1 represent those most likely to be encountered, although it is not an exhaustive list and other, rarer disorders have been reported in infants of this age. The Metabolic Biochemistry Network is a useful resource for additional reading (www.metbio.net).

Amino acid disorders	Maple syrup urine disease Non-ketotic hyperglycinaemia Tyrosinaemia type I Homocystinuria (methylene tetrahydrofolate reductase deficiency)
Urea cycle disorders	Carbamoyl phosphate synthetase deficiency Ornithine carbamoyl transferase deficiency Citrullinaemia Argininosuccinic acidaemia
Organic acid disorders	Methylmalonic acidaemia Propionic acidaemia Isovaleric acidaemia Glutaric aciduria type II (multiple acyl-CoA dehydrogenase deficiency)
Fatty acid oxidation disorders	Short chain defects Medium chain defects (e.g. MCADD) Long chain defects Carnitine transport/cycle defects
Carbohydrate disorders	Galactosaemia Glycogen storage disease type I Fructose 1,6-bisphosphatase deficiency Hereditary fructose intolerance
Energy production defects	Pyruvate dehydrogenase deficiency Pyruvate carboxylase deficiency Electron transport chain defects Mitochondrial defects (Pearson syndrome)
Peroxisomal disorders	Zellweger and pseudo-Zellweger syndromes Neonatal adrenoleucodystrophy
Purine and pyrimidine disorders	Sulphite oxidase and xanthine oxidase deficiency (molybdenum cofactor deficiency) Adenosine deaminase deficiency
Lysosomal storage disorders	GM1 gangliosidosis Niemann-Pick disease type C Krabbe leucodystrophy Lysosomal acid lipase deficiency Pompe disease Sly syndrome (MPS 7) Gaucher disease
Others	Menke syndrome Congenital adrenal hyperplasia Sulphite oxidase deficiency (isolated) Smith-Lemli-Opitz syndrome Congenital disorders of glycosylation

Note: this list is not exhaustive

Figure 10.1. Inherited metabolic disorders that present in the neonate.

Most babies with an IMD are born at or near term with normal birth weight and no abnormal features as the fetus has been protected during pregnancy. Symptoms usually develop within the first week of life, typically in the first 24-48 hours after full milk feeding is instituted.

Some IMD may result in adverse effects on fetal development. In particular, some lysosomal storage disorders can present during pregnancy with fetal ascites and as hydrops fetalis. A history of more than one pregnancy presenting in this way is suggestive of such a disorder. It is therefore important to consider metabolic disease when other commoner causes of hydrops have not been found (www.metbio.net/docs/MetBio-Guideline/Hydrops). Dysmorphism should also trigger consideration of IMD (www.metbio.net/docs/MetBio-Guideline/Dysmorphism).

The biochemical basis of these disorders is wide ranging, and for the non-specialist there is a bewildering array of tests. The best approach to investigation is to take careful note of any clues from the history, presentation and preliminary biochemical tests, and then proceed to the more specific investigations after discussion with a specialist laboratory. If the baby is acutely ill, urgent investigation is essential. Rapid recognition of IMD is important to enable prompt treatment, and thereby prevent or limit damage to the central nervous system (CNS) or other organs. Where treatment is not available, diagnosis is still important to enable prenatal diagnosis for subsequent pregnancies.

Presentation

Family history:
- consanguinity,
- family history of a similar illness,
- unexplained deaths in infancy.

For example, a history of male deaths particularly suggests an X-linked disorder such as ornithine carbamoyl transferase (OCT) deficiency.

It is particularly important to note if a previous sibling has died following a 'Reye-like' illness or episode of metabolic decompensation, as amino acid, urea cycle, organic acid and fatty acid oxidation defects can present in this way.

Examination

The classic clinical presentation is a:
- full-term baby,
- normal pregnancy and delivery,
- initial symptom-free period (few hours or weeks),
- deterioration for no obvious reason (following a change in feeding regimen, other stress factors).

The observation of a relationship between symptoms and a change in feeding regimens, e.g. changing to glucose/saline, a non-lactose milk formula or reduced protein load, adds support to the possibility of an IMD and may suggest a particular diagnosis (e.g. galactosaemia).
In most cases, however, clinical features are non-specific, e.g. poor feeding, lethargy,

vomiting, hypotonia, fits. Features that are particularly suggestive of IMD include:

- abnormal smell, e.g. sweet, musty cabbage-like, sweaty (amino acid and organic acid disorders),
- cataracts (galactosaemia),
- hyperventilation, secondary to metabolic acidosis accompanied by a high anion gap (organic acid disorders),
- ambiguous genitalia ± hyponatraemia (congenital adrenal hyperplasia see Chapter 4),
- neurological dysfunction with respiratory alkalosis ± low plasma urea (urea cycle disorders).

It is important to be aware that diagnosis of an infection does not preclude an associated IMD and that sepsis is a common accompaniment to an underlying metabolic defect.

Investigation of the sick neonate for IMD (Figure 10.2)

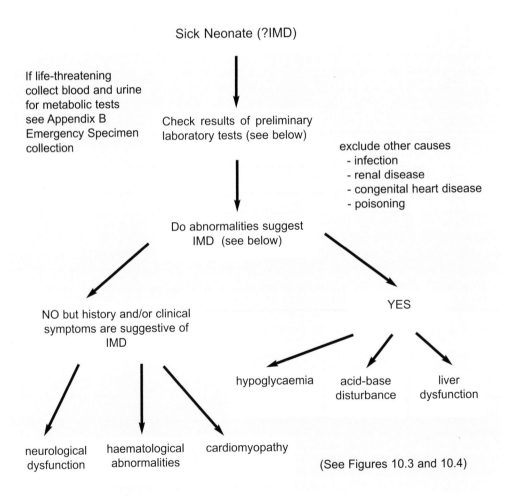

Figure 10.2. Investigation of the sick neonate for inherited metabolic disorders (IMD).

Preliminary laboratory investigations – 'Clues' to IMD

Most sick neonates will have had basic biochemical and haematological investigations carried out as part of their clinical care and these should be reviewed before deciding to undertake the more specialised tests, as certain abnormalities are suggestive of a possible IMD. Biochemical abnormalities that are suggestive of an IMD include:

- hyperammonaemia,
- hypoglycaemia (see guidelines for investigation Chapter 7),
- lactic acidosis,
- acid base disturbance (metabolic acidosis/respiratory alkalosis see Chapter 5),
- high anion gap,
- inappropriate ketonuria/absence of ketones,
- high or low plasma urate,
- high or very low plasma cholesterol (high triglycerides).

In a neonate with metabolic acidosis, calculation of the anion gap, i.e.

$$([Na^+] + [K^+]) - ([Cl^-] + [HCO_3^-]), \text{ can be helpful;}$$

- a gap > 20 mmol/L suggests an organic acidaemia,
- a normal gap is more likely to be due to renal tubular acidosis or bicarbonate loss from the gastrointestinal tract,
- urine pH below 5.5 is suggestive of an organic acid disorder, although higher pHs do not exclude the possibility of such a disorder.

In normal neonates on regular feeds, the urine test for ketones should be negative, or slightly positive if in a fasting state. A strong positive result is abnormal and indicates the need to investigate, particularly for organic acid defects. The absence of ketones in a baby who is catabolic (e.g. prolonged period without adequate feeds, stress) is suggestive of a fatty acid oxidation defect.

A normal blood pH does not exclude an elevated plasma lactate and measurement of plasma lactate should always be considered if there is hypoglycaemia or neurological dysfunction, as well as in acidotic states.

Some haematological abnormalities may also be suggestive of an IMD (Figure 10.3).

	Disorder(s)
Neutropenia	Glycogen storage type Ib Organic acidurias (methylmalonic, propionic and isovaleric) Lysinuric protein intolerance Congenital orotic aciduria Barth syndrome
Haemolytic anaemia	Neonatal haemochromatosis Cobalamin defects (haemolytic uraemia syndrome) Glycolytic enzyme defects, e.g. pyruvate kinase, glucose-6-phosphate dehydrogenase and phosphofructokinase Pearson syndrome
Megaloblastic anaemia	Cobalamin defects Methylmalonic acidaemia Homocystinuria (combined with methylmalonic acidaemia) Congenital orotic aciduria
Clotting defects	Tyrosinaemia type I Galactosaemia

Figure 10.3. Haematological abnormalities associated with IMD.

Metabolic screening (first stage) investigations

In the situation where the neonate is acutely ill, then the following investigations should be considered in order to screen for metabolic disorders. If indicated investigations should be undertaken urgently:

- ammonia (plasma)*
- lactate (plasma)*
- amino acids (urine and plasma)
- organic acids (urine)
- galactose 1-phosphate uridyl transferase (erythrocytes)
- acylcarnitines (dried blood spots and plasma).

* should be available locally

In the UK there is a network of specialist referral laboratories for tests not available locally which can be accessed for advice and diagnostic services. (http://www.metbio.net/metbioAssays.asp/). Consultation with the referral laboratory prior to specimen dispatch will identify the need for urgent analysis. Figure 10.4 lists the range of analyses used to investigate the sick neonate.

Presentation	Possible metabolic disorders	Suggested investigations
Unexplained hypoglycaemia (Chapter 7)	Organic acid disorders Fatty acid oxidation defects Amino acid disorders Glycogen storage disorders (especially type 1) Disorders of gluconeogenesis Congenital adrenal hyperplasia Congenital lactic acidosis Galactosaemia	Organic acids (U) Amino acids (U,P) 3-hydroxybutyrate (FP) Free fatty acids (FP) Carnitine and acylcarnitines (P,BS) Lactate (FP) Insulin (P,S) Cortisol (P) 17-hydroxyprogesterone (P,S) Galactose 1-phosphate uridyl transferase (B) Ammonia (P)
Acid base imbalance: - metabolic acidosis (exclude primary cardiac and respiratory disorders) - respiratory alkalosis (Chapter 5)	Organic acid disorders Congenital lactic acidosis Urea cycle disorders	Organic acids (U) Lactate (FP) Amino acids (U,P) Carnitine and acylcarnitines (P,BS) Ammonia (P) Orotic acid (U) Amino acids (U,P)
Liver dysfunction (often associated with hypoglycaemia and galactosuria)	Galactosaemia Fructose 1,6-bisphosphatase deficiency Hereditary fructose intolerance Tyrosinaemia (type I) Glycogen storage disorders (type 1) Disorders of gluconeogenesis Alpha-1-antitrypsin deficiency	Galactose 1-phosphate uridyl transferase (B) Sugars (U) Amino acids (U,P) Succinylacetone (U) Alpha-fetoprotein (P,S) Lactate (FP) Alpha-1-antitrypsin (S)
Neurological dysfunction: - seizures - depressed consciousness - hypotonia	Non-ketotic hyperglycinaemia Urea cycle disorders Xanthine/sulphite oxidase deficiency Homocystinuria (remethylation defect) Congenital lactic acidosis Peroxisomal disorders Organic acid disorders Lysosomal storage disorders Biotinidase deficiency	Amino acids (U,P,C) Orotic acid (U) Ammonia (P) Urate (P,U) Sulphite (U) Total homocysteine (P) Lactate (FP) Organic acids (U) Very long chain fatty acids (P) Leucocyte enzymes (B) Biotinidase (P)
Cardiomyopathy	Glycogen storage type II (Pompe) Fatty acid oxidation disorders Tyrosinaemia (type I) Electron transport chain disorders CDG syndrome Barth syndrome (X-linked)	Lactate (FP) 3-hydroxybutyrate (FP) Free fatty acids (FP) Oligosaccharides (U) Organic acids (U) Carnitine and acylcarnitines (P,BS) Amino acids (U,P) Transferrin isoelectric focusing (P) Cardiolipin (B)
U = urine S = serum	B = heparinised blood FP = fluoride plasma	P = plasma C = CSF BS = blood spot

Figure 10.4. Specialist investigations for IMD in the sick neonate.

Specimen collection for second stage metabolic investigations

If the baby has an episodic illness (e.g. related to a feeding regimen or associated infection) it is particularly important to collect blood and urine specimens during the acute phase as the diagnosis may be missed if specimens are collected only when the infant is 'well'.
As a minimum:
- random urine (ideally 5 mL, but smaller quantities are valuable),
- blood (at least 1 mL heparin and 1 mL fluoride oxalate),
    - plasma being separated and stored at -20°C within 30minutes of collection
    - packed red cells should be stored unfrozen at +4°C.

If the child is severely ill and deteriorating, more rigorous specimen collection is indicated (see below and Appendix B).

For all specimens, an accurate recording of date and time of collection together with the following information should be provided:
- feeding regimen at the time of and immediately prior to sampling (this is particularly important if amino acids, organic acids and sugars are requested),
- details of all drug therapy and other treatments (including blood transfusions),
- full clinical details and results of any preliminary biochemical and haematological investigations and degree of urgency. Details of drug therapy are particularly important for amino acid investigations as several antibiotics can cause interference with ninhydrin-based detection reagent.

LIFE-THREATENING ILLNESS

If an illness is progressing rapidly and death seems inevitable, it is important to consider that appropriate specimens (blood, urine, skin and tissues) should be taken for biochemical analysis to enable reliable post-mortem investigation (see Appendix B). Blood and urine should be taken pre-mortem whenever possible. Blood taken around the time of death or post-mortem will be of limited use, as lactic acidosis, hyperammonaemia and hyperaminoaci-daemia due to protein autolysis are likely to confuse the picture and make interpretation of the results at best, difficult, and often impossible. The opportunity and potential value of a post-mortem investigation should be discussed with the parents and, if consent is obtained (Human Tissue Authority), it should be undertaken as soon as possible after death to minimise specimen deterioration. For those families where a diagnosis can be made, genetic counselling and the opportunity for prenatal diagnosis for future pregnancies can be of paramount importance. In these situations great efforts in a sensitive manner should be made to obtain these important specimens.

Sudden unexplained death in infancy and metabolic disease

A small percentage of cases of sudden unexplained death in infancy (SUDI) have been associated with metabolic disorders, particularly fatty acid oxidation defects. These include medium chain acyl CoA dehydrogenase deficiency (MCADD), long chain defects and disorders of carnitine metabolism. It is therefore important to consider the possibility of metabolic disorders in infants dying suddenly and unexpectedly. Suggested guidelines for such situations are provided (see www.metbio.net/docs/MetBio-Guideline).

In situations where there are no samples for biochemical investigation from the index case, in families where there is a high degree of suspicion (e.g. fatty change in the liver, family history), further children can be investigated immediately after birth for disorders of fatty acid oxidation. Blood spot or plasma acylcarnitines and urinary organic acids collected during the first two days of life usually show the characteristic metabolites of a fat oxidation defect, although a normal result does not completely exclude the possibility of such a disorder. If tissue is available, extracted DNA can be tested for the common mutations association with MCAD and LCHAD deficiencies. Alternatively, for other defects, a skin biopsy for fibroblast culture may be required.

MANAGEMENT OF THE ACUTE SITUATION

i) Whilst awaiting results of specific investigations, management should be supportive and geared to correcting electrolyte and acid-base balance and maintaining adequate gas exchange. Regimens should be instituted to try to reduce the load on the affected metabolic pathway and induce an anabolic state as quickly as possible. Replacement of milk feeds with 10% dextrose infusion (oral or i.v.) is appropriate for most disorders, i.e. amino acid, organic acid, fat oxidation, urea cycle disorders and galactosaemia. However, this is not appropriate for the congenital lactic acidoses which are likely to be exacerbated by a high carbohydrate load.

ii) Severe hyperammonaemia should be treated without delay (see below).

iii) Several IMD have vitamin-responsive variants and the approach in some units is to give a vitamin cocktail whilst awaiting laboratory results. If this approach is used, it is crucial that the appropriate specimens (blood and urine) are taken before the vitamins are given. In practice, it is rare for an IMD presenting acutely in the neonate to be one of these vitamin-responsive types and this approach is not generally recommended.

iv) If more rigorous treatment is considered, e.g. dialysis or haemofiltration, then this will usually require that the baby be transferred to a specialised centre that is experienced in the treatment of metabolic disorders.

ANTENATAL DIAGNOSIS

Increasing numbers of metabolic disorders can be tested for in high risk families by obtaining fetal tissue (Figure 10.5). For antenatal diagnosis to be offered, the defect must have been identified in the index case either biochemically, enzymatically or at the DNA level. Usually the risk of an affected fetus for each pregnancy will be 1 in 4 as most IMDs are inherited in an autosomal recessive manner. Extensive counselling of the family, ideally before pregnancy, is essential before embarking on high risk investigations.

Technique	Collection period (weeks of gestation)	Increase in loss above normal pregnancy loss rate (%)	Test available	Key points
Chorionic villus sampling (CVS)	10-14 weeks	1-2	Metabolites (few) Enzymes DNA	Collected transcervically or transabdominally
				Slightly increased risk of fetal malformations
				Risk of maternal cell contamination
				May be difficult to get sufficient sample for enzyme testing
Amniocentesis	14-18 weeks	0.5-1 (if done earlier risk may be 7%)	Supernatant: Metabolites	Collect transabdominally
			Amniocytes: Enzymes DNA	Cells may require culture (2-6 weeks) leading to delay in diagnosis
				Small risk of maternal cell contamination
Free fetal DNA (ffDNA) in maternal blood	>6 weeks	0	DNA	Avoid maternal contamination
				Limited use currently to determine fetal sex, e.g. X-linked disorders
Fetal blood sampling	>18 weeks	2-3%	DNA	Collected transabdominally by cordocentesis, or blood vessel in fetal heart /liver
				Technically difficult

Figure 10.5. Sampling techniques for prenatal diagnosis.

The outcome of such investigations is usually to terminate the pregnancy if the fetus is found to be affected. However, in some situations, knowledge of an affected fetus is used to prepare the parents for the future. Treatment may also be started *in utero* or promptly after birth, e.g. biotin for biotinidase deficiency. Chromosome analysis is usually also performed on the ante-natal specimen.

Disorders presenting as a sick neonate

The majority of inherited metabolic disorders presenting acutely are as categorised in Figure 10.1. An overview of the most important disorders in each category is presented.

Amino acid disorders

Those defects that cause accumulation of specific amino acids in blood, urine or CSF can be diagnosed by amino acid analysis. Quantitative plasma amino acid analysis is usually essential.

Maple syrup urine disease (MSUD)

Previously this disorder was diagnosed on clinical presentation with the characteristic early presentation of feeding difficulties with worsening CNS function which ultimately could be fatal. There was a significant metabolic acidosis and hypoglycaemia and a distinctive odour of maple syrup from the urine and sweat which gave the condition its name. The disorder is due to a deficiency of the branched chain amino acid decarboxylase enzyme which results in grossly elevated concentrations of the branched chain amino acids (leucine, isoleucine and valine) in plasma and excessive excretion of the branched chain keto acid substrates of the enzyme in urine. With the introduction of newborn screening for this condition (Chapter 9), most of the characteristic neonatal classical presentations will be identified at birth. Milder variants, which may not be detected on screening, have been described but these usually present later in infancy or early childhood, with mild developmental delay.

Non-Ketotic Hyperglycinaemia (NKH)

Preliminary biochemical tests are usually normal and indication for investigation is based on the characteristic clinical picture of a neonate with severe uncontrollable seizures. In addition there is respiratory failure, hypotonia, typical burst-suppression pattern on electroencephalogram (EEG) and hiccups. The basic defect lies in the glycine cleavage system, and diagnosis is based on the finding of an elevated plasma and CSF glycine with an abnormally high CSF:plasma glycine ratio. Rapid quantitative amino acid results are required in this situation so that other disorders, perhaps treatable, can be eliminated. Hyperglycinaemia/glycinuria associated with ketonuria is strongly suggestive of an organic acid disorder (e.g. methylmalonic acidaemia) and investigation of urinary organic acids and blood spot or plasma acyl carnitines is therefore essential in this situation. Treatment for NKH is limited to sodium benzoate (which decreases blood, but not CSF, glycine concentrations) and NMDA receptor blocking medications (dextromethorphan, ketamine and felbamate) – all aid seizures control, but require careful monitoring in order to avoid toxicity.

Definitive diagnosis requires measurement of the glycine cleavage enzyme in liver or DNA analysis of the various causal genes. Prenatal diagnosis is possible by measurement of enzyme activity (uncultured CVS) or DNA analysis (cultured or uncultured CVS).

Tyrosinaemia Type I

The acute form of tyrosinaemia type I presents with severe liver disease and renal tubular dysfunction. The disease is due to a defect of the enzyme fumarylacetoacetase (Figure. 10.6) that causes accumulation of succinylacetone and secondary increase of tyrosine, methionine, 4-hydroxyphenylpyruvate and 4-hydroxyphenyllactate due to inhibition of 4-hydroxyphenylpyruvate oxidase.

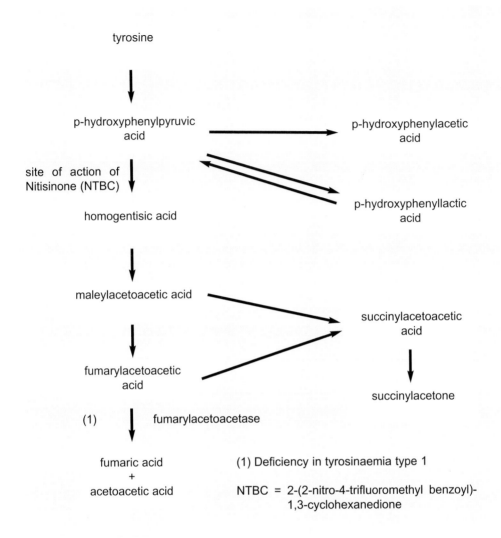

Figure 10.6. Catabolism of tyrosine.

In the neonate, the presenting feature may be hypoglycaemia progressing to fulminant liver failure. Characteristically, there is an increased plasma tyrosine concentration often associated with increased methionine and phenylalanine. It should be noted that the finding of a raised plasma tyrosine is only *suggestive* of tyrosinaemia type I. Other causes of acute liver disease, both metabolic and non-metabolic, e.g. galactosaemia and congenital viral infections, can cause increased plasma tyrosine concentrations of similar magnitude. Useful biochemical clues to support the diagnosis include a high plasma alpha-fetoprotein concentration over and above the expected neonatal range, a very high plasma alkaline phosphatase activity (>2000 IU/L) and evidence of renal tubular dysfunction. The important tests to perform in this situation are measurement of urinary succinylacetone, δ-ALA and PBG synthase or dried blood spot succinylacetone.

Definitive diagnosis requires measurement of fumarylacetoacetase in cultured skin fibroblasts or leucocytes or molecular diagnostics. There are more than 40 different mutations, of which four common ones account for more than 50% of cases. Certain mutations are more common in particular ethnic groups. For antenatal diagnosis molecular genetic analysis may be a more useful investigation than enzyme assay in some families, particularly when it is to differentiate from the pseudodeficiency state (*in vitro* enzyme deficiency with no disease expression).

Immediate treatment is with the drug Nitisinone with liver transplantation as an emergency (if there is a failure to respond), or at a later stage if hepatic malignancy develops. Nitisinone (NTBC) acts by inhibition of 4-hydroxyphenylpyruvate dioxygenase (see Figure 10.6) and should be used together with a low tyrosine and low phenylalanine diet. Without treatment, a large percentage of cases will develop hepatoma. The outcome after treatment is much improved. Nitisinone reduces the occurrence of hepatoma provided it is started in the first few weeks of life. Prenatal diagnosis is possible by measuring the enzyme or DNA analysis in chorionic villus biopsy (direct) or cultured amniotic fluid cells.

(Due to 5, 10 methylene tetrahydrofolate reductase deficiency).
Classical homocystinuria, due to cystathionine synthase deficiency, does not present in the neonate. Screening for this condition now takes place at birth.

The variant form, due to defective remethylation, (see Figure 10.7) can, however, present in the neonatal period with apnoeic episodes, fits and progressive CNS dysfunction. Diagnosis of the variant form requires detection of raised homocystine in plasma and urine. Free or total homocystine can be measured in plasma. Plasma must be deproteinised promptly if measuring free homocystine. Total homocystine measurement has the advantage of simpler sample preparation without deproteinisation. The finding of a low or low-normal plasma methionine concentration and the presence of homocystine in urine and plasma, is consistent with this defect. H owever, defects in cobalamin metabolism, methionine synthesis and maternal B_{12} deficiency should be excluded. The diagnosis can be confirmed by demonstrating the enzyme defect in cultured skin fibroblasts. Prognosis can be improved by betaine therapy, particularly if started early in the neonatal period.

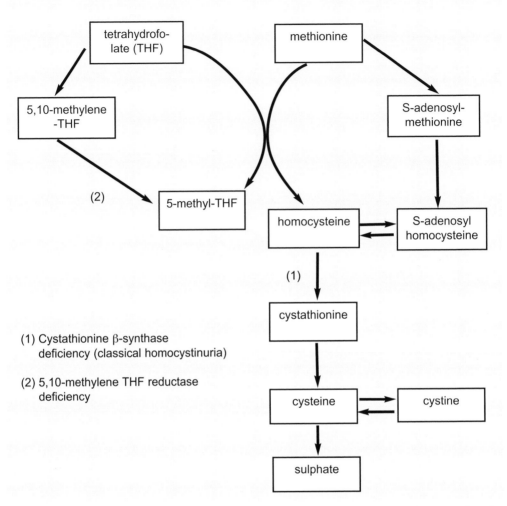

Figure 10.7. Metabolism of homocystine showing the defective enzymes in homocystinuria.

Hyperammonaemia

There are many cause of hyperammonaemia in the neonate (see Figure 10.8) including pre-analytical factors responsible for artefactually increased concentrations. In addition to disorders of intermediary metabolism ammonia can also be non-specifically increased in any sick neonate. It is important to exclude transient hyperammonaemia of the newborn. This can present as life-threatening illness in the first 48h of life indistinguishable from genuine IMD and is more likely to occur in the pre-term baby (< 36 weeks gestation). Plasma ammonia concentration is very high, usually in excess of 1500 μmol/L, and urinary orotic acid concentration is normal. The outcome is good if the condition is treated promptly and aggressively. A presumptive diagnosis is made by exclusion after careful assessment of plasma and urinary amino acids, urinary organic acids and orotic acid.

Pre-analytical	Metabolic disorders
Poor specimen quality/haemolysis	Urea cycle disorders
Difficult venepuncture	Organic acidurias (methylmalonic, propionic)
Skin contamination	Fatty acid oxidation disorders
Contaminated tube	3H syndrome (hyperammonaemia, hyperornithinaemia with homocitrullinaemia)
Delay in analysis	
	Lysinuric protein intolerance
Acquired	Hyperinsulinism (glutamate dehydrogenase deficiency)
Sick baby	Mitochondrial respiratory chain defects
Asphyxia, sepsis	Congenital lactic acidosis
Infection (urinary tract infection, GI bacterial overgrowth)	Citrin deficiency
	Ornithine aminotransferase deficiency
Liver disease	Pyruvate dehydrogenase deficicency
Parenteral nutrition (rare)	
Drugs affecting mitochondrial functioning	**Other**
	Transient hyperammonaemia of the newborn

Figure 10.8. Causes of hyperammonaemia in the neonate.

Urea cycle disorders

There are six inherited disorders of the urea cycle (Figures 10.9 and 10.10). With the exception of argininaemia, these disorders can present in the neonate with hyperammonaemia. The most common is the X-linked disorder ornithine carbamoyl transferase (OCT) deficiency with a prevalence of approximately 1 in 40,000. Plasma ammonia concentrations in excess of 800 μmol/L in the first 1-3 days of life are characteristic of the severe forms of UCD, although the ammonia concentration is dependent on protein intake and catabolic state and may be much lower than this if full milk feeding has not commenced, been reduced or withdrawn. Although babies with these conditions are well at birth, onset is usually very early (i.e. within 48h of birth) with a rapidly progressive encephalopathy.

Initial features include:
- lethargy,
- feed refusal,
- vomiting,
- irritability,
- seizures,
- tachypnoea.

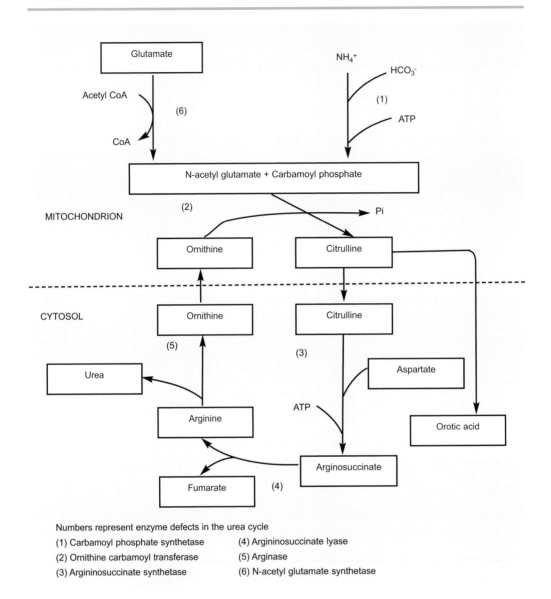

Numbers represent enzyme defects in the urea cycle
(1) Carbamoyl phosphate synthetase (4) Argininosuccinate lyase
(2) Ornithine carbamoyl transferase (5) Arginase
(3) Argininosuccinate synthetase (6) N-acetyl glutamate synthetase

Figure 10.9. Inherited disorders of the urea cycle.

Ammonia is a respiratory stimulant and the presence of a respiratory alkalosis is an important diagnostic clue. Like many other IMDs the conditions may be misdiagnosed as sepsis. A family history of male neonatal deaths particularly suggests OCT deficiency as the condition is X-linked. Liver failure may develop and pulmonary or intracranial haemorrhage can occur.

Ammonia is commonly measured on the laboratory main analyser (either wet chemistry or dry slide technology), or utilising an ammonia meter. Some of the 'single step' wet chemistry methods may be susceptible to positive interference in patients in whom there is co-existent acute liver failure (demonstrated by elevation of transaminases). Dry slide ammonia method-ology, or those methods with a two-step (blanking stage) do not appear to be susceptible to this interference. Laboratories should evaluate in-house ammonia methodology to identify likelihood of interference. If present, confirmatory analysis by an unaffected method is advised in patients with elevated ammonia and co-existent liver failure prior to the initiation of medical intervention aimed at reducing ammonia concentration.

Ammonia meters have been available for a number of years. The analytical range of meters is limited (< 286 μmol/L) and hence use should be restricted to situations where ammonia concentration is well below this threshold.

Urea cycle disorder	Urine orotic acid	Plasma	Enzyme deficiency
Carbamoyl phosphate synthetase deficiency	N	↑ glut/NH$_2$ ↑ ala ↓ cit ↓ arg	Liver
Ornithine carbamoyl transferase deficiency	↑	↑ glut/NH$_2$ ↑ ala ↓ cit ↓ arg	Liver
Citrullinaemia	↑	↑ citrulline ↑ glut/NH$_2$ ↓ arginine	Liver Fibroblasts
Argininosuccinic aciduria	↑	↑ ASA ↑ cit ↑ glut/NH$_2$ ↓ arginine	Liver Erythrocytes Fibroblasts
Argininaemia	↑	↑ arginine	Liver Erythrocytes
N-acetyl glutamate synthetase deficiency	N	↑ glut/NH$_2$ ↑ alanine	Liver

ala = alanine, arg = arginine, ASA = argininosuccinate, cit = citrulline, glut/NH$_2$ = glutamate/glutamine

Figure 10.10. Differential diagnosis of the urea cycle disorders.

Hyperammonaemia is not a diagnosis on its own. A detailed clinical history should be ascertained (particularly details of family history) to establish the cause, and additional tests should be performed (http://www.metbio.net/docs/metbio-guideline-amup).

First line:
- liver function tests: alanine aminotransferase, alkaline phosphatase, bilirubin (total and conjugated or direct), albumin
- urea, electrolytes
- blood gases
- plasma calcium
- clotting studies
- plasma glucose and lactate
- blood culture
- urine ketones (positive in organic acidurias).

Second line – specialist investigation
- plasma and urine amino acids
- urine organic acids
- urine orotic acid
- blood spot or plasma acylcarnitines.

CONFIRMATION OF UREA CYCLE DISORDERS

Definitive diagnosis requires enzyme/DNA analysis in appropriate tissue. For OCT deficiency, DNA analysis is important for carrier detection and pre-natal diagnosis, as the enzyme is not expressed in amniocytes or chorionic villus biopsy.

TREATMENT OF HYPERAMMONAEMIA

Treatment is dictated by the plasma ammonia concentration. Hyperammonaemia (greater than 150 µmol/L) requires prompt and aggressive treatment to minimise the risks of permanent neurological handicap. In severe OCT deficiency (and some other urea cycle disorders) ammonia concetrations can rise very rapidly to concentrations greater than 500 µmol/L.

Whilst awaiting the results of investigations, dietary protein should be withdrawn or reduced whilst ensuring the provision of adequate calories from other sources. Treatment with sodium benzoate and/or sodium phenylbutyrate is useful in promoting excretion of nitrogen containing compounds. With a worsening clinical state and/or rising ammonia concentration or grossly elevated concentration (> 500 µmol/L) which fails to fall significantly, aggressive therapy such as filtration or dialysis should be considered. The method of choice is continuous veno-venous haemofiltration or haemodiafiltration. Acute haemodialysis is also effective, but the benefit may be short lived. Peritoneal dialysis is less effective but can be used if haemodialysis is not immediately available. Even with early treatment, some patients with the severest types of UCD have a poor outcome, and discussion with the family about the advantages and disadvantages of embarking on aggressive treatment is required. Long-term treatment for these patients is required.

The basis of long-term treatment of the UCD is dietary protein restriction (0.8-1.5 g/kg/24h). Sodium benzoate and/or sodium phenylbutyrate therapy may also be necessary to keep plasma ammonia concentrations down to an acceptable level (< 80 µmol/L). Benzoate conjugates with glycine to form hippurate which is excreted and thereby diverts nitrogen away from the urea cycle. Sodium phenylbutyrate (or sodium phenylacetate) is converted to phenylacetylglutamine and excreted, thereby removing two nitrogen atoms. In severe cases both benzoate and phenylbutyrate can be given. Benzoic acid may be hepatotoxic and theoretically will displace bilirubin from albumin; its use, therefore, may be a particular risk in the jaundiced neonate. With the exception of argininaemia, arginine becomes an essential amino acid in patients with a UCD and supplements are required. A newer treatment for hyperammonaemia associated with organic acid disorders and N-acetylglutamate synthetase (NAGS) deficiency, is the use of carglumic acid tablets (an analog of N-acetylglutamate) which activate carbamoyl phosphate synthetase and hence excretion of ammonia through the urea cycle. Treatment regimens require regular monitoring of plasma ammonia concentration and relevant amino acids (quantitative). The outcome with treatment depends on the individual disorder, the severity of the defect and compliance with the treatment regime. For many, outcome is poor. For those patients who survive the initial hyperammonaemia, liver transplantation is an option.

Organic acid disorders

Defects of branched chain amino acid and propionyl CoA catabolism.

Organic acids are carboxylic acids of low molecular weight and are metabolites of amino acids, carbohydrates and fats. Organic acid disorders can affect several intermediary metabolic pathways, in particular the catabolism of the branched chain amino acids, leucine, isoleucine and valine (Figure 10.11.), and of propionyl CoA (Figure 10.12.). The intermediates that accumulate in these disorders, with the exception of MSUD, do not react with ninhydrin and cannot be diagnosed by amino acid analysis. Specific methods for organic acids using gas chromatography-mass spectrometry are essential. Over 50 disorders caused by a primary biochemical defect of organic acid metabolism have been described and their combined incidence is probably at least as great as that of the amino acid disorders. There are often other metabolic abnormalities associated with the acidosis. For presentation, diagnosis and treatment of these disorders see Figure 10.13.

Whilst awaiting results of investigations, dietary protein should be withdrawn.

Unfortunately, despite treatment, patients who have presented in the neonatal period continue to have intermittent crises of ketoacidosis and, generally, the long-term outcome is poor. A few patients with methylmalonic acidaemia and propionic acidaemias have had liver transplantation. Patients who have survived have some improvement, although mortality associated with the procedure has been high.

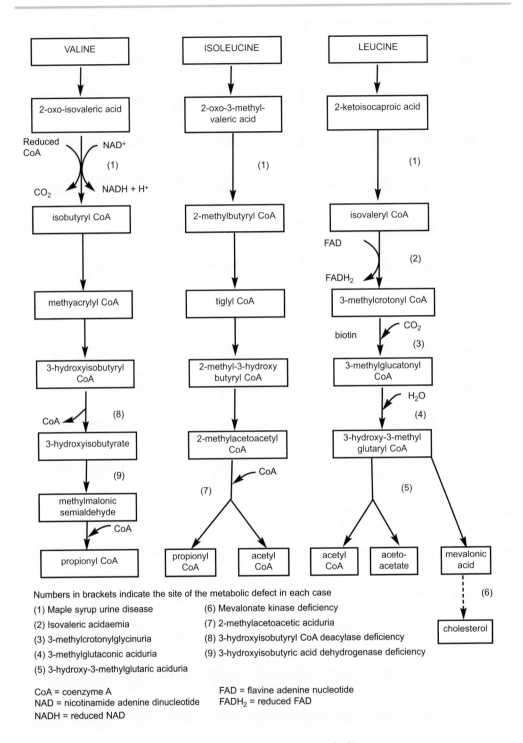

Numbers in brackets indicate the site of the metabolic defect in each case

(1) Maple syrup urine disease
(2) Isovaleric acidaemia
(3) 3-methylcrotonylglycinuria
(4) 3-methylglutaconic aciduria
(5) 3-hydroxy-3-methylglutaric aciduria

(6) Mevalonate kinase deficiency
(7) 2-methylacetoacetic aciduria
(8) 3-hydroxyisobutyryl CoA deacylase deficiency
(9) 3-hydroxyisobutyric acid dehydrogenase deficiency

CoA = coenzyme A
NAD = nicotinamide adenine dinucleotide
NADH = reduced NAD

FAD = flavine adenine nucleotide
$FADH_2$ = reduced FAD

Figure 10.11. Disorders of branched chain amino acid catabolism.

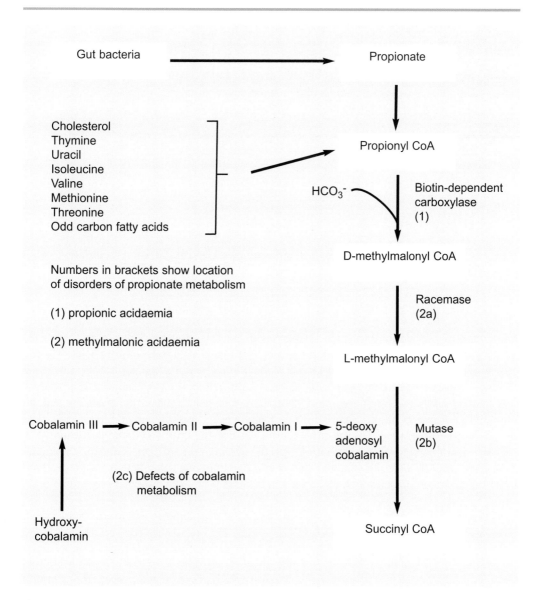

Figure 10.12. Formation and metabolism of propionyl coenzyme A (CoA).

Clinical presentation	Non-diagnostic lab features	Diagnostic tests	Treatment
Severe metabolic acidosis Lethargy Vomiting Hypotonia	Hypoglycaemia Hyperammonaemia Hypocalcaemia Ketonuria Hyperlactataemia Hyperuricaemia Neutropenia Increased plasma and urine glycine	Urine organic acids Blood spot and plasma carnitine species, eg. propionylcarnitine (Samples should be collected whilst acidotic and before institution of dietary protein restriction)	Dietary protein restriction (0.8-1.5 g/kg/day) Artificial amino acid mixture

Figure 10.13. Branched chain amino acid and propionyl CoA catabolism: presentation, diagnosis and treatment.

Disorders of fatty acid transport and oxidation

Mitochondrial β-oxidation of fatty acids plays a major role in energy production, especially during periods of fasting. It is a complex process that involves uptake of fatty acids into the cell, activation to the acyl CoA and then transport into the mitochondria, which requires a carnitine transport cycle (see Figures 10.14 and 10.15). Within the mitochondria, the β-oxidation spiral requires a series of enzymes with carbon chain length specificity. There are a range of inherited disorders due to defects in the carnitine cycle and the β-oxidation process. The defects of the β-oxidation process differ on the basis of the fatty acid chain length which is affected. The commonest disorder described is the defect of the medium chain acyl CoA dehydrogenase (MCAD) which is now included in the neonatal screening bloodspot programme (see Chapter 9). For presentation, diagnosis and treatment of these disorders see Figure 10.16.

Clinical severity varies widely in fatty acid oxidation defects. Some of the disorders are candidates for prenatal diagnosis.

Diagnosis of these conditions can be very difficult, as investigations may be completely normal when the infant is well and abnormalities may only become evident when the infant is stressed by fasting when fatty acid esters and corresponding dicarboxylic acids accumulate. It is particularly important to investigate newborn sibs of known cases by looking for characteristic metabolites in blood (acylcarnitines) and urine (organic acids) which have been collected within the first 72h of life when the baby is stressed from the birth process.

Syndromes of maternal illness during pregnancy, e.g. hepatic encephalopathy, liver dysfunction and low platelets (HELLP) and acute fatty liver of pregnancy (AFLP), have been associated with a fetus affected by some of these defects (in particular LCHAD).

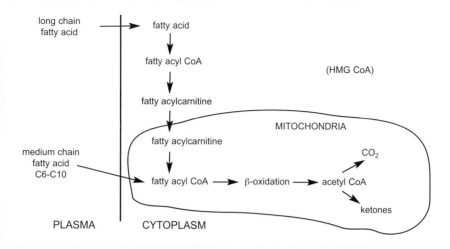

Figures 10.14. Fatty acid uptake, activation and β-oxidation.

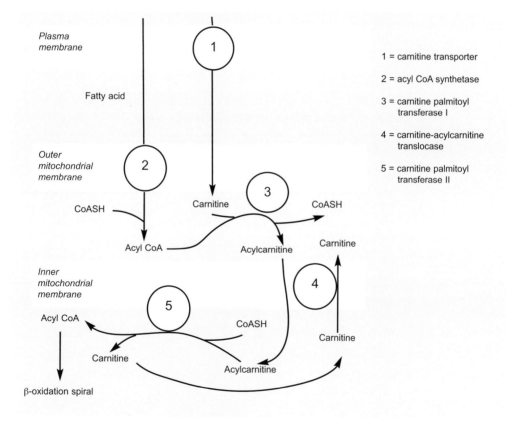

1 = carnitine transporter

2 = acyl CoA synthetase

3 = carnitine palmitoyl transferase I

4 = carnitine-acylcarnitine translocase

5 = carnitine palmitoyl transferase II

Figure 10.15. The carnitine transport cycle.

Clinical presentation	Non-diagnostic lab features	Diagnostic tests	Treatment
Malformations and facial dysmorphism	Hypoketotic hypoglycaemia	Collected at time of illness:	Avoidance of fasting
Cardiac arrhythmias and conduction defects	High ratio of plasma free fatty acids: 3-hydroxybutyrate	Urinary organic acids (fatty acid esters and corresponding dicarboxylic acids,	Medium Chain Triglyceride (MCT) diet
Cardiomyopathy	+/-Hyperammonaemia e.g. CPT II and	e.g. sebacic,	
Lethargy, coma and hypotonia	translocase deficiency	suberic and adipic acids accumulate	
Sudden infant death	+/-Metabolic acidosis	(see Figure 10.17). Dried blood spot and plasma acylcarnitines DNA test (e.g. MCADD)	

Figure 10.16. Fatty acid transport and oxidation disorders: presentation, diagnosis and treatment.

Fatty acids with chain lengths as below

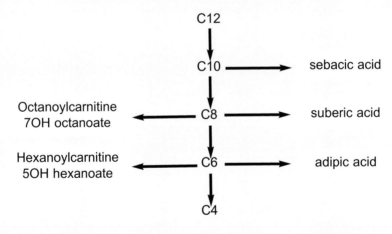

Figure 10.17. Medium chain fatty acid metabolism in fat oxidation defects.

Carbohydrate disorders

Galactosaemia

Classic galactosaemia, due to galactose 1-phosphate uridyl transferase (gal 1-PUT) deficiency (Figure 10.18), characteristically presents in the first week of life. Some countries have neonatal screening programmes. Where this is not the case, initial diagnosis relies on clinical acumen. For presentation, diagnosis and treatment see Figure 10.19.

If the diagnosis is suspected, the baby should be taken off lactose whilst awaiting the results of the screening test. An abnormal screening test should always be confirmed with a quantitative enzyme assay as the heterozygous state cannot always be reliably differentiated, and also several enzyme variants (e.g. Duarte allele) exist. Epimerase deficiency (Figure 10.18) has been described in a few cases and can present with a similar clinical picture to transferase deficiency; this deficiency should be considered if there is persistent galactosaemia and a normal gal 1-PUT.

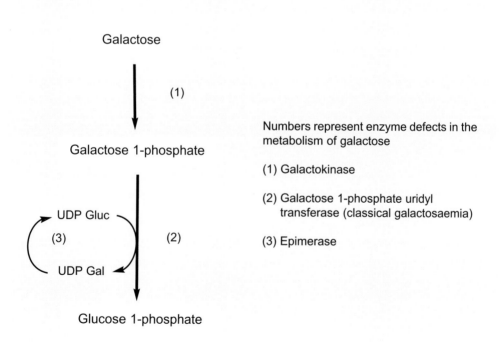

Numbers represent enzyme defects in the metabolism of galactose

(1) Galactokinase

(2) Galactose 1-phosphate uridyl transferase (classical galactosaemia)

(3) Epimerase

Figure 10.18. Disorders of galactose metabolism.

Clinical presentation	Non-diagnostic lab features	Diagnostic tests	Treatment
Failure to thrive	Hypoglycaemia	Erythrocyte galactosaemia screen (Beutler)	Galactose- (& lactose) free diet
Hepatomegaly	Hyperbilirubinaemia (initially unconjugated)		
Vomiting		Galactose 1-phosphate uridyl transferase (gal 1-PUT) in erythrocytes	Dietary compliance should be monitored by measurement of erythrocyte galactose 1-phosphate
	Abnormal liver enzymes		
Lethargy			
Oedema	Coagulopathy		
Ascites	Hypophosphataemia	Also:	
Cataracts	Aminoaciduria	Urine sugars	
Liver failure	Hyperphenylalaninemia	Urine galactitol	
Sepsis (E.coli)		Mutation analysis	
Death			

Figure 10.19. Galactosaemia: presentation, diagnosis and treatment

Persistent galactosuria in a baby must be taken seriously and a diagnosis pursued vigorously – the neonatologist and clinical biochemist should be aware of the possibility of a false negative result typically due to preceding blood transfusion or removal of lactose from infant feeds. If the baby has a classic galactosaemia picture with galactosuria, tyrosinaemia type I and hereditary fructose intolerance should be considered as part of the differential diagnosis. Recovery from the acute life-threatening stage is usually rapid and complete. Cognitive outcome appears to relate to genotype rather than metabolic control. In the UK, homozygosity for the Q188R mutation is invariably associated with a relatively poor outcome.

Glycogen storage disease (GSD) type I

This is a group of disorders caused by a deficiency of glucose 6-phosphatase. There have been cases described where a baby has had unexplained hypoglycaemic episodes soon after birth, from which there was apparent full recovery until presentation several months later with unexplained hepatomegaly. Such cases stress the importance of adequately investigating neonatal hypoglycaemia (Chapter 7). The presentation, diagnosis and treatment of GSD I are shown in Figure 10.20.

The important biochemical features are as indicated in Figure 10.20. Definitive diagnosis is provided by histological investigation and specific tissue enzyme measurements. As the child gets older, the frequency of hypoglycaemic attacks usually declines. However, in the longer term patients can develop impairment of renal and liver function and follow-up with relevant biochemical and clinical monitoring is required.

Clinical presentation	Non-diagnostic lab features	Diagnostic tests	Treatment
Metabolic acidosis	Hypoglycaemia	DNA	Minimise/prevent hypoglycaemia by:
+/- hepatomegaly	Lactic acidosis	Glucose-6-phosphatase activity (in liver – as	Carbohydrate-rich diet eg. cornstarch,
	Elevated liver enzymes	enzyme is not present in blood cells or	frequent feeds, continuous tube
	+/- Neutropenia	fibroblasts)	feeding
	Elevated triglycerides	Further tests to diagnose subtypes	
	Elevated cholesterol	of GSD type I	
	Elevated urate		
	Liver biopsy: Excess glycogen and steatosis		

Figure 10.20. Glycogen storage disease type I: presentation, diagnosis and treatment.

Disorders of fructose metabolism

HEREDITARY FRUCTOSE INTOLERANCE (HFI)

This disorder only presents after exposure to fructose (or sucrose) and is therefore very rare in neonates. Presentation is very similar to galactosaemia and removal of the dietary sugar results in rapid clinical and biochemical improvement. Biochemical features include hypophos-phataemia, hypoglycaemia and increased plasma lactate concentration. The diagnosis may be suspected from detailed nutritional history, clinical picture, the finding of a positive test for urinary reducing substances and aminoaciduria.

Measurement of the enzyme fructose 1,6-diphosphate aldolase activity in liver tissue is required for definitive diagnosis. One specific mutation (A149P) in the gene encoding the enzyme is relatively common in North West Europeans and may therefore provide a useful approach to diagnosis.

FRUCTOSE 1,6-BISPHOSPHATASE DEFICIENCY

In contrast to HFI, dietary ingestion of fructose is not a prerequisite to presentation. Acute presentation in the neonate is usually within the first few days as a life-threatening illness with hypoglycaemia, metabolic (lactic) acidosis, convulsions and hepatomegaly. Diagnosis requires measurement of the enzyme in leucocytes or liver.

Lactic acidosis

There are several non-specific causes of lactic acidosis (Figure 10.21). When considering meta-bolic causes of lactic acidosis, it is therefore important to ensure that the baby is well perfused and has an adequate blood volume and blood pressure. Lactate is usually measured in venous blood, although concentrations in free flowing capillary blood correlate well with venous blood measurement. Blood for lactate measurement is stable for at least three hours at room temperature if taken into fluoride/oxalate preservative; it is less stable in heparin.

Lactate concentration	Causes
up to 20 mmol/L	Severe respiratory failure
greater than 10 mmol/L	Hypoxia - excessive muscular activity - seizure Circulatory - hypoplastic left heart - intraventricular haemorrhage
2-4 mmol/L	Infection Dehydration Liver dysfunction Immaturity Anaemia

Figure 10.21. Non-specific causes of high blood lactate.

If non-specific causes have been excluded, a persistent and significantly elevated lactate (i.e. > 3 mmol/L) requires further investigation for the possibility of a congenital lactic acidosis or other IMDs. This is particularly likely if associated with hypoglycaemia and/or hyperammon-aemia. Differential diagnoses include:
- glycogen storage disorder type I,
- organic acid disorders,
- fatty acid oxidation defects,
- disorders of pyruvate metabolism (pyruvate dehydrogenase deficiency),
- disorders of gluconeogenesis (phosphoenolpyruvate carboxykinase, pyruvate carboxylase, fructose 1,6-bisphosphatase deficiencies),
- electron transport chain defects/mitochondrial disorders.

Further tests will be directed by clinical history and should include consideration of blood spot or plasma acylcarnitines, urinary organic acids, plasma urate, plasma creatine kinase, plasma and urine amino acids, fasting blood glucose, plasma 3-hydroxybutyrate and free fatty acids and liver enzymes (Figure 10.4). The results of these tests may be useful in establishing the significance of a mild or intermittent lactic acidosis and in guiding further investigations. CSF lactate is important if neurological features are predominant. Mitochondrial DNA and electron transport disorders should be considered in the differential diagnosis of a sick newborn with lactic acidosis, especially if there is hypotonia; this will require further investigations including muscle biopsy.

Urinary organic acids may not show an increased lactate if the plasma lactate does not exceed 7 mmol/L. Normal urinary organic acids, therefore, do not preclude the possibility of a significantly increased plasma lactate.

Peroxisomal disorders

The peroxisome is a subcellular organelle containing many enzyme systems. Functions include biosynthesis of plasmalogens (essential neuronal lipid compounds), catalase activity, oxidation of very long, long and medium chain fatty acids and phytanic acid, and metabolism of pipecolic acid (a metabolite of lysine oxidation). Several inherited metabolic disorders have been described due to single or multiple defects in peroxisomal function. The classic disorder of this group is Zellweger syndrome which presents at birth and has a poor prognosis with affected patients often dying within the first year of life (Figure 10.22).

Clinical presentation (at birth or shortly after)	Non-diagnostic lab features	Diagnostic tests	Treatment
Dysmorphism	Elevated bilirubin	Plasma very long chain fatty acids (VLCFA)	Anticonvulsants for seizures
Hypotonia	Abnormal LFTs		
Liver dysfunction	Coagulopathy	Plasma bile acids	Vitamin K for coagulopathy
Hepatomegaly		DNA (PEX gene mutation)	
Developmental delay			Gastrostomy to improve nutritional intake
Seizures			
Calcific stippling of epiphyses (radiology)			

Figure 10.22. Zellweger syndrome.

Purine and pyrimidine disorders

Purine and pyrimidines supply the basic components of DNA and RNA as well as important intracellular pools, e.g. ATP. Several inherited metabolic disorders of purine or pyrimidine metabolism have been described, affecting the functioning of the CNS, kidney and immune system and, hence, having a wide range of clinical presentations. The most severe disorder presenting in the neonatal period is xanthine oxidase/sulphite oxidase deficiency due to a deficiency of their enzyme co-factor – molybdenum. Over 100 patients have been reported in a wide range of ethnic groups. The disorder presents with intractable seizures and can be suspected by the finding of a low plasma urate concentration and low urinary urate:creatinine ratio. Lesch-Nyhan syndrome can present, albeit rarely, in the neonatal period with characteristically high plasma and urine urate concentrations; presentation at this age is with an orange/red 'sand' in the nappy and/or haematuria. In rare cases hypotonia has been recognised shortly after birth. Adenosine deaminase deficiency, associated with severe combined immune deficiency (SCID), manifests at birth with diarrhoea, failure to thrive and candidiasis.

Others

Smith-Lemli-Opitz (SLO) syndrome

Smith-Lemli-Opitz syndrome is an inborn error of cholesterol metabolism due to deficiency of 7-dehydrocholesterol reductase as a result of mutations in the DHCR7 gene. It is relatively common, with estimates of incidence ranging from 1 in 40,000 to 1 in 20,000.

Affected individuals have facial dysmorphia that correlates with the severity of biochemical and physical abnormalities. In the severe form, patients have a distinctive facial appearance with congenital microcephaly and ptosis. There are usually feeding problems and hypotonia. Some patients present with a severe lethal form in the newborn period from complications of visceral malformations. Due to the role of cholesterol in steroid hormone production individuals may also have endocrine problems, including adrenal insufficiency.

Biochemical diagnosis requires measurement of plasma 7-dehydrocholesterol. Cholesterol concentrations may be low or normal (~10% of those with SLO), but the ratio of 7-dehydrocholesterol: cholesterol is high. Mutation analysis of DHCR7 can be used as a confirmatory test or where there are equivocal biochemical results. Once the mutation is identified it can be used to determine carrier status in at risk relatives or allow prenatal testing. Dietary management with cholesterol replacement therapy has been used with reported benefits of improved behaviour and better growth in some patients.

Congenital disorders of glycosylation (CDG)

These are a family of genetic disorders characterised by a deficiency of the carbohydrate moiety (glycan) of glycoproteins and other glycoconjugates. The commonest type is due to phosphomannomutase deficiency (type 1A) and is a multisystem disease, presenting in the neonate with dysmorphism, CNS dysfunction and involvement of several different organs, e.g. liver failure, pericardial effusion and nephrotic syndrome. Patients with type 1B due to a defect in their microsomal glucose 6-phosphate transporter system, usually manifest with a gastroenterological presentation. Biochemical diagnosis requires demonstration of a characteristically abnormal transferrin electrophoresis pattern in plasma. There are associated abnormalities of several plasma glycoproteins (e.g. deficiencies of clotting factors and hormone binding glycoproteins). The specific enzyme defect of phosphomannomutase can be demonstrated in fibroblasts. No effective treatment is available for type 1A. For type 1B, treatment with mannose may be effective.

The dysmorphic baby and inherited metabolic disorders

Dysmorphic features in the newborn baby usually suggest an intrauterine insult, e.g. infection, drug exposure, chromosome abnormality, or a genetic 'syndrome' without a known biochemical cause. In some cases, however, the malformation or dysmorphism can be associated with a biochemical disorder (see Figure 10.23 and www.metbio.net/docs/MetBio-Guideline for investigation of dysmorphism).

The neonate with dysmorphic features should have a careful and detailed examination to assess CNS function, and a sample taken for chromosome analysis. Neurological and/or radiological abnormalities may suggest particular biochemical defects and the need for more specific investigations.

It is likely that an increasing number of syndromes will be found to have a biochemical basis and clinicians need to be aware of these possibilities and investigate accordingly.

	Dysmorphic features	Other features	1st line and diagnostic investigations
Maternal PKU	Microcephaly	Congenital heart disease	Plasma phenylalanine in the mother
Congenital lactic acidosis (pyruvate dehydrogenase deficiency)	Abnormal facies Microcephaly	Acidosis Hypotonia Seizures Abnormal brain (absence of corpus callosum)	Blood (& CSF) lactate Fibroblast studies Pyruvate oxidation DNA analysis
Zellweger syndrome and related disorders	High forehead Shallow supra-orbital ridges Epicanthic folds Abnormal ear helices High arched palate Micrognathia Large fontanelle	Hypotonia Hepatomegaly Seizures Calcific stippling of epiphyses	Plasma VLCFA C26:C24 fatty acid ratio Bile acids Red cell membrane plasmalogens Platelet and fibroblast dihydroxyacetone phosphate acyl transferase
Glutaric aciduria type II (multiple acyl CoA dehydrogenase deficiency)	Macrocephaly Abnormal facies	Hypotonia Hypoglycaemia Polycystic kidneys	Urine organic acids Plasma acylcarnitines Lymphocyte/fibroblast fatty acid oxidation studies
Sulphite/xanthine oxidase deficiency (molybdenum cofactor deficiency)	Abnormal facies	Seizures Hypotonia	Plasma urate Urinary urate:creatinine ratio Plasma/urine S-sulphocysteine Fibroblast sulphite oxidase assay. Mutation screening of molybdenum cofactor synthesis genes or sulphite oxidase genes.
Congenital adrenal hyperplasia	Ambiguous genitalia in females	Salt loss Recurrent vomiting Dehydration Hyponatraemia	Plasma 17-hydroxy-progesterone Urine steroid profile
Congenital hypothyroidism	Coarse facies	Jaundice	Plasma TSH and free T4
GM2 gangliosidosis	Frontal bossing Depressed nasal bridge Low set ears	Feeding difficulties Hypoactive Hypotonia Oedema	Urinary oligosaccharides Leucocyte/fibroblast β-galactosidase
Mucolipidosis 2 (I cell disease)	Coarse facies Depressed nasal bridge Large tongue	Restricted joint movement Radiological changes	Plasma arylsulphatase A (I cell screen) Mutation Analysis

Figure 10.23. Metabolic disorders that may present with dysmorphic features in the neonate (Cont...).

	Dysmorphic features	Other features	1st line and Diagnostic investigations
Mucolipidosis I (Sialidosis)	Coarse facies Depressed nasal bridge	Radiological changes Cherry red spot Myoclonus	Urine oligosaccharides Fibroblast α-neuraminidase and β-galactosidase
Mucopolysaccharidosis VII (Sly disease)	Coarse facies Depressed nasal bridge Large tongue	Hydrops fetalis Hepatomegaly	Urine GAGs Plasma/Leucocyte/ fibroblast β-glucuronidase
Multiple sulphatase deficiency (Austin variant)	Coarse facies Depressed nasal bridge Large tongue	Icthyosis Hepatomegaly Radiological changes	Urine GAGs Leucocyte/fibroblast sulphatase
Menke's disease	Abnormal facies	Hypothermia Fine hair Trichorrhexis nodosa Seizures	Plasma copper and caeruloplasmin
Congenital disorders of glycosylation	Coarse facies Dysmorphism	Multisystem	Plasma transferrin isoforms
Cholesterol synthesis defects eg. Smith-Lemli-Opitz	Microcephaly Facial dysmorphism Syndactyly	Hypotonia	Plasma 7-dehydro-cholesterol Plasma sterols Mutation analysis e.g. 7- DHCR gene
Mevalonate kinase deficiency	Abnormal facies	Hepatosplenomegaly Anaemia Recurrent infections	Urine organic acids Mevalonate kinase assay or mutation analysis.

GAGs = Glycosaminoglycans

Figure 10.23 (Cont...). Metabolic disorders that may present with dysmorphic features in the neonate.

Inherited metabolic disorders and seizures

There are numerous causes of seizures in the neonate (Figure 10.24). Seizures are also a feature of several inherited metabolic disorders (Figure 10.25). Clues that seizures may be metabolic in origin include:
- peculiar odour,
- intractable seizures occurring after the first 72 hours,
- normal prenatal and delivery history,
- emergence of food intolerance,
- increasing lethargy.

- Hypoxic-ischaemic encephalopathy
- Cerebrovascular accident/arterial or venous infarction
- Intraparenchymal cerebral haemorrhage
- Subdural haemorrhage
- Subarachnoid haemorrhage
- Infective encephalitis, e.g. Herpes
- Meningitis, e.g. E coli or Group B Streptococcus
- Congenital CNS malformations, e.g. lissencephaly, microgyria
- Hydrocephalus (any cause)

Figure 10.24. Neonatal seizures: Non-metabolic causes.

- Hypoglycaemia (see Chapter 7)
- Hypocalcaemia (see Chapter 8)
- Non-ketotic hyperglycinaemia
- Urea cycle defects
- Homocystinuria (remethylation defect)
- Zellweger's syndrome (peroxisomal defects)
- Molybdenum cofactor deficiency and isolated sulphite oxidase deficiency
- Pyridoxine and pyridoxal phosphate responsive seizures
- Glucose transporter 1 deficiency
- Biotinidase deficiency
- Glutaric aciduria type 1 (see Chapter 9)
- Tyrosine hydroxylase deficiency
- 3-Phosphoglycerate dehydrogenase deficiency
- Aromatic amino acid decarboxylase deficiency (neurotransmitter disorders)
- Pterin disorders
- Menkes syndrome
- γ-Aminobutyrate transaminase deficiency
- Familial neonatal seizures

Figure 10.25. Neonatal seizures: Metabolic causes.

Seizures may be the presenting feature in a primary disorder of the glucose transporter (GLUT) found primarily in the CNS, and responsible for glucose transfer across the blood brain barrier. Glucose transporter 1 deficiency usually presents in early infancy with seizures and developmental delay, and patients become progressively microcephalic. The characteristic abnormalities are a low concentration of glucose in CSF and a reduced CSF/blood glucose ratio. Seizures respond well to the institution of a ketogenic diet.

Benign familial neonatal convulsions is a dominant epilepsy syndrome presenting in the first week of life. The seizures usually remit within the first six months of life, although 10% of patients have seizures when older. It is caused by a mutation in one of the potassium channel genes. Some neonatal seizures, which may start *in utero*, and are resistant to conventional anticonvulsants, are due to pyridoxine dependency.

Pregnancy and IMD

It is now well established that, for certain metabolic disorders, there are complications associated with pregnancy (see Chapter 3). These may manifest as risks to the mother, detrimental effects on the fetus, or both. The best example of such a condition is phenylketonuria. Clinicians, particularly obstetricians, geneticists and biochemists, need to be aware of the potential for complications during pregnancy in this group of disorders.

Further reading

http://www.metbio.net/metbioGuidelines.asp/
- Biochemical Investigation of Fits and Seizures for Inherited Metabolic Disorders
- Diagnosis of inherited metabolic disease in children with dysmorphic features
- Investigation of Hyperammonaemia
- Investigation of hypoglycaemia in infants and children
- Metabolic investigations of sudden infant death
- Neonatal Jaundice in Inherited Metabolic Disorders

http://www.metbio.net/docs/MetBio-TrainingDoc-TURA758503-05-09-2009.pdf

http://www.metbio.net/docs/MetBio-Presentation-KAME741213-21-01-2011.pdf

http://www.safeguardingshropshireschildren.org.uk/scb/files/west-midlands-sudi-guidance.pdf

www.hta.gov.uk/legislationpoliciesandcodesofpractice/codesofpractice.cfm (July 2014)
http://www.orpha.net

Bennett MJ, Renaldo P, Strauss AW. Inborn errors of mitochondrial fatty acid oxidation. Crit Rev Clin Lab Sci 2000; **37**: 1-44.

Brown GK. Glucose transporters: Structure, function and consequences of deficiency. J Inher Metab Dis 2000; **23**: 237-246.

Chakrapani A, Cleary MA, Wraith JE. Detection of inborn errors of metabolism in the newborn. Arch Dis Child Neonatal Ed. 2001; **84**: F205-210.

Herrera D, Hutchin T, Fullerton D, Gray G. Non-specific interference in the measurement of plasma ammonia. Ann Clin Biochem 2010; **47**: 81-83.

Kim SZ, Kupke KG, Ierardi-Curto L, Holme E, Greter J, *et al.* Hepatocellular carcinoma despite long-term survival in chronic tyrosinaemia I. J Inherit Metab Dis 2000; **23**: 791-804.

Leonard JV, Morris AAM. Inborn errors of metabolism around time of birth. Lancet 2000; **356**: 583-587.

Maestri NE, Clissold D, Brusilow SW. Neonatal onset ornithine transcarbamylase deficiency: A retrospective analysis. J Ped 1999; **134:** 268-272.

Nowaczyk MJM. Smith-Lemli-Opitz Syndrome. 1998 Nov 13 [Updated 2013 Jun 20]. In: Pagon RA, Adam MP, Ardinger HH, *et al.*, editors. GeneReviews® [Internet]. Seattle (WA): University of Washington, Seattle; 1993-2014.
Available from: http://www.ncbi.nlm.nih.gov/books/NBK1143/

Shield JPH, Wadsworth EJK, MacDonald A, Stephenson A, Tyfield L, Holton JAB *et al.* The relationship of genotype to cognitive outcome in galactosaemia. Arch Dis Child 2000; **83:** 248-250.

Stacpoole PW, Bunch ST, Neuberger RE *et al.* The importance of cerebrospinal fluid lactate in the evaluation of congenital lactic acidosis. J Ped 1999; **134:** 99-102.

Van den Berghe. Disorders of gluconeogenesis. J Inher Metab Dis 1996; **19:** 470-477.

Wraith JE. Ornithine carbamoyltransferase deficiency. Arch Dis Child 2001; **84:** 84-88.

Chapter 11
Haematology and the neonate

Summary

- Disorders of erythrocytes, leucocytes, platelets and of the haemostatic and thrombotic system can present in the neonate.

- Anaemia is a common disorder in neonates and most commonly arises from blood loss.

- Haemolytic disease of the newborn due to rhesus incompatability is an important cause of anaemia and jaundice.

- Blood transfusion is the mainstay of management of neonatal anaemia and is not without risk.

- Immune mediated disorders of neutrophils and platelets cause neutropenia and thrombocytopenia respectively.

- Neonatal haemostasis and thrombosis is dependent upon various procoagulants, anticoagulants and fibrinolysis proteins that make up the haemostatic system, as well as platelets and vascular components.

- The most common disorders of the haemostatic system in the neonate are haemorrhagic disease of the newborn and disseminated intravascular coagulation.

Haematopoiesis

Fetal haematopoiesis

Haematopoiesis begins in early embryonic development, taking place first in the yolk sac, and then from six weeks until 6-7 months gestation, in the liver. Whilst the liver continues to produce blood cells until about two weeks after birth, from the third trimester onwards the principal site of haematopoiesis is the bone marrow as it is throughout childhood and adult life. The most important stimulus for erythropoiesis is the hormone erythropoietin (EPO) which, in the fetus, is produced in the liver. As gestation advances, EPO production gradually switches to the kidney; however the liver remains the principal source until after birth.

As the site of haematopoiesis changes during gestation, so too does the type of haemoglobin synthesised – a process known as 'haemoglobin switching'. Developmentally there are embryonic, fetal and adult haemoglobins, each of which is adapted to their particular oxygen requirements. Haemoglobin is made up of two matching chains of proteins, which are named after Greek letters of the alphabet.

- In the hepatic phase of haematopoiesis, fetal haemoglobin (HbF) ($\alpha_2\gamma_2$) predominates. As the bone marrow becomes the main site of haematopoiesis there is a gradual shift to production of adult type haemoglobin (HbA) ($\alpha_2\beta_2$), starting at around 34 weeks gestation and continuing into infancy.

- At full term, about 20% of circulating haemoglobin is HbA and by six months of age HbF makes up less than 1% of the total.

Neonatal haematopoiesis

A number of physiological changes occur at birth which affect erythropoiesis in the neonatal period. The switch in erythropoietin (EPO) production, from the liver to the kidney, together with the rise in arterial oxygen concentrations post-delivery, causes a rapid decline in EPO production. Consequently, erythropoiesis virtually halts by the end of the first week, with a resultant fall in red cell and haemoglobin production. In term infants, the haemoglobin reaches a nadir of around 90-100 g/L at 8-10 weeks of age (physiological anaemia of the newborn). In preterm infants, this nadir may occur earlier and is exaggerated, with the haemo-globin falling as low as 70-80 g/L (physiological anaemia of prematurity). The cause of this exaggerated nadir is likely to be multifactorial:

- Preterm babies still have the liver as the primary site of EPO production, which is relatively insensitive to the effects of anaemia and hypoxia compared with the kidney.

- Preterm neonates are likely to have increased requirements due to rapid growth, increased blood loss due to blood sampling, and decreased red cell survival.

Compensation for the reduced oxygen carrying capacity, due to the physiological fall in haemoglobin and red cell production, is achieved by changes in the oxygen affinity and releasing capacity of haemoglobin.

HbF has a higher affinity for oxygen than HbA. This benefits the fetus as a higher oxygen content in the blood can be achieved in the environment of a low partial pressure of oxygen (PaO_2) within the placenta. However, after birth, when the PaO_2 rises, this is no longer an advantage.

The affinity with which haemoglobin binds to oxygen is affected by a number of factors as shown in the oxygen dissociation curve (Figure 5.2).

- In term infants, the switch to the production of HbA, together with an increase in 2,3-bisphosphoglycerate (facilitates oxygen transport) in the erythrocytes, shifts the oxygen disassociation curve to the right and facilitate 'unloading' of oxygen to tissues. This increase in delivery of oxygen to tissues more than compensates for the decreased oxygen carrying capacity associated with the physiological fall in haemoglobin concentration.

- Factors that increase the affinity of haemoglobin for oxygen shift the curve to the left and potentially decrease the availability of oxygen to the tissues.

Neonatal anaemia

Neonatal anaemia may be classified according to the mechanism of anaemia or timing of onset (Figure 11.1). It can be due to blood loss which is the most common cause, increased red cell breakdown or decreased red cell production. Anaemia can occur before birth, during the first 24 hours of life or after 24 hours.

Mechanism	Haematological causes	Onset
Blood loss	Fetomaternal haemorrhage	*In utero* or at delivery
	Twin-to-twin transfusion	*In utero*
	Placenta previa/abruption	*In utero* or at delivery
	Umbilical cord rupture	At delivery
	Obstetric accidents	At delivery
	Iatrogenic: blood tests	Post-natal
	Internal haemorrhage: intra- and extracranial, intra-abdominal, other	Pre- and post-natal depending on cause
Increased red cell destruction	Immune haemolysis: Rhesus/ Kell	*In utero*
	Infection: congenital/acquired	*In utero* and post-delivery depending on cause
	Red cell membrane disorders: Hereditary spherocytosis/ elliptocytosis,	Usually after first 24 hours
	Red cell enzyme disorders: G6PD deficiency, PK deficiency	Usually after first 24 hours
	Abnormal haemoglobins: α-thalassaemia, others	*In utero* and post-delivery depending on cause
	Microangiopathic haemolytic anaemia	Post-delivery
Decreased red cell production	Congenital red cell aplasia	*In utero* and post-delivery
	Parvovirus B19 infection	*In utero* and post-delivery
	Congenital leukaemia	*In utero* and post-delivery
	Physiological anaemia of prematurity	Post-delivery

Figure 11.1. Causes of neonatal anaemia.

Blood loss

This is the most common cause of neonatal anaemia. Blood loss may be acute or chronic; symptoms depend on the volume and rate of blood loss. The full blood count (FBC) and blood film may be helpful in distinguishing acute from chronic blood loss:

- in acute blood loss the red cells are normochromic and normocytic,

- in chronic blood loss there are hypochromic, microcytic red cells with anisopoikilocytosis on the blood film.

Note that in acute blood loss haemoglobin may be normal initially, before falling rapidly.

Intrauterine blood loss due to feto-maternal haemorrhage arises when blood cells from the fetus pass across the placenta into the maternal circulation. These bleeds can occur in any pregnancy, especially during the third trimester (including during labour or delivery). Invasive obstetric procedures such as amniocentesis or fetal blood sampling are important risk factors. In severe cases, fetomaternal haemorrhage may result in hydrops fetalis.

The degree of fetomaternal bleed can be crudely estimated by the Kleihauer (or acid-elution) test on maternal blood. The test discriminates fetal from adult red cells by using acid to elute adult haemoglobin, but not fetal haemoglobin, from the cells. After staining, fetal cells appear pink and adult cells appear ghost-like. The ratio of fetal to adult cells is used to estimate fetal blood loss in mL.

Twin-to-twin transfusion can rarely occur when identical twins share the same placenta (monochorion). An unbalanced flow of blood between the two fetuses leads to one becoming fluid overloaded and the other anaemic. Usually the condition is detected by antenatal ultrasound.

In preterm babies the commonest cause of blood loss is from iatrogenic blood sampling, so sampling frequency and volume should be kept to a minimum. Many NNUs electively replace sampling volumes after 10% of blood volume has been taken.

Increased red cell destruction

This can present as anaemia where the rate of haemolysis exceeds the rate of red cell production, or as unconjugated hyperbilirubinaemia (see Chapter 7).

The neonatal red cell membrane has increased mechanical fragility. Neonatal red cells are also more susceptible to oxidant-induced damage. These factors contribute to the shortened lifespan of the neonatal red cells: 60-70 days for term neonates and 35-50 days for preterm infants, compared with 120 days for the adult red cell.

Factors causing haemolysis may be immune, intrinsic to the red cell (relating to the haemoglobin, red cell membrane or red cell enzymes), or mechanical. Laboratory findings indicative of haemolysis include unconjugated hyperbilirubinaemia and reticulocytosis. Other findings, such as a positive direct antiglobulin test (DAT), or characteristic red cell morphological features also help in delineating the underlying cause.

Immune haemolysis

The most common causes of haemolytic disease of the newborn are the blood group incompatibilities involving the ABO, Rhesus (Rh), Kell or Duffy systems. It may present as fetal or neonatal anaemia or neonatal jaundice presenting on the first day of life.

ABO incompatibility rarely causes significant clinical haemolysis. The greatest risk is where the mother is blood group O and the baby blood group A (occasionally B). Haemolysis occurs due to maternal anti-A (or anti-B) IgG antibodies crossing the placenta and binding to the fetal blood cells. The direct antiglobulin test (DAT) is usually positive; spherocytes are a prominent feature of the blood film.

In contrast Rhesus incompatibility can present with severe haemolytic disease. There are five distinct antigen types in the Rhesus system – C, D, E, c and e; D is most important. The term 'Rhesus-positive' refers to a person who has at least one copy of the D antigen. Where a mother, who is RhD negative, is carrying a baby who is RhD positive, leakage of fetal blood into the maternal circulation may provoke maternal IgG antibody production. The antibodies can pass across the placenta and act against the fetal cells. The first appearance of these antibodies rarely produces an affected baby, but subsequent pregnancies are at risk as re-exposure to RhD positive fetal red cells may produce a heightened antibody response in a previously sensitised mother. A similar process can occur in pregnancies with other red cell incompatibilities (e.g. Kell, Duffy).

Rhesus haemolytic disease of the newborn can be prevented by immunoprophylaxis with anti-D immunoglobulin. Non-sensitised Rh (D)-negative women in the UK are routinely given prophylactic anti-D immune globulin (Ig) at 28 and 34 weeks gestation. Additional doses are given following any possible sensitising event during the pregnancy, and then on delivery if the neonate is found to be Rh (D) positive.

For pregnant women in whom allo-antibodies have already developed, early detection of the type, specificity and level of the antibody is important, followed by serial monitoring of antibody titres. Red cell genotyping of fetal DNA extracted non-invasively from maternal plasma can also help to identify if the fetus or neonate is at risk.

Pregnancies at risk of haemolytic disease of the fetus and newborn (fetal antigen positive with rising maternal antibody titres or history of significantly affected pregnancies) should have serial monitoring in specialised fetal medicine units. Non-invasive techniques now allow for monitoring of fetal anaemia using Doppler ultrasound to assess the fetal middle cerebral artery peak systolic velocities (MCA PSV). Invasive procedures such as fetal blood sampling and intrauterine transfusion (IUT) are required if the MCA PSV rises above a threshold of 1.5 multiples of the median or if there are other signs of fetal anaemia (such as polyhydramnios or cardiomegaly).

The timing of delivery depends on the potential risk of anaemia in the baby. Where antibody titres remain stable, delivery may take place between 37-38 weeks gestation. Earlier delivery is required where there is a greater risk of anaemia.

At delivery, cord blood is taken for haemoglobin, bilirubin, blood group and DAT. Although a positive DAT indicates that the neonatal red cells are covered with antibodies it does not predict the severity of haemolysis.

Management of the newborn depends on the degree of anaemia or haemolysis.

- Providing that cord Hb is >120 g/L, the main risk is jaundice. Serum bilirubin should be checked four-hourly and phototherapy started promptly. Exchange transfusion may be needed if bilirubin rises above the exchange threshold for gestation (see Chapter 7).

- If the baby has received IUT and is anaemic at delivery a 'top-up' transfusion may be more appropriate.

- Babies with red cell alloimmunisation may also develop hepatosplenomegaly. There may be cardiomegaly, ascites and oedema, and the baby may need resuscitation and respiratory support. In these babies the risk of bilirubin encephalopathy is high and early exchange transfusion is indicated.

Babies affected by any form of isoimmunisation are discharged home on oral folic acid supplements (1 mg daily), and should be monitored for development of late anaemia for 12 weeks, or until the haemoglobin starts to rise.

Non-immune haemolysis

Infection (intrauterine and postnatally acquired) is an important cause of neonatal anaemia due to increased red cell turnover (Chapter 12).

RED CELL MEMBRANE DEFECTS

Abnormalities of the red cell membrane or constituent enzymes as well as disorders of haemoglobin synthesis can result in haemolysis. The red cell membrane is important for maintaining the shape and deformability of the red cell. Some conditions are associated with abnormally shaped red cells that are less deformable and more prone to extravascular haemolysis.

Hereditary spherocytosis is the commonest congenital red cell membrane defect. The inheritance is usually autosomal dominant, and the diagnosis is suggested either by family history, or by the presence of numerous spherocytes in the neonatal blood film. Anaemia is usually mild, the DAT is negative and hyperbilirubinaemia is the most likely presenting feature. A definitive diagnosis can usually be made after the neonatal period using the eosin-5-maleimide (EMA) binding dye test (routine test only in larger centres). Rarer inherited red cell membrane disorders include congenital elliptocytosis (clinical presentation similar to hereditary spherocytosis) and hereditary pyropoikilocytosis (HPP), which causes more severe anaemia with microcytosis, requiring regular transfusion.

RED CELL ENZYME DEFICIENCIES

The congenital red cell enzyme deficiencies of glucose 6-phosphate dehydrogenase (G6PD) and pyruvate kinase (PK) may cause early neonatal jaundice, neonatal anaemia, or in severe cases hydrops fetalis. G6PD is the commonest red cell enzyme deficiency, making cells more prone to oxidative damage secondary to precipitants such as drugs or infections. It is an X-linked disorder with disease expression in males and homozygous females. The disorder occurs most frequently in those of Mediterranean, African and Asian origin. Approximately 20% of infants with G6PD develop neonatal jaundice. The diagnosis is confirmed by enzyme assay; care is required in interpreting results of assays performed during the acute haemolytic episode, where results may be falsely high in the presence of reticulocytosis. In populations where the prevalence of G6PD deficiency is high, neonatal screening has been effective in reducing the frequency of neonatal kernicterus associated with hyperbilirubinaemia. In lower prevalence populations all infants with first day jaundice, or with plasma bilirubin exceeding the phototherapy threshold, should be screened for G6PD deficiency. Ongoing management involves education of families with affected infants on possible precipitants (especially drugs) to avoid and when to seek medical attention. PK deficiency may cause early onset hyper-bilirubinaemia (usually on the day one of life), and kernicterus. Hydrops fetalis due to severe intrauterine haemolysis has also been reported. Diagnosis is by enzyme assay and the blood film may show echinocytes.

Haemoglobin disorders

Haemoglobin abnormalities causing haemolysis in the neonatal period are primarily related to α- or γ-chains; synthesis of β-chains is limited during the first few weeks of life.

In α-thalassaemia deletion of α-globin genes results in reduced α-chain synthesis.

- When all 4 α-globin genes are deleted (α-thalassaemia major), no HbF or HbA can be produced and the fetus is unlikely to survive.

- Deletion of 3 α-globin genes produces haemoglobin H (HbH) disease, which may manifest as severe microcytic haemolytic anaemia in the neonatal period.

- Deletion of 2 α-globin genes is known as alpha thalassaemia trait, and may be associated with mild anaemia.

- Deletion of 1 α-globin gene is usually asymptomatic.

The manifestations of β-thalassaemisa do not normally occur until around three months of age. Occasionally a bleed or other disorder in a fetus or newborn with β-thalassaemisa leads to anaemia because the red cells cannot be replaced with cells containing HbF, and the baby cannot produce HbA. This is known as $\gamma\beta$-thalassaemisa.

Other causes of non-immune neonatal haemolysis

These include fragmentation syndromes, such as disseminated intravascular coagulation (DIC), Kasabach-Merritt syndrome and congenital thrombotic thrombocytopenic purpura.

Decreased red cell production

The commonest cause of anaemia due to decreased red cell production, is physiological anaemia of prematurity (see above). Congenital infection, especially human parvovirus B19, may cause inhibition of erythropoiesis.

Congenital bone marrow disorders causing red cell aplasia are rare, and may not present until after the neonatal period. Causes include:
- Diamond-Blackfan anaemia,
- Congenital dyserythropoietic anaemia,
- Pearson syndrome,
- Congenital leukaemia (causing bone marrow infiltration and suppression of normal haematopoiesis),
- Transient myeloproliferative disease associated with Down syndrome,
- Osteopetrosis.

Diagnostic approach to the cause of neonatal anaemia

First line investigations to the cause of neonatal anaemia include:
- FBC and blood film,
- Reticulocyte count,
- Bilirubin,
- Direct antiglobulin test (DAT),
- Neonatal and maternal blood group and maternal antibody screen.

Further tests may then be indicated depending on findings. A suggested schema is shown in Figure 11.2.

Management of anaemia

The mainstay of management of anaemia is blood transfusion although this is not without risk. The aim of a transfusion is to decrease the symptoms of anaemia and ensure adequate tissue oxygenation. Indications for blood replacement in anaemic babies must take account of both the measured haemoglobin concentration and the clinical state of the baby (British Committee for Standards in Haematology (BCSH) 2004). NNUs may have their own transfusion thresholds for different clinical situations. In all cases, samples for investigation of the anaemia must be taken prior to transfusion.

Exchange transfusions should be with group O blood or blood that is ABO-compatible with maternal and neonatal plasma, and either RhD negative or of the same RhD type as the neonate.

Intrauterine transfusion may be indicated for the treatment or prevention of severe fetal anaemia or to allow the pregnancy to advance to a gestation where survival of the neonate may be achieved. There is a risk of fetal loss or premature delivery with the procedure and so it should only be undertaken in specialised centres, with parents counselled on the risks and benefits of the procedure.

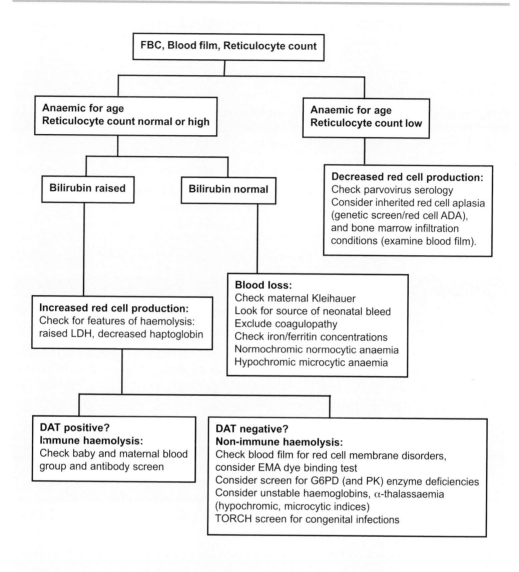

Figure 11.2. Diagnostic approach to neonatal anaemia.

Adjuncts to transfusion include:

• Folic acid administered to babies with haemolysis and to preterm infants.

• Iron supplementation may be required for preterm infants who are exclusively breast-fed (especially if not previously transfused) and for those with a history of chronic blood loss.

• Recombinant human erythropoietin (r-HuEPO) has also been used in the treatment of anaemia of prematurity. However, although numerous studies have been undertaken it is unclear that this treatment is clinically effective in reducing the need for transfusions, or cost-effective. r-HuEPO may have other benefits, including a lower incidence of necrotising enterocolitis and reduced risk of brain injury.

Neonatal polycythaemia

This is defined as a venous haematocrit of >65%. Apparent polycythaemia from a capillary sample should always be confirmed on a free flowing venous blood, as squeezing the baby's heel may produce apparent haemoconcentration.

Causes of polycythaemia include:
- Acute or chronic fetal hypoxia, e.g. in fetuses with abnormal growth (growth-restricted babies or infants of diabetic mothers). This leads to increased erythropoietin production, which in turn causes increased red cell production and polycythaemia.

- Delayed cord clamping at birth allowing maternal-fetal transfusion from the placenta.

- Twin-to-twin transfusions.

- Chromosomal abnormalities such as Trisomy 21.

The polycythaemic baby appears plethoric, and is likely to develop jaundice. Signs of hyper-viscosity may include cardiac failure, respiratory distress and neurological signs. The under-lying cause of polycythaemia is usually clear after taking a history and examining the baby, and further specific investigations are not usually necessary.

Treatment depends on the absolute haematocrit and presence of signs and symptoms. It is very unusual for signs or symptoms to be present with a venous haematocrit below 70%. Many clinicians will treat an asymptomatic baby with a haematocrit between 70 and 75% with rehydration alone, but electively seek to reduce the haematocrit by dilutional exchange trans-fusion at values above this or if any symptoms of hyperviscosity are present.

Neonatal leucocyte disorders

Leucocyte production in the fetus, like red cells, occurs initially in the yolk sac, moving sequen-tially to the liver and spleen and then to the bone marrow. At birth, the total white cell count is high, falling by about 25% in the first four weeks. The neutrophil count rises immediately after birth, peaking at 12 hours then falls to a steady level from 60 hours onwards. Knowledge of postnatal age is therefore very important in interpreting neutrophil count results. Gestational age, birth weight and altitude also influence the neutrophil count.

Neonatal neutrophil disorders

Causes of neutrophilia and neutropenia in the neonate are shown in Figure 11.3. The commonest causes of neutrophil count variation are infection, drugs and neonatal stress (secondary to bleeding, asphyxia).

Neutropenia	Neutropenia or neutrophilia
Alloimmune neutropenia	Infection
Maternal pre-eclampsia	Periventricular haemorrhage
Metabolic disorders	Asphyxia
Severe congential neutropenia (Kostmann syndrome)	Drugs
Reticular dysgenesis	
Cartilage-hair hypoplasia	
Hyper-IgM syndrome	
Schwachman-Diamond syndrome	

Figure 11.3. Causes of neonatal neutropenia and neutrophilia.

Neonatal alloimmune neutropenia refers to a situation where maternal sensitisation to fetal neutrophil antigens (paternally inherited and different from maternal neutrophil antigens) occurs. Maternal neutrophil IgG antibodies cross the placenta and cause immune-mediated destruction of the fetal neutrophils. Transient neonatal neutropenia occurs until the maternal antibodies are cleared.

Neonatal platelet disorders

The normal platelet count range for preterm and term infants is generally the same as for adults (150-450 x10^9/L), although a small number of healthy neonates have counts from 100-150 x10^9/L at birth that spontaneously increase over time. Thrombocytopenia (platelet count <100 x 10^9/L) of some degree is most frequent in sick neonates with an incidence of up to 35% reported in NNU admission.

The cause of thrombocytopenia (Figure 11.4) may be due to inadequate production, increased destruction or sequestration or a combination of both. Neonatal thrombocytopenia can occur antenatally, within the first 72 hours of life or later.

Signs of bleeding due to thrombocytopenia include mucocutaneous bleeding, bruising, petechiae and purpura. The most serious consequence of neonatal thrombocytopenia is intracranial haemorrhage (ICH), which may have lasting neurological sequelae.

The risk of serious haemorrhage is not solely related to the degree of thrombocytopenia. Infants who are sick (for example with NEC or sepsis) are more likely to bleed than those with severe thrombocytopenia secondary to IUGR or pregnancy-induced hypertension.

General management of neonatal thrombocytopenia

The mainstay of treatment of neonatal thrombocytopenia is platelet transfusion. A frequently used schema for determining when transfusion is indicated is that of Roberts and Murray (2003).

Neonatal immune thrombocytopenia

Neonatal alloimmune thrombocytopenia (NAIT) is a rare but important cause of severe thrombocytopenia in the newborn. It is analogous to haemolytic disease of the newborn, with the development of maternal IgG antibodies, directed against paternal antigens present on fetal but not maternal platelets, which can then cross the placenta and cause fetal thrombocytopenia. Unlike haemolytic disease of the newborn, severe thrombocytopenia may develop in the first-born child. The baby is otherwise healthy and the maternal platelet count is normal. Maternal antibodies can cross the placenta from 14 weeks gestation; thus fetal thrombocytopenia may occur, and babies are typically thrombocytopenic at birth. As the maternal antibody falls after birth, the platelet count returns to normal over a period of 2-4 weeks. The most serious complication of NAIT is intracranial haemorrhage (ICH), which may be clinically silent. Any baby with low platelets and/or suspected NAIT should have cranial ultrasound imaging.

The diagnosis may be suspected in an otherwise healthy infant with moderate to severe thrombocytopenia. There may be a previously affected pregnancy. Laboratory diagnosis is performed by the National Blood Service. Ideally samples should be collected from the mother, father and baby. Confirmation of NAIT is based on demonstration of a maternal platelet antibody specific for paternal platelet antigens, with an absence of that platelet antigen in the mother. In Caucasians the majority of NAIT cases are caused by maternal antibodies directed against the human platelet antigen (HPA)-1a.

The most important treatment in the management of neonates with NAIT and bleeding symptoms or severe thrombocytopenia is transfusion of compatible, antigen-negative platelets. BCSH guidelines indicate that transfusion is indicated when the platelet count falls to <30 $x10^9$/L.

When NAIT is diagnosed *in utero*, maternal intravenous immunoglobulin (IVIG), with or without steroids, or intrauterine transfusion of compatible platelets may be indicated under specialist multidisciplinary guidance.

Neonatal autoimmune thrombocytopenia

This may occur in association with maternal autoimmune disease, e.g. idiopathic thrombocytopenia purpura (ITP) or systemic lupus erythematosus (SLE). Maternally-derived antibodies are directed against antigens common to neonatal and maternal platelets. Unlike NAIT the platelet count may be normal at birth, with the nadir occurring a few days after birth, hence it is important to monitor the FBC post-delivery until a sustained rise in platelet count is seen. Note that there is no correlation between maternal and neonatal platelet counts. Neonatal thrombocytopenia secondary to maternal ITP is seldom severe and the risk of ICH is low.

Cause/Mechanism	Clinical features	Onset Time
Immune:		
Neonatal alloimmune thrombocytopenia (NAIT)	Previous affected child in 50% of cases. Mother normal platelet count	Fetal/ Early
Maternal ITP	Maternal platelet count normal or low. Baby otherwise healthy	Fetal/Early/Late
Infection:		
Congenital infection (Toxoplasmosis, CMV, Rubella)	May be other features of congenital infection	Fetal/Early/Late
Perinatal Infection (E. Coli, GBS)	Likely maternal infection	Early
Late onset systemic infection (bacterial, candida	Other signs of sepsis, neutropenia, DIC	Late
Genetic/ Inherited:		
Chromosomal disorders (Trisomy 13, 18, 21; Turner syn.)	Other clinical features of syndrome	Fetal
Congenital thrombocytopenia (TAR, CAMT, Fanconi Anaemia, MYH9-related thrombocytopenia, Wiskott-Aldrich)	Other clinical features of syndrome. May progress to aplastic anaemia (CAMT, FA) May have large platelets (MYH9-related)	Fetal/Early/Late
Inherited Metabolic Diseases (MMA, PA)	See chapter 10	Early/Late
Miscellaneous:		
Maternal drug ingestion (Quinine, hydralazine, tolbutamide)	Mother may also be thrombocytopenic	Fetal/Early
DIC	Complicates severe neonatal illness	Early/Late
Necrotising enterocolitis	If severe may be poor prognostic factor	Late
Renal vein thrombosis	Triad of haematuria, palpable kidney, thrombocytopenia	Early
IUGR		Early
Perinatal asphyxia		Early
Pregnancy induced hypertension		Early
Kasabach-Merritt syndrome	Cavernous haemangioma	Early/Late
Bone marrow replacement (Congenital leukaemia, TMD)	Other haematological features Trisomy 21 and GATA1 mutation (TMD)	Fetal/Early

Figure 11.4. Causes of neonatal thrombocytopenia.

Neonatal haemostasis and thrombosis

Haemostasis and thrombosis in neonates depends on the various pro-coagulants, anticoagulants and fibrinolysis proteins that make up the haemostatic system, as well as platelets and vascular components. A balance between anticoagulant and pro-coagulant factors is maintained in the immature neonatal haemostatic system which ensures that there are generally few problems for the healthy neonate.

Coagulation proteins are synthesised by the fetus. At term, plasma concentrations of the vitamin K-dependent factors (II, VII, IX, X) and contact factors are approximately equal to half adult values, while those of fibrinogen, factor VIII, factor V and von Willebrand factor are at similar concentrations to those found in adults. Most haemostatic parameters reach adult values by age six months, even in preterm infants. Prior to this time, care should be taken to interpret the results of routine coagulation screens and specific factor assays using reference ranges (ideally established by local laboratories) that are based on both gestational and postnatal age, and also take account of postnatal vitamin K administration.

The routine coagulation screen commonly consists of the Prothrombin Time (PT) and the Activated Partial Thromboplastin Time (APTT). In addition, the Thrombin Time (TT) and fibrinogen concentration are routinely measured in many laboratories.

- The PT is a measure of the extrinsic and common pathways of the coagulation cascade (see figure 11.5). PT is affected by deficiencies in Factors VII, II (prothrombin), V, X or fibrinogen.

- The APTT is a measure of the intrinsic and common pathways, and is prolonged in deficiencies of Factors XII, XI, IX, VIII,V, X, II (prothrombin) or fibrinogen.

- The TT is a measure of fibrin formation and is affected by low concentrations or abnormally functioning fibrinogen or other inhibitors of fibrin formation (such as fibrin degradation products).

Together with the platelet count, blood film and clinical history of the patient, these routine coagulation screens can help to determine the risk of bleeding in the neonate, identify possible causes of abnormalities and indicate which further investigations are required.

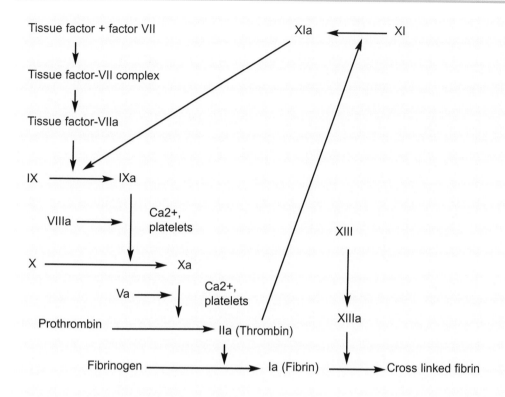

Figure 11.5. The clotting cascade.

Coagulation disorders

CONGENITAL COAGULATION DEFICIENCIES

The majority of haemostatic problems in the neonate are acquired. However congenital bleeding disorders may present in the neonatal period, sometimes without a previous family history (30% of haemophilia cases occur due to new mutations). Where a family history of haemostatic problems is known, the pregnancy and delivery must be managed to reduce risks to the mother and the baby. Close liaison between obstetric, neonatal and haematology services is key. Post-delivery, cord blood or venous samples should be taken to confirm the diagnosis of the bleeding disorder.

Haemophilia A (Factor VIII deficiency), factor V or fibrinogen deficiencies can be reliably diagnosed in the neonatal period, as levels at birth should be within the normal range in both term and preterm infants. Diagnosis of haemophilia B (factor IX deficiency) is more difficult, unless deficiency is severe, because normal values are lower in neonates.

In the absence of a positive family history, congenital bleeding disorders in the neonate may be suspected by the pattern of bleeding. Characteristic features are continuous oozing or haematoma formation associated with procedures such as venepuncture, heel pricks or intramuscular (IM) injections. Bleeding post-ventouse or forceps delivery may also be seen. Umbilical bleeding is relatively uncommon. If seen, factor XIII deficiency and low concentrations of fibrinogen should be considered.

Treatment of neonates with significant bleeding and a suspected congenital bleeding disorder should initially be with fresh frozen plasma (FFP), until the underlying factor deficiency is known. IM injections should be avoided and vitamin K given orally. Once the diagnosis is established, specific treatment may be given prophylactically or for bleeding episodes, as advised by an appropriately experienced haematologist.

ACQUIRED COAGULATION DISORDERS IN THE NEONATE

The commonest acquired disorders of haemostasis in the neonate are haemorrhagic disease of the newborn and disseminated intravascular coagulation (DIC).

Haemorrhagic disease of the newborn is caused by vitamin K deficiency. It was first described as self-limiting bleeding occurring between the first and fifth days of life, associated with low plasma concentrations of prothrombin. Up to 1% of babies were affected before routine postnatal vitamin K supplementation was introduced. Vitamin K is synthesised by the gastrointestinal flora; concentrations are low at birth, because the gastrointestinal tract is initially sterile. Breast milk is a poor source of the vitamin, so unfed or breast-fed infants or those with underlying hepatic pathology and reduced ability to manufacture coagulation proteins are particularly at risk of deficiency.

- Early haemorrhagic disease may present in the first 24 hours, particularly if the mother was taking anticonvulsant drugs. Bleeding is rare but can be serious, including ICH.

- Classic haemorrhagic disease occurs between 1 and 7 days and is characterised by cord or post-circumcision oozing in a baby who has not received vitamin K at birth.

- Late disease occurs at one to three months of age, in exclusively breast-fed infants or babies with underlying malabsorption or liver problems such as cystic fibrosis or α1-antitrypsin deficiency.

PT and PTT are prolonged and concentrations of vitamin K dependent factors (II, VII, IX, and X) are low, but are corrected within hours by administration of 1 mg of intravenous vitamin K. Fresh frozen plasma should be given in addition to vitamin K if there is active bleeding. Clotting factor concentrations (of vitamin K dependent factors II, VII, IX, X) may also be measured when the diagnosis is suspected, to aid diagnosis.

In the UK, all babies receive vitamin K at birth with parental consent, usually 1 mg Konakion intramuscularly; in well term babies there is the option of 2 mg oral Konakion (Konakion MM Paediatric) followed by further oral doses for as long as exclusive breast feeding continues. Infants on prolonged total parenteral nutrition or who have chronic malabsorption should receive weekly parenteral Konakion (1 to 2 mg).

Disseminated intravascular coagulation (DIC) results from activation and dysregulation of haemostatic systems, with generation of products of haemostasis and haemolysis and consumption of haemostatic components. In the neonate, the usual presentation is with bleeding rather than thrombosis. DIC can be initiated by vascular injury, trauma, hypoxia, or sepsis especially with Gram-negative bacteria. Diagnosis depends on clinical features and laboratory tests: reduced platelet count (invariably), prolonged PT and APTT, low fibrinogen concentration and elevated fibrin degradation products.

Treatment depends on managing the underlying condition and most babies with DIC will survive. Active bleeding should be treated with FFP. Platelet transfusions may also be required if the platelet count is less than 50×10^9/L.

Differential diagnosis of clotting problems

A family history of coagulation factor deficiencies, or of easy bruising or bleeding with operations or procedures in close family members is suggestive as is a maternal history of thrombocytopenia or SLE or any illness that could have caused congenital infection.

Observations on examination of the baby include the presence of petechiae which are suggestive of platelet deficiency or dysfunction, or a vascular problem. Bleeding from organs suggests a more generalised clotting failure. If generally unwell, the clotting problem may be secondary to systemic disease.

Initial laboratory investigations (Figure 11.6) should include FBC, blood film, PT and APTT, with further investigation as indicated by these results.

Thrombotic disorders

Thrombotic events in neonates are relatively uncommon, occurring mainly in sick or preterm infants. Risk factors for neonatal thrombosis include intravascular catheters, septicaemia, dehydration, maternal diabetes and asphyxia. Treatment is controversial and should always be planned in conjunction with an appropriately experienced haematologist. Often supportive treatment is all that is required; therapeutic interventions with anticoagulants (unfractionated or low molecular weight heparin) or even thrombolysis may be indicated where there is organ dysfunction or a limb is threatened.

Congenital homozygous disorders causing thrombosis in the neonatal period are rare. Most serious of these is deficiency of protein C or protein S, which can cause the life-threatening condition *purpura fulminans* within hours or days of birth. Cerebral and renal vein thromboses are characteristic, as are ocular manifestations. Laboratory tests are suggestive of DIC and the diagnosis is confirmed by low activity of protein C (or S). Treatment is with FFP to replace the deficient factor. If protein C deficiency is confirmed, replacement using protein C concentrate is recommended.

	Platelets	PT	APTT	Likely diagnosis
Sick infants	Decreased	Increased	Increased	Disseminated intravascular coagulation
	Decreased	Normal	Normal	Platelet consumption (infection, necrotising enterocolitis, renal vein thrombosis)
	Normal	Increased	Increased	Liver disease
	Normal	Normal	Normal	Compromised vascular integrity (hypoxia, prematurity, acidosis, hyperosmolality)
Healthy infants	Decreased	Normal	Normal	Immune (auto or allo) thrombocytopenia Occult infection Thrombosis
	Normal	Increased	Increased	Vitamin K deficiency
	Normal	Normal	Increased	Hereditary clotting factor deficiencies
	Normal	Normal	Normal	Local factors (trauma, anatomical abnormality) Qualitative platelet abnormality Factor XIII deficiency

Figure 11.6. Laboratory test results in the bleeding infant.

Haematological indices in the neonate

Reference ranges for haematological indices at birth are available for term and preterm babies (See appendix: Haematological reference ranges). These ranges are often based on historical studies and compiled from a number of sources. Care should be taken to interpret the results of routine screens and assays against reference ranges (ideally established by local laboratories) that are based on both gestational and postnatal age. Factors that can affect results include the method of blood collection. Capillary blood samples give consistently higher haemoglobin results than those collected by the venous or arterial route. Poor-flowing capillary samples may produce spurious results, for example an inaccurate haemoglobin value or a falsely low platelet count due to platelet clumping in the blood sample. Delayed cord clamping allows more complete transfusion of the placental blood volume and increases the infant blood volume by up to 50%.

Further reading

British Committee for Standards in Haematology http://www.bcshguidelines.com/

Transfusion guidelines for neonates and older children. Brit J Haem 2004 **124:** 433-453. http://www.bcshguidelines.com/documents/transfusion_Neonates_bjh_124_4_2004.pdf.

Roberts I, Murray N. Neonatal thrombocytopenia: causes and management. Arch Dis Child Fetal Neonatal Ed. 2003; **88:** F359–F364.

Chapter 12
Congenital and neonatal infections

Summary

- Congenital infections are caused by microorganisms that are transmitted from the mother to the unborn fetus or newborn infant during the pregnancy up to and including the time of delivery.

- Various strategies are used to prevent congenital infections, ranging from maternal antenatal serological screening for a range of infections to assessment of women at the onset of labour for the risk of having a group B streptococcus infected baby.

- Group B streptococcus (GBS) is the commonest cause of early-onset neonatal sepsis (infection presenting within 72 hours of birth), with an incidence of 1:2000 live births.

- Around 10% of all newborn babies are commenced on intravenous antibiotics because of concern that they may have a bacterial infection, although the incidence of true neonatal sepsis is probably only around 0.1-0.2%.

- In the UK NICE Guidance has been produced with the aims of prioritising the treatment of sick newborn babies, minimising impacts on healthy women and babies, and using antibiotics judiciously.

- Late-onset neonatal sepsis (presenting 72 hours or more after birth) is caused by a much wider range of microorganisms, and occurs mainly amongst babies being cared for in neonatal intensive care units.

Introduction

There is considerable overlap between important pathogens that are acquired before, during and after birth. Nevertheless, it is useful to classify infections as being congenital or neonatal, because different approaches to the diagnosis and prevention of the same infection are required depending on the timing of acquisition by the baby. Congenital infections are caused by microorganisms that are transmitted from the mother to the unborn fetus or newborn infant during the pregnancy up to and including the time of delivery (Chapter 3). Infections can be acquired through transplacental spread of systemic maternal infections or from the genital tract once the membranes have ruptured. Most congenitally acquired bacterial infections present as early-onset neonatal sepsis, the investigation and management of which is similar to late-onset sepsis: early- and late-onset neonatal sepsis are considered together in this chapter. Neonatal infections are acquired after delivery; the neonate is then exposed to a wide range of microorganisms originating from its mother, healthcare staff, family and visitors, and the hospital and home environments.

Congenital infections

DIAGNOSIS OF CONGENITAL INFECTIONS: GENERAL PRINCIPLES:

Early diagnosis of some maternal infections during pregnancy allows measures to be taken to prevent the baby acquiring the infection. For this reason, screening during pregnancy is routinely offered for a number of infections (see Figure 12.1). Congenital infections for which there is no screening programme may be identified as a result of investigations of maternal illness. However, many fetal infections are only diagnosed after abnormalities are detected in antenatal scans or after birth.

Infection	Screening method	Rationale/Action
Infections for which screening is routinely offered in the UK		
Rubella	Antibody detection	Non-immune women offered immunisation after delivery (since rubella vaccine is a live vaccine it is contraindicated in pregnancy)
Syphilis	Antibody detection	Antimicrobial therapy given where evidence of active infection to prevent congenital syphilis
Hepatitis B	Detection of viral surface antigen (HbsAg)	Immunisation of neonate to prevent mother-to-baby transmission
HIV	Antibody detection	Preventative measures before, during and after delivery greatly reduce risk of mother-to-baby transmission
Asymptomatic bacteriuria	Culture	Prevention of maternal pyelonephritis and preterm delivery
Infections for which screening is routinely offered in some countries, but not in the UK		
Toxoplasmosis	Repeated testing of sero-negative women	Antimicrobial therapy given to women who seroconvert during pregnancy may prevent or limit fetal damage
Group B streptococcus	Culture or PCR of vaginal and rectal swabs	Intra-partum antimicrobial prophylaxis given to carriers
Infections for which screening is offered to selected groups in the UK		
Chlamydia trachomatis	Nucleic acid amplification tests (NAATs), e.g. PCR	Women aged under 25 years are given details of their local National Chlamydia Screening Programme. Treatment will prevent mother-to-baby transmission
Antibiotic-resistant bacteria (e.g. MRSA, carbapenemase-producing Enterobacteriaceae)	Culture or PCR	Women at increased risk of having these infections are tested; isolation ± decolonisation treatment of affected mothers and their babies

Figure 12.1. Infection screening during pregnancy.

DIAGNOSIS OF CONGENITAL INFECTION DURING PREGNANCY

Investigation usually begins with serological testing of the mother, since fetal infection cannot occur without maternal infection. Serodiagnosis is usually based on:

- Detection of specific IgM; IgM class antibodies appear soonest after infection, and usually disappear after only a few weeks.

- Demonstration of seroconversion (that is appearance of specific antibodies in the blood of a person who previously did not have those antibodies). Laboratories must retain sera collected from women at their booking antenatal appointment; retrieving these samples for testing in parallel with sera collected later in pregnancy is often helpful in demonstrating that seroconversion has occurred during pregnancy.

If there is no evidence of maternal infection, no further action is required.

Where maternal infection is demonstrated, further investigations are required to determine whether infection has been transmitted to the fetus. Fetal infection can only be diagnosed *in utero* by testing of amniotic fluid or fetal blood. Nucleic acid amplification techniques are now the mainstay of detection of fetal infection, and have largely superseded traditional methods such as culture and serology that are less sensitive.

DIAGNOSIS OF CONGENITAL INFECTIONS AFTER DELIVERY

These are diagnosed by testing of samples collected from the infant: cord blood should **NOT** be used because it may be mixed with maternal blood. There are two approaches to diagnosis:

- Serodiagnosis depends on distinguishing between antibodies that have been produced by the baby and passively acquired antibodies of maternal origin. This may be done by:
    - detection of specific IgM antibodies, which do not cross the placenta or occur in breast milk,
    - demonstration of a rising antibody titre in the infant after birth, or
    - demonstration of persistence of antibody beyond the age when passively acquired antibodies would be expected to have been lost. Traditionally, antibodies persisting beyond six months of age were considered diagnostic of fetal infection. However, with highly sensitive techniques, such as enzyme immunoassay for anti-HIV antibodies, passive antibody may be detected for a year or more.

- Direct detection of the pathogen in samples from the infant, usually by nucleic acid amplification techniques.

TORCH infections

TORCH is the acronym for the four most common, congenitally acquired infections. These are:
- Toxoplasma gondii
- Rubella
- Cytomegalovirus
- Herpes simplex virus.

Transplacental transmission of these infections is more likely when maternal infection occurs later in pregnancy (when placental blood flow is higher), but fetal damage is generally more severe when infection is transmitted in early pregnancy.

Toxoplasmosis

Toxoplasma gondii is a protozoan parasite whose definitive host is the cat. Oocysts excreted in cat faeces sporulate to form infectious sporocysts that are ingested by secondary hosts (virtually any animal or bird, including farm livestock) in which parasitaemia and tissue invasion occurs. The life cycle is completed when a cat predates secondary hosts such as rodents or birds. Humans may acquire infection by:

- Contact with or consumption of raw or undercooked meat, especially lamb.

- Direct or indirect (for example eating raw vegetables) contact with cat faeces.

- Contact with sheep at lambing.

- Mother to fetus transmission *in utero.*

- Very rarely, toxoplasmosis by blood transfusion or organ transplantation.

Epidemiology

In the UK, seroprevalence rates rise from 20% at age 20 years to 50-60% by age 60, with a risk of infection during pregnancy of 0.5% to 0.7%. In some other countries, such as France, toxoplasmosis is more common and occurs at an earlier age, such that as many as 80% of pregnant women are sero-positive.

Congenital toxoplasmosis is rare:
- Around 50 infants are born each year in the UK with overt congenital infection.

- Another 400 infected babies are born each year who are asymptomatic at birth. Many of these will develop chorioretinitis (usually bilateral) in later life, with a peak incidence in the second or third decades.

Clinical features

Toxoplasmosis in adults usually causes no, or only subclinical, illness. Maternal infection may result in spontaneous abortion, stillbirth or congenital infection. The risk of congenital infection increases from under 10% in the first trimester to 70% in the third. However, the risk of serious effects decreases from 75% to 5% between the first and third trimesters. The classic triad of severe congenital infection is chorioretinitis, hydrocephalus, and intracranial calcifications. Other signs include intrauterine growth restriction, hepatitis, splenomegaly, lymphadenopathy and myocarditis.

Diagnosis and management *in utero*

- Screening is undertaken in some countries, but not in the UK, where both the prevalence and incidence of toxoplasmosis are low.

- Detection of IgM antibodies to *T. gondii* is usually the first indicator of possible maternal infection. However, this is not diagnostic of acute toxoplasmosis during pregnancy because anti-toxoplasma IgM remains detectable for many months after acute infection.

- Consider starting therapy with spiramycin immediately (to prevent spread of organisms across the placenta from mother to fetus) pending the results of further investigations to determine the timing of the maternal infection and whether fetal infection has occurred.

- Offer amniocentesis to identify *Toxoplasma gondii* in the amniotic fluid by polymerase chain reaction if:
    - Maternal primary infection during pregnancy cannot be excluded, or
    - Abnormal ultrasound findings (intracranial calcification, microcephaly, hydro-cephalus, ascites, hepatosplenomegaly, or severe intrauterine growth restriction).

- Do not offer amniocentesis at less than 18 weeks' gestation or less than four weeks after suspected acute maternal infection (risk of false-negative results).

- Offer treatment with a combination of pyrimethamine, sulfadiazine, and folinic acid for women in whom fetal infection is confirmed or is highly suspected (usually by a positive amniotic fluid polymerase chain reaction).

Neonatal diagnosis and management

- Neonatal infection is usually diagnosed by PCR on neonatal blood. Only around one third of congenitally infected neonates produce a detectable IgM response.

- Infected newborns are usually prescribed pyrimethamine and sulphonamide for 12 months, although efficacy is uncertain.

Rubella

Rubella is a highly infectious viral illness that is spread by the respiratory route. After an incubation period of 14-23 days, rubella presents with mild constitutional upset, a skin rash, lymphadenopathy and occasionally arthropathy. Patients may be infectious for up to seven days before, and four days after, onset of the rash.

Epidemiology

Childhood immunisation (MMR) has led to rubella becoming an uncommon illness; fewer than 100 cases are diagnosed in the UK each year. Congenital rubella is extremely rare. At least 90% of pregnant women are immune; however, reinfections can occur even in the presence of immunity, and these can damage the fetus.

Clinical features

Rubella presents with a rash and lymphadenopathy; arthralgia may also occur in adults. When rubella is contracted by a woman during the first 12 weeks of pregnancy the fetus is virtually always severely affected. Thereafter the risk decreases rapidly, from 17% between 13 and 16 weeks to nil by 20 weeks. The classic triad of manifestations in congenital rubella is cataracts, heart disease and deafness.

- Maternal infection is diagnosed by demonstration of specific IgM in blood or oral fluid, or by PCR detection of viral RNA in oral fluid or a throat swab.

- *In utero* diagnosis of fetal infection with rubella is rarely necessary, but viral RNA can be detected in amniotic fluid by PCR.

- Termination of the pregnancy is usually offered to women who acquire rubella during the first twelve weeks of pregnancy. The risk of congenital defects declines rapidly during the subsequent 4-6 weeks, and careful counselling is required to help women infected at this stage to decide whether to continue with their pregnancies.

NEONATAL DIAGNOSIS AND MANAGEMENT

- After birth, congenital rubella can be confirmed by demonstration of specific IgM, or by detection of viral RNA in urine or throat swab.

- There is no specific anti-viral therapy for rubella.

Cytomegalovirus

Cytomegalovirus (CMV) is not very infectious, and is usually only spread by prolonged close contact with infected body fluids, such as saliva, semen, blood and urine.

EPIDEMIOLOGY

In the UK, around 40% of individuals have detectable antibody by the age of 20 years, and around 1% of susceptible pregnant women acquire primary infection with CMV (that is 5-7 infections per thousand pregnancies). Most cases of congenital CMV follow maternal primary infection, but there is a small and unquantified risk of congenital infection where a woman experiences a reactivation or reinfection during pregnancy. Each year around 120 congenitally infected infants have defects at birth, and a further 175 who appear normal at birth will develop defects during the first year of life.

CLINICAL FEATURES

Most primary infections in healthy individuals outside the neonatal period are asymptomatic, or cause mild non-specific and self-limiting illness. Occasionally CMV causes more severe symptoms, such as a glandular fever-like illness or hepatitis. When a pregnant woman experiences a primary infection with CMV the risk of transmission to the fetus is around 40%. At least 85% of infected babies will have no adverse effects. Around 5% will be symptomatic at birth; clinical manifestations include hepatosplenomegaly, thrombocytopenia, prolonged neonatal jaundice, pneumonitis, growth retardation, microcephaly and cerebral calcification. A further 5-10%, although asymptomatic at birth, will develop long-term sequelae (usually cognitive, motor, visual or hearing defects).

DIAGNOSIS AND MANAGEMENT *IN UTERO*

- Detection of maternal IgM anti-CMV antibodies is suggestive of acute infection, but does not distinguish between primary and recurrent infections. Demonstration of seroconversion or IgG avidity testing can help assess the likelihood of primary infection during pregnancy.

- Fetal infection is usually diagnosed by detection of CMV in amniotic fluid by polymerase chain reaction.

- There are reports of treating infected women during pregnancy with CMV immunoglobulin and/or ganciclovir, but it is unclear whether these approaches are protective to the baby.

NEONATAL DIAGNOSIS AND MANAGEMENT

Congenital infection in the neonate can be diagnosed by detection of IgM antibodies or detection of virus in a throat swab, blood or urine by PCR within 2-3 weeks of birth. Positive tests in babies older than 2-3 weeks are not diagnostic of congenital infection (CMV infections can be acquired intrapartum or post-natally, and these infections are usually benign). A retrospective diagnosis of congenital CMV infection can be made by retrieving the surplus neonatal screening blood spot sample for testing.

A six-week course of ganciclovir may prevent hearing loss and improve developmental outcomes in infants born with symptomatic congenital CMV infection; however, it is not clear that this benefit is sustained at one year; longer treatment courses (up to one year) using oral valganciclovir may give a better outcome.

Herpes simplex viruses

Although herpes simplex viruses (HSV) are classified as one of the TORCH organisms, transplacental transmission of HSV is rare. Most neonatal herpes infections are acquired at the time of delivery through an infected birth canal. Infections can also be acquired post-natally.

Two types of HSV cause mucocutaneous herpes in humans. HSV-I is mainly associated with orolabial herpes and HSV-II with genital herpes, although this demarcation is not absolute. After primary infection with HSV the infection usually becomes latent, and may later reactivate. HSV are transmitted by close contact. The risk of serious neonatal infection is greatest if the mother has active lesions of a primary herpes infection at the time of vaginal delivery. Where the mother has had a previous primary infection the baby will be protected by passive immunity; serious infections in these neonates are uncommon, even if the mother has active recurrent disease at the time of delivery.

EPIDEMIOLOGY

The overall rate of genital HSV infection varies from country to country. Intrauterine HSV infections are very rare. The risk of infection during delivery is highest where the mother has a primary genital infection; these babies have a 50% risk of infection, compared with <5% in cases of recurrent infection present at the time of delivery. In many cases of neonatal infection there is no evidence of active genital herpes in the mother.

CLINICAL FEATURES

Intrauterine HSV infections often result in fetal death. Features in infants surviving *in utero* primary herpes virus infections include skin lesions and scars, chorioretinitis, microcephaly, and microphthalmia. The most serious form of neonatal HSV infection is disseminated disease, where the virus is found in multiple organs, including the brain, liver and skin. Infants may also present with localised neurological or mucocutaneous disease.

DIAGNOSIS AND MANAGEMENT *IN UTERO*

Recurrent genital herpes can usually be diagnosed clinically, without recourse to laboratory tests. Where it is necessary to confirm maternal infection PCR is the diagnostic test of choice. Investigations for fetal infection are not usually indicated. Maternal herpes simplex infection should be treated with acyclovir.

NEONATAL DIAGNOSIS AND MANAGEMENT

PCR carried out on blood and/or CSF is the mainstay of diagnosis. Neonatal infections are treated with aciclovir. However, even with treatment, serious neonatal herpes infection is associated with a high rate of serious morbidity and mortality.

Congenital syphilis

Syphilis is a sexually transmitted infection caused by the highly delicate spiral bacterium (spirochaete), *Treponema pallidum*.

EPIDEMIOLOGY

In the past decade the number of diagnoses of infectious syphilis in women in the UK has risen five-fold to around 500 cases per year. As a result, congenital syphilis has re-emerged, and it is estimated that there are around ten cases per year.

CLINICAL FEATURES

Without treatment, syphilis in adults runs a course over many years that is divided into a number of stages. A mother with untreated syphilis can infect her fetus. The risk of vertical transmission during the first year after infection is 80-90%, and diminishes rapidly thereafter until after four years transmission is rare. Without interventions, up to 50% of babies with congenital syphilis die *in utero* or post-natally. Symptomatic congenital syphilis in survivors is classified into early and late stages. Early congenital syphilis is a generalised infection that usually presents between two and twelve weeks of age with features such as rhinitis, skin rash and hepatosplenomegaly. Late congenital syphilis usually presents at age six to fourteen years with local infections of sites such as eyes, ears, bones and central nervous system. Lesions of early and late congenital syphilis heal to leave characteristic stigmata such as nasal, dental and bony deformities, blindness and deafness.

DIAGNOSIS AND MANAGEMENT

Serology is the mainstay of diagnosis of syphilis in the mother and the baby. There are two types of serological test:
- Non-treponemal tests (e.g. Venereal Disease Research Laboratory (VDRL), Rapid Plasma Reagin, (RPR)) measure antibody against a cardiolipin antigen that is not specific for *T.pallidum*. These tests are useful because the results tend to correlate with disease activity.

- Treponemal tests (e.g. *Treponema pallidum* Particle Agglutination (TPPA), Fluorescent Treponemal Antibody Absorption (FTA-ABS), enzyme immunoassays (EIAs)) that measure specific anti-treponemal antibodies and tend to remain positive for life.

A positive IgM EIA test, and/or a sustained four-fold or greater difference of VDRL/RPR titre or TPPA titre above that of the mother, is diagnostic of congenital infection. Congenital syphilis in symptomatic babies can also be diagnosed by detection of *T.pallidum* in material from lesions, or in nasal discharge, by dark ground microscopy or by PCR.

To exclude congenital syphilis in a baby born to a mother who may have been infectious during pregnancy, repeat:
- The IgM at three months (in case the infant's immune response is delayed or suppressed),

and
- All positive tests at three, six and 12 months of age, or until all tests become negative.

Congenital syphilis should be treated in consultation with a Genitourinary Medicine specialist. The standard treatment is a ten-day course of intravenous benzylpenicillin at a dose of 50,000 units/kg 12-hourly in the first week of life, and 50,000 units/kg 8-hourly thereafter.

Human parvovirus B19

Human parvovirus B19 (HPV B19) replicates rapidly in erythroid progenitor cells. Transmission is via the respiratory route, but HPV B19 is much less infectious than many other respiratory viruses.

EPIDEMIOLOGY
Approximately 50-60% of individuals will have already been infected with parvovirus B19 by the time they reach adulthood. Infection is seasonal, with increases in infection in spring and early summer, with additional increases in incidence occurring every 3-4 years.

CLINICAL FEATURES
After an incubation period of 6-15 days the early symptoms of HPV B19 infection are non-specific, and indistinguishable from those of other respiratory viruses. In around half of cases the illness is biphasic, the initial viraemic phase being followed by a skin rash (classically giving the appearance of slapped cheeks) and/or arthropathy.

When HPV B19 infection occurs during the first 20 weeks of pregnancy there is a 10% risk of fetal loss, and between 9 and 20 weeks a further 3% risk of hydrops fetalis. Infections after 20 weeks of gestation do not cause serious morbidity, but are occasionally associated with transient anaemia in the mother or newborn. HPV B19 is not known to cause developmental abnormalities.

DIAGNOSIS AND MANAGEMENT *IN UTERO*
Detection of maternal IgM anti-HPV B19 antibodies is diagnostic of recent infection, but because the window of IgM seropositivity is short (typically six weeks) these antibodies may have disappeared by the time fetal HPV B19 infection is suspected. Demonstration of sero-

conversion, or of IgM anti-HPV B19 antibodies in the antenatal booking blood sample, are also diagnostic. Where necessary, fetal infection can be confirmed by detection of HPV B19 in amniotic fluid, or in fetal blood, by polymerase chain reaction. Fetal anaemia and hydrops is treated by intrauterine blood transfusion; the prognosis is excellent.

NEONATAL DIAGNOSIS AND MANAGEMENT

Diagnosis and therapy are rarely required after delivery. IgM anti-HPV B19 antibodies or just IgM is detected in fewer than 50% of congenitally-infected neonates with intrauterine infection. HPV B19 may be detected in neonatal blood by polymerase chain reaction.

Neonatal infections

Serious systemic sepsis

The vast majority of neonatal sepsis cases are caused by bacteria. Yeasts (mainly *Candida spp.*) are an important, but relatively infrequent, cause of NICU-acquired infections, and a small number of viruses can cause systemic infection that mimics bacterial or fungal sepsis. Infections are usually classified as 'early-onset' (infections that present within the first 72 hours of life), or 'late-onset' (presenting after 72 hours). The distinction is important, because most early-onset infections are acquired from the mother around the time of delivery. The sources of, and therefore the microbial causes of, late-onset neonatal sepsis are much broader (Figure 12.2).

Species	Typical species distribution (%) in infections that are:	
	Early-onset (< 72 hours)	Late-onset (> 72 hours)
Gram-positive bacteria		
Group B streptococcus	30-50	5
Streptococcus pneumonia	5-10	0-5
Staphylococcus aureus	5-10	10-15
Enterococci	0-5	5-10
Coagulase-negative staphylococci	0-5	15-50
Listeria monocytogenes	0-2	-
Gram-negative bacteria		
E. coli	10-30	10-15
Haemophilus influenzae	0-5	-
Klebsiella	0-5	10-25
Enterobacter	-	5-10
Pseudomonas aeruginosa	-	5-10
Yeasts		
Candida	-	5-15

Figure 12.2. Pattern of bacterial and fungal infections in neonatal intensive care units.

Important viral causes of systemic infection include herpes simplex viruses (see earlier), varicella zoster virus, enteroviruses (e.g. Coxsackie and ECHO viruses) and parechoviruses.

Many more babies are commenced empirically on antibiotics than prove to have bacterial sepsis. In the UK around 10% of newborn babies are commenced on intravenous antibiotics, whereas culture-proven early-onset sepsis is only confirmed in 1-2% of those. Similarly, there is almost certainly a large disparity between numbers of cases of suspected and proven late-onset sepsis.

The incidence and causes of late-onset neonatal bacterial and fungal sepsis will depend on risk factors:
- low birth weight,
- extreme prematurity,
- ventilatory support,
- presence of intravascular devices,
- administration of parenteral nutrition,
- additional risk factors for invasive fungal infection include broad-spectrum antibiotic therapy and hyperglycaemia.

Neonatal systemic viral infections are rare. A British Paediatric Surveillance Unit survey suggested that the incidence of disseminated neonatal herpes simplex infection in the UK is under two cases per 100 000 live births. There are no reliable estimates of the incidence of other viral infections.

The clinical signs of neonatal sepsis are often non-specific (Figure 12.3) as also observed in neonates with suspected inherited metabolic disease (Chapter 10). The presence of one does not exclude the other. Although patients may have an associated focus of infection, such as meningitis or pneumonia, localising signs are rarely seen because of the rapidly progressive nature of the illness. Pointers to a viral cause of neonatal sepsis include a history of viral illness (often trivial) in contacts of the baby and skin rash.

Decreased activity	Lethargy
Temperature instability	Vomiting
Respiratory distress	Jaundice
Irritability	Hepatomegaly
Poor feeding	Thrombocytopenia
Altered skin colour	Seizures
Skin rashes	

Figure 12.3. Clinical signs of systemic neonatal sepsis.

Laboratory services must be able to promptly diagnose and report evidence of sepsis in neonates. Through timely reporting of negative results laboratories can also support timely discontinuation of antibiotics in babies who prove not to have sepsis. The NICE Guidance on antibiotics for early-onset neonatal infection recommends cessation of antibiotic therapy if the baby's clinical condition is reassuring, and the following laboratory test results are obtained:

- CRP concentrations at presentation and 18-24 h later both < 10 mg/L.
- Negative blood culture results 36 hours after antibiotics were started.

Although the NICE Guideline only deals with early-onset infection, a similar approach could be used as guidance for cessation of antibiotics in older babies.

Blood cultures: Blood cultures are mandatory in the investigation of any unwell neonate. Blood culture media specially formulated for paediatrics should be used. These are designed to support the growth of common paediatric pathogens and to cope with relatively small blood volumes. Because anaerobic bacteraemia is very uncommon in infants, anaerobic blood cultures are rarely necessary. Although blood cultures are usually maintained in the laboratory for 5-7 days, at least 90% of isolates are detected within the first 36 hours.

The drawback of blood cultures is that after signalling positive it conventionally takes at least a further 24 hours before the isolate can be identified and antimicrobial susceptibilities are available. Recent technological developments can reduce this delay, which can be critical in guiding antibiotic treatment.

- Use of microbial identification, and antibiotic susceptibility testing systems (e.g. BioMerieux Vitek2™) that can produce same day results when inoculated directly from blood culture bottles.

- Use of PCR-based systems (e.g. BioMerieux FilmArray™) that can detect key pathogens and antibiotic resistances directly from blood culture bottles within 60 minutes after the blood culture signals positive. However, the limited information on antimicrobial susceptibilities that these systems provide may be of limited clinical value.

- Many laboratories now use Matrix-Assisted Laser Desorption/Ionization – Time of Flight (MALDI-TOF) systems for routine identification of bacterial and fungal isolates. This mass spectrometry technology can provide clear species identification of cultures within minutes, and can also be used to rapidly identify microorganisms directly on positive blood culture broths. This speeds up bacterial identification, but no antibiotic susceptibility results are generated; the contribution of this technology to antibiotic stewardship, especially in neonatology, is as yet uncertain.

- PCR tests that can detect bacteria and fungi directly in blood (e.g. Roche SeptiFast™) without incubation in a blood culture bottle are also commercially available. However these methods currently require larger sample volumes than are easily obtained from neonates (minimum 1.5 mL); may not be sensitive or specific predictors of neonatal sepsis; and once again give little or no information on antimicrobial susceptibilities.

Examination of CSF is desirable in all neonates with suspected systemic sepsis. However, it is now common practice to await the results of blood cultures, and perform lumbar puncture only on infants with confirmed bloodstream infection. The interpretation of the results of CSF analyses can be difficult in the neonate. During the first week of life the white cell count may be as high as 32 cells/mm^3, and it only gradually decreases thereafter. Both the normal CSF protein concentration and CSF:blood glucose ratio may also be considerably higher than in adults (Appendix Biochemical Reference Values). PCR is already routinely used to diagnose meningococcal and pneumococcal meningitis (the most important bacterial causes of meningitis in older age groups), and is likely to become increasingly important in investigating suspected bacterial meningitis in neonates.

OTHER SAMPLES

Endotracheal tube aspirates from septic neonates who are ventilated should be collected for microscopy and culture. Bacteriological examination of upper respiratory tract samples, such as oropharyngeal secretions, is usually of no value in the diagnosis of infection, and is not recommended. Do not routinely collect a urine sample for microscopy and culture from neonates with suspected early-onset sepsis, but urine testing should be part of the investigation of older babies with sepsis.

OTHER LABORATORY TESTS

Most biochemical and haematological tests are of no value in predicting or excluding a diagnosis of neonatal sepsis. However, a full biochemical and haematological profile should be obtained to assess the severity of the patient's condition and guide supportive therapies. Measurement of C-reactive protein (CRP) at the time of commencing antibiotics, and again 18-24 hours later, may be useful in confirming (where one or both values are elevated), or ruling out (where both values are within normal limits) infection.

Haematological	Neutropenia or neutrophilia
	Increased immature:total neutrophil ratio
	Thrombocytopenia
	Deranged clotting
Biochemical	Hyperglycaemia or hypoglycaemia
	Hyperbilirubinaemia
	Deranged liver function tests
	Elevated C-reactive protein; procalcitonin
	Elevated plasma lactate

Figure 12.4. Changes in haematological and biochemical parameters in neonates with systemic sepsis.

The mainstay of diagnosis of systemic viral infections is detection of viral nucleic acid in blood and/or CSF by PCR. Virus can often be detected in other sites, such as material from skin lesions, throat swabs, faeces, but there is usually no additional benefit from sampling these sites.

Neonates who develop chickenpox should be treated with aciclovir as soon as possible.

Treatment

Antibiotic therapy must be commenced as soon as possible and always within one hour of the decision to treat. Blood cultures should be collected before the first dose of antibiotics is given, but all other investigations can be undertaken after the first dose has been given.

In all cases of suspected neonatal sepsis, empirical antibiotic therapy should be reviewed after 36-48 hours, taking account of clinical progress and laboratory test results, and at least every 24 h thereafter. Treatment may need to be altered because of unexpected antibiotic resistance, to optimise antibiotic delivery to the site of infection, or because of a failure of clinical response. When cultures are negative, and the patient's condition is satisfactory, cessation of antibiotic therapy should be considered.

EARLY-ONSET NEONATAL SEPSIS

- The NICE Guideline recommends using benzylpenicillin together with an aminoglycoside such as gentamicin.

- Use of cephalosporins as first-line empiric therapy for neonatal sepsis is not recommended because of the risk of adverse effects, including:
    - Selection of antibiotic-resistant Enterobacteriaceae.
    - Selection of MRSA.
    - Increased risk of candidiasis.

- A second agent with activity against Gram-negative bacteria (usually a third generation cephalosporin, such as cefotaxime) should be substituted for benzyl penicillin where Gram-negative bacterial sepsis or meningitis is strongly suspected.

- Substitute ampicillin or amoxicillin for benzylpenicillin in cases of listeriosis.

LATE-ONSET NEONATAL SEPSIS

- The choice of antibiotics should take account of:
    - Local antibiotic resistance patterns.
    - The individual patient's previous microbiology results and antibiotic therapy.
    - Any evidence of a potential focus of infection (e.g. presence of an intravascular device increases the likelihood of coagulase-negative staphylococcal infection).

- Broad-spectrum cover is required, encompassing Gram-negative bacteria, streptococci and *Staphylococcus aureus.*
    - Flucloxacillin (or a glycopeptide, such as vancomycin, where flucloxacillin-resistant

Gram-positive bacteria are suspected), together with an aminoglycoside such as gentamicin is recommended as empiric therapy.

- Flucloxacillin can be replaced by cefotaxime where Gram-negative bacterial sepsis or meningitis is strongly suspected.

- In NICUs where antibiotic-resistant Gram-negative bacteria are prevalent, a carbapenem (usually meropenem) may be required, combined with a glycopeptide where necessary.

Eye infections

Sticky eyes are a common problem in the neonate, and are not always caused by infection.

BACTERIAL CONJUNCTIVITIS

- *Staphylococcus aureus* is the most common cause. Other causes include group B streptococci; *Streptococcus pneumonia; Haemophilus influenzae.*

- *Neisseria gonorrhoeae* and *C.trachomatis* can cause ophthalmia neonatorum; these infections are acquired from the maternal genital tract at the time of delivery. Gonococcal ophthalmia almost always develops within a week (usually 1-4 days) of delivery. Chlamydial ophthalmia usually has a longer incubation period, and may present at any time from 2-30 days after delivery.

VIRAL CONJUNCTIVITIS

- Viruses such as enteroviruses and adenoviruses are occasional causes of neonatal conjunctivitis and can cause outbreaks in NNUs.

DIAGNOSIS

Mild conjunctivitis is usually self-limiting, and investigation is not usually necessary. Swabs are recommended in severe cases, or where there has been no response to initial treatment. Separate swabs are usually required for investigating suspected gonococcal, chlamydial and viral infections; the local laboratory will provide swabs that are compatible with their analysers.

Bacteria seen in Gram stained preparations can sometimes be presumptively identified on the basis of their morphological appearance. Demonstration of inflammatory cells in the absence of bacteria is suggestive of a chlamydial or viral aetiology. Most bacteria that cause conjunctivitis can be cultured from clinical samples within 24 hours. *N.gonorrhoeae* can be detected by culture, but along with *C.trachomatis* and viruses is usually detected using nucleic acid amplification techniques such as PCR.

TREATMENT

Mild conjunctivitis usually resolves without antimicrobial therapy. Topical treatment with chloramphenicol or gentamicin drops suffices for most cases of purulent conjunctivitis. Systemic antibiotic therapy is indicated for ophthalmia neonatorum (see above).

Umbilical cord and skin infections

Infections of the umbilical cord stump and skin occur quite frequently. *S.aureus* is the most common cause of both. The presence of flare or cellulitis around the umbilicus is suggestive of streptococcal infection. Umbilical cord stump infections with mixed coliforms and anaerobic bacteria are also common, but usually respond to conservative management. Cutaneous candidiasis is most often seen in the napkin area, and should be suspected where the rash is florid and confluent, involving the skin flexures.

INVESTIGATIONS

Swabs should be collected from the infected areas. If the skin is dry, the swab should be moistened first with sterile water or saline to enhance microbial pickup and survival during transport to the laboratory. Gram staining of skin swabs is not usually helpful, because it is often impossible to distinguish between commensal and pathogenic bacteria. A preliminary culture result is usually available within 24 hours.

TREATMENT

Mild infections may respond to washing with water and a mild soap or antiseptic. Topical nystatin or miconazole are recommended for candidiasis. Indications for systemic antibiotic therapy include widespread infection, cellulitis, and evidence of systemic upset. Flucloxacillin will suffice in most situations. Consider adding benzylpenicillin if cellulitis is present (to improve cover against streptococci), or gentamicin if the patient is seriously unwell.

Gastrointestinal tract infections

Infective gastroenteritis is very uncommon in neonates in developed countries. When gastroenteritis does occur it is more likely to be viral in aetiology (especially rotavirus). Viral gastroenteritis is much more readily transmissible than bacterial gastroenteritis, and without control measures, outbreaks affecting patients, visitors and staff can occur.

INVESTIGATIONS

Microscopy and bacterial culture is generally of little use in the investigation of diarrhoea in neonates. Rotavirus testing should be considered, especially during the rotavirus season (late winter-spring). This is usually done by antigen testing; be aware that some commercially available kits can give false positive results on neonatal stool samples. Other viruses can be tested for by PCR.

TREATMENT

Fluid replacement is the mainstay of management of infective gastroenteritis.

Necrotising enterocolitis (NEC)

The exact cause of NEC remains unknown, but a number of factors are likely to contribute to the initial mucosal damage that culminates in necrosis of the bowel wall, including immaturity, inadequate tissue oxygenation, disruption of intestinal mucosal integrity, formula feeding, hyperosmolar load to the intestine and bacterial overgrowth and translocation. Whether or not bacteria are involved in the primary aetiological process, systemic bacterial infection as a result of translocation of bacteria across the abnormal bowel wall is common. Babies with suspected NEC should have a blood culture taken before commencing broad-spectrum antibiotic therapy (such as penicillin, gentamicin and metronidazole).

Respiratory tract infections

Babies who develop ventilator-associated pneumonia should be investigated and treated as for any baby with systemic sepsis (see earlier). There are some other important causes of respiratory tract infection in neonates.

Chlamydia trachomatis pneumonia is rare. It usually presents at four to six weeks of age with gradual onset dyspnoea, but usually no fever and little or no cough. Up to half of patients with untreated chlamydial ophthalmia may subsequently develop pneumonia, but pneumonia is not always preceded by conjunctivitis.

Genital tract mycoplasmas, especially *Ureaplasma urealyticum*, have been implicated as neonatal pathogens, although their true significance is uncertain. *U.urealyticum* may be an occasional cause of congenital pneumonia in low birth weight neonates, but in many cases isolation of *U.ureaplasma* in respiratory tract samples probably represents colonisation only. Special culture techniques are required for mycoplasmas. Where indicated, treatment is with erythromycin.

Pertussis is an important, but uncommon cause of serious neonatal infection. The classical presentation is where a newborn baby is discharged to a household where there older individuals with upper respiratory tract infections that are undiagnosed as pertussis. Diagnosis is by PCR, but is often delayed because the possibility of pertussis is not considered. Lymphocytosis is another laboratory marker of pertussis. Treatment is with clarithromycin.

Like older infants, neonates can get viral upper respiratory tract infections such as RSV, parainfluenza and influenza viruses. Outbreaks of these infections occur from time to time in NICUs. Diagnosis is by testing a nasopharyngeal aspirate by testing for viral antigens (EIA or immunofluorescence) or preferably by PCR. Influenza is treated with oseltamivir; for other infections only supportive treatment is available.

Bloodborne viral infections in the neonate

Hepatitis B

Hepatitis B virus has three important antigens, HBsAg, HBcAg and HBeAg. HBsAg and HBeAg together with the antibodies formed against the three main antigens are used, along with detection of viral DNA, as markers of the various stages of hepatitis B infection (Figure 12.5).

Following infection, a significant proportion of individuals fail to eliminate the virus and become carriers; the risk of long-term carriage is much higher in congenitally infected individuals. Not only do carriers represent an infectious risk to others, but they are at risk of developing serious long-term sequelae, including chronic hepatitis, cirrhosis and hepatocellular carcinoma.

Marker	Significance
HBsAg	Acute or chronic hepatitis B
Anti-HBs	Immunity to hepatitis B
Anti-HBc (total)	Past or current hepatitis B
Anti-HBc (IgM)	High titre: acute infection Low titre: chronic infection
HBeAg	Active viral replication High infectivity
Anti-HBe	Low infectivity
HBV DNA polymerase	Active viral replication
HBV DNA	Active viral replication Infectivity depends on viral load

Figure 12.5. Significance of serological markers of hepatitis B.

Hepatitis B is hyperendemic in south-east Asia and parts of Africa, where up to 90% of the population is infected. By contrast, in areas of low endemicity (including northern Europe and North America) carriage rates are under 1%. However, carriage rates in immigrant women tend to parallel rates in their countries of origin.

Without interventions, the risk of transmission to the baby from a mother who is a hepatitis B carrier depends on her HBeAg and anti-HBe status:
- Mother HBeAg positive: over 90%.
- Mother negative for HBeAg and anti-HBe: 10%.
- Mother anti-HBe positive: <5%.

Most neonatal infections are perinatally acquired, with intrauterine infections accounting for fewer than 5% of cases. Thus, where a mother has hepatitis B, immunisation of the newborn can prevent almost all cases of vertical transmission.

- All babies born to HBsAg-positive mothers commence a course of vaccination against hepatitis B at birth.

- In addition, babies whose mothers are HBeAg positive, HBsAg positive without e markers, or who had acute hepatitis B during pregnancy are given hepatitis B immunoglobulin (HBIG) at birth.

• Hepatitis B infected mothers may breast feed, provided that their babies have been appropriately immunised.

Although immunisation gives over 95% protection, infants should be tested for serological evidence of hepatitis B infection at intervals during at least the first year of life.

Hepatitis C

Hepatitis C is another blood-borne viral hepatitis often associated with chronic viral carriage. The seroprevalence in the general UK population is around 0.01%, but is higher in some southern European countries. Mother to infant transmission of hepatitis C occurs relatively infrequently (well under 10% in most studies), but high maternal viral load and co-infection with HIV are important risk factors. No interventions are routinely used to prevent vertical transmission of hepatitis C, and hepatitis C positive mothers can normally be allowed to breastfeed their baby. Infants born to hepatitis C infected mothers should receive serological follow-up: persistence of anti-hepatitis C antibodies and/or detection of viral genome by PCR are diagnostic of infection.

Human T cell lymphotropic virus-I (HTLV-I)

HTLV-I is endemic in the Caribbean, Japan, South America and parts of Africa. The infection is very rare in the UK other than in people originating from those endemic areas. Over 95% of people with this virus are unaffected, but HTLV-I infection can cause serious conditions, e.g. adult T cell lymphoma (ATLL), HTLV-I associated myelopathy/tropical spastic paraparesis (HAM/TSP). Up to one in four children born to HTLV-I-positive mothers become infected, usually through prolonged breast feeding. If a woman is known to be HTLV-I infected she should not breastfeed her baby.

HIV

The antenatal HIV screening programme has been extremely successful in almost eliminating neonatal HIV infection in the UK. Where a mother is found to be HIV-positive anti-retroviral treatment is given to the mother, with the aim of suppressing her plasma viral load to unde-tectable levels, and to the neonate. Delivery by Caesarean section is not usually necessary where the maternal viral load is undetectable. HIV positive mothers are still advised not to breast feed, even if their viral load is undetectable.

Babies born to HIV-positive mothers require laboratory follow-up to confirm that vertical transmission of infection has not occurred (Figure 12.6). The gold standard test for HIV infec-tion in infancy is HIV DNA PCR on peripheral blood lymphocytes, although there is growing evidence that conventional PCR tests for amplification of viral RNA are at least as accurate.

Although an unexpected diagnosis of HIV infection is unlikely to be made in a baby whose mother received antenatal care in the UK, it is important to be mindful of the possibility of HIV infection in babies born overseas. HIV infected infants tend to have high viral loads and progress rapidly to symptomatic disease. They may then present with non-specific symptoms and signs such as failure to thrive, diarrhoea, anaemia, lymphadenopathy and hepatosplenomegaly. Alternatively, they may present with an unusually severe episode of infection with a recognised neonatal pathogen such as candida, cytomegalovirus or herpes simplex virus, or with an opportunistic infection such as Pneumocystis carinii pneumonia.

Antibody tests are of limited value in diagnosing HIV infection in infants because passively transferred anti-HIV antibodies remain detectable for up to 18 months. Diagnosis is usually made by detection of viral DNA/RNA by PCR.

Timing of sample	Tests required	Rationale
Around the time of birth (not cord blood)	HIV DNA/RNA	May permit detection of infections that have been acquired *in utero*
6 weeks	HIV DNA/RNA	Many perinatally acquired infections are diagnosable by this stage
3 months	HIV DNA/RNA	Most infections are diagnosable by this stage
18-24 months	HIV DNA/RNA Anti-HIV antibodies	Most uninfected children will have lost anti-HIV by this stage

Figure 12.6. Recommended testing schedule for infants born to HIV-positive mothers.

Further reading

British HIV Association guidelines for the management of HIV infection in pregnant women 2012 (2014 interim review). HIV Medicine 2014; **15 (Suppl. 4):** 1-77.

Del Pizzo J. Congenital infections (TORCH). Pediatrics in Review 2011; **32:** 537-542.

NICE Clinical Guideline 149. Antibiotics for early-onset neonatal infection: Antibiotics for the prevention and treatment of early-onset neonatal infection. August 2012.

Pinninti SG, Kimberlin DW. Management of neonatal herpes simplex virus infection and expo-sure. Arch Dis Child Fetal Neonatal Ed 2014; **99:** F240-F244.

Remington JS, Klein JO, Wilson CB, Nizet V, Maldonado Y. Infectious Diseases of the Fetus and Newborn, 7th Edition. Elsevier, New York, 2011.

Chapter 13
Infection prevention and control in the neonatal unit

Summary

- Babies on NNUs are at very high risk of infection, both because of their innate immaturity and the invasive procedures that they undergo during high dependency and intensive care.

- Consistent application of good infection prevention and control measures can prevent a substantial proportion of, but not all, NNU-acquired infections.

- Admission screening and surveillance cultures can play an important role in controlling important NNU pathogens such as MRSA and antibiotic-resistant Gram-negative bacteria.

- Infection surveillance on NNUs is an important quality measure that allows comparisons between NNUs, and also allows early identification of local infection problems.

- Even with the best infection control measures in place outbreaks of infection will occur from time to time.

- It is important that possible outbreaks of infection are immediately reported to the Infection Prevention & Control Team so that control measures can be implemented as soon as possible.

Introduction

The Neonatal Unit (NNU) presents many infection prevention and control challenges. At birth, a baby's immune system is immature, making it more susceptible to infection. Preterm neonates are particularly susceptible to infection because their immune system is even less mature, and their skin, which normally provides a natural barrier to infection, is also poorly developed. Consequently the risk of neonatal infection is inversely proportional to birth weight and gestational age. Babies on an NNU also share the same risk factors for infection as any other group of patients receiving high dependency or intensive care, e.g. ventilatory support, intravascular devices, administration of parenteral nutrition. Infections can be serious, with high rates of mortality and long-term morbidity. Colonisation and infections with antibiotic-resistant bacteria are becoming an increasing problem; without good infection control these bacteria can very easily becoming entrenched in NNUs. Multidrug-resistant, extensively drug-resistant and pan drug-resistant Gram-negative bacteria present a particular threat. Outbreaks of infection in NNUs are more common, and more likely to be the focus of media attention, than in other hospital settings. Before admission of the neonate to the NNU, she/he will only have been exposed to a few different microorganisms, mostly from the mother's genital tract. Almost all infections acquired at the time of delivery present in the first two to three days of life. After that, any infections are likely to be caused by microorganisms acquired after delivery. There are many possible sources of infection on the NNU, including other babies, the environment, family and other visitors.

General principles of infection prevention and control

In recent years the governments of many countries have published cleanliness and infection control criteria that are required to maintain good standards of infection prevention and control in hospitals. In England the statutory requirements for the management of infection prevention and control are enshrined in the Health and Social Care Act (2008), and compliance is regulated by the Care Quality Commission (CQC). Scotland, Wales, and Northern Ireland each have similar independent regulatory standards for infection prevention and control. Elements of these standards that are especially relevant to NNUs are shown in Figure 13.1.

Infection surveillance and benchmarking on the NNU

A programme of infection surveillance is an important quality measure of neonatal care. However, because NNU babies often have many risk factors for infection, and these may change by the day, any comparison of infection rates must take account of risk factors.

Infection surveillance may be organism- or condition-based.
- Organism-based surveillance involves determining the number of cases or incidence of specific hospital pathogens, e.g. *Staphylcococcus aureus*, Gram-negative bacteria.
- Condition-based surveillance is the collection of incidence data on certain types of infection, most commonly bloodstream infections, central venous catheter-related infections, ventilator-associated pneumonia: these three types of infection account for 80-90% of all serious NNU-acquired infections.

Infection surveillance can be undertaken on an individual NNU or on a multicentre basis. Single NNU-based surveillance is relatively easy, quick and inexpensive to establish. It can promptly identify changes in the pattern of infections that need to be investigated and measure the impact of any initiatives to prevent NNU-acquired infections. Multicentre surveillance allows comparison of performance with other NNUs. However it requires consistency in the definition of infections and requires stratification of risk factors for infection between centres to ensure that data are comparable. Consequently this type of surveillance is much more difficult and time-consuming to establish, and is mainly of use in measuring long-term infection prevention performance, rather than identifying immediate risks.

Element	Considerations for NNUs
An infection prevention and control team (IPCT) consisting of specialist nursing and medical expertise.	Infection Control link nurses provide a link between the NNU and the IPCT.
Provision of a clean and appropriate environment	Adequate space between cots. Medical equipment and consumables kept at the cot side restricted to the minimum required for that patient. Regular monitoring of cleanliness standards.
Hand hygiene facilities	Available throughout the unit and at the point of care.
A programme of risk assessment and audit of infection prevention and control practices	Must include hand hygiene and care bundles for elements of intensive care (e.g. central line and ventilator care).
Provision of adequate isolation facilities	Difficult or impossible to provide in all circumstances. Should be clear guidance on cohort isolation (where babies with the same infection are nursed together) and priorities for isolation (when demand for single rooms exceeds availability).
Early identification of patients who have, or are at risk of developing, an infection	Close liaison with microbiology laboratory, so that important preliminary and final results are communicated promptly. Infection screening: as a minimum all babies should be screened for MRSA; many NNUs screen for other bacteria, e.g. antibiotic-resistant Gram-negative bacteria.
Sharing information about infectious risks to anyone providing care for a patient	Communication of Infectious risks when patients transferred between NNUs.
Policies and procedures	Tailored to the needs of neonatal care Antibiotic prescribing policy to support good antibiotic stewardship.
Staff involvement and training	All staff appropriately trained on the above policies and procedures.
Visitors	Restrictions on visitors with transmissible infections.

Figure 13.1. Elements of an effective infection prevention and control infrastructure relevant to NNUs.

Antibiotic stewardship on the NNU

Antibiotics must be used wisely in babies to avoid the selection and spread of antibiotic resistance. The rapid emergence and world-wide spread of Gram-negative bacteria that are resistant to most or all standard antibiotics used to treat neonates is of particular concern. These bacteria are categorised as follows:

- Multidrug-resistant (MDR): resistant to at least one agent in three or more antimicrobial categories.

- Extensively drug-resistant (XDR): resistant to at least one agent in all but two or fewer antimicrobial categories.

- Pan drug-resistant (PDR): resistant to all agents in all antimicrobial categories.

MDR and XDR Gram-negative bacteria are now not infrequently encountered in UK NNUs, and around half of units have a screening programme to identify colonised babies. An appropriate approach to antibiotic stewardship should:

- Avoid using antibiotics unless there is reasonable evidence of bacterial infection.

- Regularly review antibiotic therapy and stop antibiotics as soon as it is clinically safe to do so.

- Use narrow-spectrum agents where possible.

- Avoid large scale use of cephalosporins (potent selectors of MDR and XDR bacteria).

Prevention, investigation and management of outbreaks of infection

An understanding of the risks and routes of transmission of different infections allows design of strategies to prevent spread of infection in NNUs (Figures 13.2 and 13.3). However, even in NNUs with excellent infection control practices, outbreaks of infection inevitably occur from time to time.

An outbreak is defined as the occurrence of an unexpectedly high number of cases of an infection. The occurrence of a single case of an uncommon and serious infection may therefore constitute an outbreak, but more usually the term relates to two or more cases of infection that are linked. Sources of infection include:
- Another person: a patient, a member of staff, a family member, or other visitor.
- The NNU environment: e.g. water-, food- or air-borne.
Suspected outbreaks of infection must be reported immediately to the IPCT so that investigation can begin, and controls instituted, as soon as possible. Most outbreaks are small and can be controlled by the IPCT and NNU staff without causing significant disruption. For more serious outbreaks, a multidisciplinary Outbreak Control Group may be required to direct the management of the incident.

Microorganism	The risks on NNUs	Routes of spread	Control measures
Staphylococcus aureus (MSSA)	One of the commonest causes of NNU-acquired infections	Directly from baby-to-baby or adult-to-baby Indirectly via contaminated equipment or the environment	Good general infection prevention and control Early identification and treatment of localised infections to prevent systemic infection developing
Staphylococcus aureus (MRSA)	Infections are difficult to treat. Outbreaks can have a serious reputational impact	As for MSSA	Screening of babies Isolation of all cases Topical decolonisation therapy
Antibiotic-resistant *Enterobacteriaceae*	Infections are difficult to treat Outbreaks can have a serious reputational impact	As for MSSA	Isolation of colonised or infected cases Some NNUs screen babies
Pseudomonas aeruginosa	Infections have a high mortality rate Outbreaks can have a serious reputational impact	As for MSSA Contaminated water systems are another important source	Water safety plan Isolation of colonised or infected cases
Acinetobacter baumanii	Infections are difficult to treat	Directly from baby-to-baby Environmental contamination is an important source	Isolation of colonised or infected cases Effective environmental cleaning

Figure 13.2. Routes of spread and infection control measures for important neonatal bacterial pathogens.

Microorganism	The risks on NNUs	Routes of spread	Control measures
Herpes simplex viruses	Life-threatening systemic neonatal infection	Directly from baby-to-baby. More commonly from adult-to-baby	Isolation of cases in a single cubicle. Offer treatment with topical aciclovir to adults with orolabial herpes; follow local policy on whether contact with babies is allowed
Cytomegalovirus	Main risk is of transmission from a congenitally infected baby to a pregnant staff member	Transmission requires **close** contact with body fluids (urine, respiratory secretions)	Pregnant staff should, if possible, avoid contact with body fluids from a CMV-infected baby, although the risk is low
Varicella zoster virus (chickenpox and shingles)	Life-threatening systemic neonatal infection	Chickenpox is transmitted via respiratory secretions and vesicle fluid; shingles (less infectious) via vesicle fluid only	Isolation of cases in a single cubicle Use of VZIG for non-immune contacts Exclude non-immune staff/visitors who are contacts of chickenpox
Infants born to mothers with blood-borne virus infections (hepatitis B, hepatitis C, HIV)	If baby is infected, risk of transmission to others Risk of transmission from mother-to-baby after delivery (e.g. via breast milk) Risk of staff member-to-baby transmission during exposure prone procedures	Via mucous membrane or percutaneous exposure to blood and body fluids	Avoid inoculation injuries from infected babies HIV-positive mothers should not breast feed Health care workers who know or suspect that they have one of these infections must inform their Occupational Health service *immediately.*

Figure 13.3. Routes of spread and infection control measures for important neonatal viral pathogens.

Further reading

Department of Health. The Health and Social Care Act 2008 Code of Practice on the prevention and control of infections and related guidance. Published December 2010.

National Institute for Health and Care Excellence. PH36: Prevention and control of healthcare-associated infections: Quality improvement guide. Issued November 2011.

National Institute for Health and Care Excellence. CG 149. Antibiotics for early-onset neonatal infection: Antibiotics for the prevention and treatment of early-onset neonatal infection. Issued August 2012.

Chapter 14
Nutrition

Summary

- Adequate nutritional intake is vital for neonates to facilitate growth.

- For the majority of healthy term neonates, breast milk is the best nourishment.

- For mothers unable to breast feed directly, their own expressed breast milk, or donor breast milk, may be used. These approaches carry additional microbiological risks that must be considered and reduced.

- For those infants whose nutritional requirements cannot be met by the enteral route, parenteral nutrition is an essential component of care.

- There is limited requirement for biochemistry in monitoring breast feeding; jaundice although common is self-limiting and benign.

- In contrast there is an important role for the laboratory in the monitoring of parenteral nutrition.

Breast feeding

Breast milk is the best nourishment for healthy term babies, and usually also for babies who may be separated from their mothers on Neonatal Units. It is nutritionally complete, protects against infection and necrotising enterocolitis, and promotes neurological development. Allergies in later infancy may also be less common in babies fed with breast milk.

Women are advised to breastfeed their baby exclusively for six months and to continue to breastfeed after six months as part of a balanced diet.

The mother's own fresh milk is optimal in terms of nutritional availability and biological activity. However, where a supply of fresh milk cannot be maintained for infants who are hospitalised, stored mother's milk or milk from an unrelated donor (the former being preferred) may be used.

There are some uncommon but important biochemical and microbiological issues relating to breast feeding, including breast milk jaundice and the risk of transmission of infection via breast milk; microbiology issues become more important with stored milk, and are most important with donor breast milk. In addition, breast milk may be contraindicated for some babies with, or at risk of, rare inherited metabolic disorders (see Chapter 10); potentially harmful drugs that are secreted in breast milk are discussed in Chapter 15.

Jaundice associated with breast feeding

Breast feeding can be associated with unconjugated hyperbilirubinaemia in the first postnatal days (breast feeding jaundice), or persisting beyond the first two weeks of life (breast milk jaundice). Whilst jaundice can be a common complication of breast feeding, it is generally benign, and breast feeding can and should continue without any interruption in most cases. However, it is always important to consider the possibility of a pathological cause for jaundice before attributing it to breast feeding (see Chapter 6).

Breast feeding by vegan mothers

Animal products are the main source of vitamin B_{12}. Vegans, therefore, have low body stores of B_{12}, and babies who are exclusively breast-fed by vegan mothers are at risk of B_{12} deficiency. Clinical problems usually only occur in infants who have been exclusively breast-fed for at least six months, when they may present with anaemia or neurological signs. Investigations will reveal macrocytic anaemia, methylmalonic aciduria and low serum B_{12} concentrations, and sometimes hyperammonaemia and homocystinuria. Treatment is with B_{12} injections, and full recovery can be expected.

Infections

Breast milk is not sterile, making it a potential means of transmission of infection to babies. Expressed breast milk is associated with additional microbiological risks because of the additional handling and storage involved. Donor breast milk presents a further hazard of transmission of serious blood-borne viral infections from the donor to recipient.

BACTERIAL INFECTIONS

It is rare for babies to contract a bacterial infection during breastfeeding, even when the mother has infectious mastitis; indeed mothers with mastitis are encouraged to continue trying to breastfeed. A woman with untreated syphilis could infect her baby via breast milk, but because the antenatal screening programme includes serological testing for syphilis this is very unlikely to occur where a woman has received her antenatal care in the UK.

VIRAL INFECTIONS

Although on a global scale breast feeding is an important route of transmission of some viral infections, breast milk is often not a very efficient means of transmission of infection, and the risk to the individual breast-fed baby is often low. Especially in developing countries, this risk may be outweighed by the nutritional and anti-infective benefits to the infant from breast feeding. Important determinants of the risk of transmission include the stage of maternal infection, and the duration of breast feeding. There are only a small number of maternal viral infections where breastfeeding is contraindicated.

Human immunodeficiency viruses (HIV)

Breast feeding may more than double the risk of mother to infant transmission of HIV. The risk of infection is proportional to the maternal viral load. In the UK and other developed countries breast feeding is not recommended, even by mothers whose viral load has been rendered undetectable by highly active anti-retroviral therapy. If a mother insists on breast feeding (for example for religious reasons), then she should be encouraged to do so for as short a period as possible, and given advice on how to avoid inflammatory breast conditions that may increase the risk of HIV transmission.

Cytomegalovirus (CMV)
There is a high incidence of post-partum transmission of CMV to infants of seropositive mothers; breast feeding probably accounts for one third of these cases. Most such infections are asymptomatic, even in preterm babies, presumably because babies will be protected by passive immunity from their mothers.

Human T-cell leukaemia virus type I (HTLV-I)
HTLV-I is a retrovirus that is endemic in areas such as southern Japan, the Caribbean and West Africa. In the UK, HTLV-I is uncommon, and occurs mainly amongst immigrants from endemic areas. The vast majority of carriers develop no related disease, but HTLV-I can cause two serious conditions; an aggressive T-cell malignancy, adult T-cell leukaemia/lymphoma (ATLL) and a progressive demyelinating disease, tropical spastic paraparesis (TSP).

Breast feeding appears to be the major route of transmission of HTLV-I; at least 25% of infants breast-fed by seropositive mothers will become infected during the first year of life. Therefore when a mother is known to be infected with HTLV-I, breast feeding is not advised.

Breast feeding and immunisation
Both inactivated and live vaccines included in the routine immunisation schedule, and most other vaccines, can be safely administered to breast feeding mothers. However, as a precaution it is recommended that some travellers' vaccines (Japanese encephalitis, yellow fever) should generally be avoided.

Expressed breast milk
Mothers who are separated from their babies should be encouraged to express milk for feeding to their babies. Feeding of expressed breast milk (EBM) entails considerably more handling of the milk than direct breast feeding, creating opportunities to introduce microbial contamination. These risks are best managed using Hazard Analysis and Critical Control Point (HACCP) principles. This is a systematic preventive approach to managing hazards in food handling that assures that the product that is consumed is safe without routine microbiological testing. Measures to optimise the collection, storage and handling of EBM for feeding a mother's own baby are outlined in Figure 14.1.

	Measure	**Rationale**
Collection	Encourage good hygiene in the mother	Minimises risk of contamination with bacteria from maternal skin
	Clean and disinfect or sterilise collection kit after use	Minimises risk of contamination with bacteria of maternal or environmental origin
	Store cleaned collection kit dry	Prevents bacterial multiplication
	Collect milk in volumes as close as possible to required feed size, but not less than 15-20 mL	Excess volumes result in waste. Very small volumes contain higher bacterial counts
	Use suitable containers	Considerations include ease of cleaning (if not disposable); suitability for freezing; minimisation of immunoglobulin loss
	Refrigerate milk as soon as possible after collection	Inhibits bacterial multiplication
	Ensure that samples are clearly labelled	Ensures milk is given to the correct infant and within the defined shelf life
Storage	Milk that is to be used within 48 hours may be stored refrigerated	Microbial multiplication is minimal during this time
	Freeze milk that is to be stored for over 48 hours	Prevents microbial multiplication during prolonged storage
Administration	Ensure that the infant receives the correct milk	Maternal viral infections can be transmitted via breast milk. Accidental administration of breast milk to the wrong infant should be managed as an inoculation injury
	Where possible frozen milk should be thawed in the refrigerator	Low temperature minimises microbial multiplication
	Dispose of unused frozen milk that has been thawed after 12 hours	Microbial counts in frozen milk may be higher, giving risk of rapid multiplication after thawing

Figure 14.1. Recommended measures to optimise the collection, storage and administration of expressed breast milk.

Donor breast milk

Microbiological safety is a key consideration in the use of donor breast milk. In England a NICE Clinical Guideline on the safe and effective operation of donor milk banks was published in 2010. Key elements of the Guidance are shown in Figure 14.2. All donor milk administered in the NHS should be from milk banks that can demonstrate adherence to this guidance.

Quality assurance

- Use Hazard Analysis and Critical Control Point (HACCP) principles in all processes during collection, handling and storage.

- Ensure that all equipment is used according to the manufacturer's instructions, and appropriately validated, calibrated and maintained.

- Ensure that all milk bank staff receive appropriate ongoing training.

Screening and selecting donors

- Follow a stepped screening process to exclude potential donors who are unsuitable because of risk of infection:

    – Provide information to allow women to self-screen.

    – Ask specific questions to assess risk.

    – Undertake serological testing for: HIV 1 and 2; hepatitis B and C; HTLV I and II; syphilis.

Handling donor milk at the milk bank

- Before pasteurisation, test a sample from each batch of pooled donor milk for microbial contamination and discard if samples exceed a count of:

    – 10^5 colony-forming units (CFU)/mL for total viable microorganisms **or**

    – 10^4 CFU/mL for *Enterobacteriaceae* **or**

    – 10^4 CFU/mL for *Staphylococcus aureus*.

- Regularly test pasteurised donor milk for microbial contamination. Base the testing schedule on the volume and throughput of milk.

Tracking and tracing

- Ensure donor milk containers are clearly labelled at all stages.

- Clearly identify milk that is ready to be used.

- Only supply donor milk to hospitals or neonatal units that agree to comply with the tracking procedures for milk outlined by the milk bank.

Figure 14.2. Key elements of safe donor breast milk banking included in the NICE Clinical Guideline.

Parenteral nutrition

Maintaining nutritional intake is vital for babies and there is much greater recognition of the importance of appropriate nutrition in the neonatal period. Growth failure on the neonatal unit is associated with long-term growth failure and poorer neurodevelopmental outcome. The problem is particularly severe for preterm babies who have very little calorific energy reserve i.e. liver glycogen with virtually all of their carbohydrate, protein and fat in a structural role. Parenteral nutrition (PN) is an important component of the care of babies who are unable to obtain sufficient nutrition via the enteral route, including:

- Preterm infants.

- Low birth weight infants born at term.

- Term infants with compromised gastrointestinal function (e.g. protracted diarrhoea, short bowel syndrome).

Most preterm babies require PN for no more than 2-3 weeks until enteral feeds are established. Some babies, usually those with surgical abnormalities of the GI tract, require PN for considerably longer. Home parenteral nutrition is now well established for those patients requiring long-term support.

Administration of PN is a complex procedure that should be overseen by an experienced multi-disciplinary specialist team of clinicians, dieticians, pharmacists, nurses, biochemists and microbiologists.

Indications for parenteral nutrition

The risks and benefits of administering PN must be carefully balanced. Important complications of PN include infection, cholestatic jaundice and metabolic disturbance. As PN use is becoming increasingly common, it is vital to be aware of these and be vigilant in identifying them. However, important risks from not administering PN promptly include under-nutrition, growth failure and potential neurodevelopmental impairment. PN should be prescribed where it is judged that the neonate will be unable to absorb sufficient nutrients enterally to prevent catabolism. This assessment will depend on how much enteral feed the baby can safely tolerate and whether there are any additional stress factors, e.g. sepsis, respiratory difficulties, severe intra-uterine growth retardation. As a rule, PN is only beneficial when it is administered for at least seven days.

ABSOLUTE INDICATIONS FOR PN
- Any infant born < 30 weeks gestation or < 1000g birth weight.

- Intestinal failure, bowel obstruction, severe necrotising enterocolitis.

- Infants up to 1500 g who are unlikely to achieve full enteral feeds by day seven.

- Infants >1500 g who are likely to require PN for at least seven days

Whenever possible minimal enteral feeding (MEF) or trophic feeding (typically 10-20 mL/kg/day of expressed breast milk feed given nasogastrically) should be used as an adjunct to PN as this will:

- Protect against sepsis.

- Reduce the risk of cholestasis.

- Promote faster growth.

- Reduce the time required to establish full enteral feeding.

- Protect the gut mucosa from degeneration associated with prolonged fasting.

Requirements for parenteral nutrition

Where PN is indicated it should be started as soon as possible; NNUs should have immediate access to standard bags to facilitate this. A standard bag is ready made to a standard formula for a particular group of patients. They have a number of advantages:
i)   availability,
ii)   safety (able to do end point testing),
iii)   longer stability.

Disadvantages
i)   access to aseptic pharmacy facilities required in order to add the full range of
         necessary trace elements: this lessens shelf-life to seven days after addition,
ii)   some standard bags only contain selenium and zinc as trace elements as these do not
         affect the stability.

The volume of PN administered needs to be considered in the context of the overall fluid requirement of babies. PN can be prepared in a more concentrated form where an increase in calories is required, or where babies are fluid restricted. The fluid requirement of extremely preterm infants nursed on maximally humidified incubators is 60-80 mL/kg/24h, increasing to 100-120 mL/kg/24h in week two. If measures to reduce transcutaneous water loss are not taken, fluid requirements for extremely preterm infants could be greater than 150 mL/kg/24h. The volume of the PN are increased gradually, usually over about 3-4 days so that by day five the baby should be receiving maximum volume of PN. Lipid (administered separately) is started on day 0 and increased slowly due to intolerance in extremely preterm infants.

In term infants, an intake of at least 110 kcal/kg body weight/24h is required to promote anabolism whilst growth of preterm infants is possible on a significantly lower caloric intake. The average energy intake for preterm infants is around 80 kcal/kg/24h. The energy component is provided as glucose (0.4 kcal/mL @ 10%) and lipid (1.1 kcal/mL @ 10%). Protein should only be utilised for tissue growth, and not as an energy substitute. Moreover, it is important that it is given in the correct ratio to carbohydrate and fat to ensure body growth is appropriate in composition. 1-2 g/kg/24h of protein, along with at least 70 kcal/kg/24h of non-protein calories, will prevent catabolism of body protein. The aim is to deliver at least 3 g/kg/24h of protein. Very preterm babies can tolerate up to 4 g/kg/24h protein without adverse biochemical or clinical consequences.

ADMINISTRATION

PN is usually administered via central venous lines as they allow higher concentrations of glucose to be administered without causing extravasation injury (from the hyperosmolar solution) and are associated with a lower risk of infection. The lipid and glucose/amino acid components are delivered separately. This allows for the easy identification of precipitates and for increased electrolyte administration. A bacterial filter (0.22 µM) is used on the aqueous side only. Since lipid solutions are sheared by filters of this size, a larger pore-size filter may be used although this will not filter out bacteria.

Nutrient sources and the composition of intravenous solutions

Parenteral nutrition for preterm babies is designed to reproduce *in utero* growth and regimens need to take account of the differing needs of the term or preterm baby. The basic composition of a nutritionally complete regimen is summarised in Figure 14.3

Laboratory medicine-related complications of parenteral administration

Infection

Infection is an important complication of PN; most infections can be prevented with good infection control practices.

Parenteral nutrition must be prepared in an aseptic facility in order to minimize risks of microbiological, particulate and pyrogen contamination.

Catheter-related blood stream infection (CRBSI) is an important complication of intravenous feeding; infection can reach the catheter tip via the catheter track from the skin, endo-luminally from the hub, or occasionally via the bloodstream from infection at another anatomic site.

Use of care bundles can reduce the incidence at least ten-fold, to around 3-4 infections per thousand catheter days.

Component	Notes
Carbohydrate (Glucose)	• Solutions >12.5% must be given via a central vein. • Preterm infants are often relatively glucose-intolerant (and insulin infusion may be required). MEF, through a trophic action on gut hormones, may allow higher concentrations to be tolerated. • Glucose in excess of energy requirements is converted into endogenous lipid resulting in a fatty liver.
Lipid	• Parenteral lipid emulsions (e.g. Intralipid) are isotonic fluids that provide essential fatty acids, are energy rich and decrease the osmolality of the PN solution. • Parenteral lipid should be introduced gradually, particularly in babies who are pre-term or small for gestation, in those at risk from chronic lung disease, and in those with jaundice or liver dysfunction. • The lipid component may cause hepatic impairment; SMOF (blend of Soya oil, Medium chain triglycerides, Olive oil and Fish oils) lipid have potential benefits over soya-only based lipid (Intralipid). • Lipid is usually run over 24 hours in preterm babies to improve tolerance. If blood for laboratory analysis appears lipaemic, the lipid needs to be switched off and sample collection repeated in 4 hours. • Extremely preterm (due to reduced activity of lipoprotein lipase) and septic infants may develop intolerance to lipid. • High triglycerides can cause unexplained thrombocytopaenia. • Fatty acids can displace bilirubin from albumin resulting in increased free, unconjugated hyperbilirubinaemia.
Protein supplied as elemental amino acids	• Amino acids are essential precursors for proteins (and, thus, growth), neurotransmitters, as transport molecules, and in cell signalling. • A balanced mixture of L-amino acids (including adequate essential amino acids) is required; the optimal proportions of different amino acids are uncertain, and there is considerable variability among commercial preparations. • Preterm infants require more amino acids, and probably in different proportions.
Vitamins	• Water-soluble and fat-soluble preparations are given in doses appropriate to the baby's weight.
Minerals	• Electrolyte concentrations, particularly sodium, can fluctuate widely and rapidly in neonates. • The precipitation of the inorganic salts of calcium and phosphate due to limited solubility may make provision of the full requirements impossible, particularly in pre-term infants. Cysteine can be added to neonatal PN to lower the pH and increase calcium and phosphate solubility. Glucose 1-phosphate and calcium glycerophosphate, which have greater solubility, have also been used to increase the calcium and phosphate concentrations of intravenous feeding solutions.
Trace elements (chromium, copper, iodine, manganese, molybdenum, selenium, zinc, etc.)	• Where indicated, these are provided as a supplement based on body weight. • Routine supplements may not supply enough trace elements for preterm infants on long term PN (i.e. > four weeks), especially if there are abnormal losses of fluid from the gut.

Figure 14.3. Components of a nutritionally complete PN regimen for neonates.

These are summarised in Figure 14.4.

Frequent complications

>
> *Electrolyte abnormalities
> *Glucose abnormalities
> *Conjugated hyperbilirubinaemia
> *Hypophosphataemia, hypocalcaemia and hypomagnesaemia
> Acid base disturbances

Less frequent complications

>
> *Hyperlipidaemia (raised cholesterol and triglycerides)
> *Hyperphenylalaninaemia (± hypertyrosinaemia)
> Hyperammonaemia
> Zinc, copper or selenium deficiency
> Carnitine deficiency
> Essential fatty acids deficiency

* particularly important in extreme preterm infants

Figure 14.4. Metabolic complications of parenteral nutrition in neonates.

Electrolyte abnormalities
Maintaining sodium, potassium and chloride within normal limits is one of the main challenges in administering PN to neonates. Higher early sodium intake may be associated with early hypernatraemia and increased oxygen requirements to 28 days. Similarly, hyperkalaemia is a common complication in the first 48 hours of life; minimal potassium concentration of starter PN is therefore recommended. Later, hyponatraemia and hypokalaemia may occur, especially in those with continuing abnormal fluid and electrolyte losses, e.g. diarrhoea, upper gastro-intestinal fluid loss or renal losses. Hyperchloraemia is common, and is associated with acidosis; the incidence of hyperchloraemia and acidosis can be reduced by partly replacing chloride with acetate (metabolised to bicarbonate) in PN.

Glucose abnormalities
Hyperglycaemia and glycosuria (> 0.5% measured by strip tests) may occur in very low birth weight babies and six-hourly blood glucose monitoring and urine testing for glucose is recom-mended. Reported adverse effects of hyperglycaemia include death, intraventricular haemor-rhage, bacterial and fungal infections, retinopathy of prematurity and necrotizing enterocol-itis. Hyperglycaemia is managed initially by reducing the carbohydrate concentration to avoid an osmotic diuresis. The neonate may subsequently require an insulin infusion to ensure adequate energy intake, especially if of very low birth weight or if steroids are being given for lung disease. Hyperglycaemia in term infants or previously stable infants is uncommon and when it occurs is suggestive of infection or other stress, accidental over-supply or a complica-tion of steroid therapy in premature neonates. With refractory hypoglycaemia, consider administration problems (e.g. leak, disconnected catheter), hypopituitarism and hyper-

insulinism (see chapter 7).

Conjugated Hyperbilirubinaemia
Hyperbilirubinaemia occurs in some neonates, particularly if on PN for more than 14 days. Intralipid 20% is derived from soya beans and is primarily made up of omega-6 polyunsaturated fatty acids. These are pro-inflammatory and can result in the production of free radicals which in turn can cause oxidative damage to cells. It also contains phytosterols which are directly hepatotoxic. It is thought that these two constituents of Intralipid contribute to parenteral nutrition associated liver disease (PNLD). SMOF lipid is a blend of Soya oil, Medium chain triglycerides, Olive oil and Fish oils. Fish oil contains primarily omega-3 polyunsaturated fatty acids which are anti-inflammatory and potentially hepato-protective. It does not contain phytosterols. Studies are ongoing to establish the benefits of SMOF lipid in preventing PNLD. Whilst conjugated hyperbilirubinaemia secondary to cholestasis is a known complication of prolonged parenteral nutrition, it is important to exclude other underlying causes (e.g. biliary atresia, neonatal hepatitis.

Calcium, phosphate and magnesium
Higher intakes of calcium and phosphate increase mineral retention, bone mineral content and bone strength. However, the quantity of calcium and phosphate that can be added to PN is constrained by the precipitation of calcium phosphate salts. Hypophosphataemia is very common in those receiving prolonged PN and therefore oral vitamin D (with routine vitamin supplementation) and phosphate supplements are needed for those infants at risk of bone disease of prematurity before PN is discontinued. Plasma magnesium concentration should also be measured if there is refractory hypocalcaemia. Because clearance of magnesium by neonates is reduced, supplementation should be given only when plasma concentrations are low (see chapter 8).

Acid-base disturbances
Mild acid-base disturbances are common, particularly with increased duration of PN and are generally safely ignored. Clinical signs are rare unless the base deficit exceeds 5 mmol/L. In very immature infants, it is common to see base deficit exceed 10 mmol/L, presumably due to renal immaturity; this may require bicarbonate treatment.

Hyperlipidaemia
Hypercholesterolaemia has been noted in some babies receiving Intralipid. The phospholipid present as an emulsifier has been implicated as the cause, and its intake can be reduced by giving the Intralipid as a 20% rather than a 10% emulsion, since the former preparation has a lower proportion of phospholipid. The significance of this hypercholesterolaemia is not known. Hypertriglyceridaemia should not occur if the rate of lipid infusion is controlled appropriately. If triglyceride concentrations exceed 2.8 mmol/L, the lipid intake should be reduced.

Amino acids
Amino acid imbalances were more of a problem when products formulated for adults were used for neonates. Considerations now relate mainly to long-term PN when taurine deficiency may be associated with an abnormal electroretinogram, although this appears to be reversible.

Hyperammonaemia
Hyperammonaemia is a rare complication with the currently available nitrogen sources and if liver function is normal. If, however, the baby becomes lethargic or develops fits, plasma ammonia concentration should be measured.

Trace elements deficiency and toxicity
These are essential micronutrients in many metabolic processes, and include chromium, copper, iodine, manganese, molybdenum, selenium and zinc. If PN is supplemental or required for only two weeks, only zinc needs to be added to the infusion. If PN continues for longer than a month, other trace metals need to be added. Zinc, copper and selenium are the most important deficiencies in neonates receiving PN (Figure 14.5); the risk is highest in surgical babies with increased gastrointestinal losses. Manganese deficiency in neonates receiving PN has not been described. In contrast copper and manganese may need to be with-held if the neonate develops PN-associated liver disease because copper is potentially hepa-totoxic and manganese, which is potentially neurotoxic, is dependent on a patent biliary tract for excretion. Selenium deficiency may be a risk factor for chronic neonatal lung disease, retinopathy of prematurity and sepsis. Note that plasma selenium concentration is an indi-cator of recent intake, whereas erythrocyte glutathione peroxidase activity or whole blood selenium is a better marker of overall selenium status. Iodine deficiency and excess have been reported in preterm infants, with iodine excess associated with transient hypothyroidism. Chromium deficiency has rarely been reported; excess chromium intake may be associated with renal impairment.

Zinc	Dermatitis (symmetrical periorifacial)
	Alopecia
	Diarrhoea
	Immune deficiency
Copper	Hypochromic anaemia
	Neutropenia
Selenium	Cardiomyopathy
	Skeletal myopathy

Figure 14.5. Important clinical effects of key trace element deficiencies.

Other trace metal requirements include iron supplementation. This is not provided intra-venously because of the possible increased risk of infection and because iron needs may be met with blood transfusions. Some elements may unintentionally be given in excess of requirements, as contaminants, particularly of amino acid solutions. There is still concern about aluminium accumulation in preterm infants after prolonged IV feeding and its associa-tion with impaired neurological development and metabolic bone disease. In very long-term PN, consideration should be given to measurement of aluminium.

Carnitine Deficiency
Preterm infants have limited carnitine storage and biosynthesis; supplementation should be considered in babies receiving PN for more than two weeks.

Haematological complications
Anaemia and dysfunction of thrombocytes or neutrophils can occur. Note that hyperlipidemia can cause spurious elevation of the haemoglobin concentration.

Laboratory monitoring of parenteral nutrition

There are numerous guidelines for biochemical monitoring, most of them based on little hard scientific data. With increasing experience and availability of more appropriate products for neonates, biochemical complications are less common, and less frequent monitoring may be required. Unnecessary blood sampling is traumatic to the baby and creates an added risk of infection and anaemia. For clinically stable infants who are being monitored *solely* because they are receiving parenteral nutrition, a conservative approach to monitoring is recommended (Figure 14.6). However, in an infant who is clinically unstable, is very preterm, or has major organ failure or unusual fluid losses, more frequent or extensive monitoring is needed. For example preterm infants will require additional monitoring of glucose (blood and urine) and plasma phosphate. In babies with no particular susceptibility to acid-base disturbances, routine hydrogen ion and blood gas measurements are not indicated. Nor is there a role for osmolality measurements as it is usually more informative to measure individual analytes. If there is particular concern about lipid clearance, e.g. due to liver dysfunction, plasma triglyceride and non-esterified fatty acid concentrations should be measured; visual lipaemia provides an insensitive assessment and does not correlate well with quantitative measurements.

Timing	Body Fluid	Tests
Pre-PN	Blood/plasma	Sodium, potassium, urea, creatinine, bilirubin, phosphate
	Urine	Sodium, potassium
Throughout PN With short-term PN (<2 weeks), this basic biochemical and haematological monitoring usually suffices	Blood/plasma	Sodium, potassium, urea, creatinine: daily initially until stable Phosphate, calcium, alkaline phosphatase, ALT, bilirubin (total and conjugated): once weekly. More frequent phosphate monitoring will be required if plasma concentration is low. Glucose: daily first week or more frequently if unstable or preterm. Can be reduced thereafter unless glucose intake is being increased or baby is preterm Apparently low glucose results by a strip method (i.e. < 2 mmol/L) MUST be confirmed with a laboratory result Haemoglobin, haematocrit, WBC and differential, platelets: weekly Triglycerides: weekly as lipid content increases
	Urine	Sodium, potassium, glucose: as required
Additional tests after three weeks PN	Blood	Selenium, zinc, copper, manganese: three weekly
Long-term PN		After 4 weeks fat soluble vitamins (A,E,D), B12 and folate, ferritin (NB. copper is a positive acute phase reactant, whilst vitamin A, zinc and selenium are negative acute phase reactants. Simultaneous CRP can aid interpretation of results.)

Figure 14.6. Protocol for routine biochemical and haematological monitoring of term neonates on PN.

Further Reading

Bolisetty S, Osborn D, Sinn J, Lui K. Australasian Neonatal Parenteral Nutrition Consensus Group. Standardised neonatal parenteral nutrition formulations – an Australasian group consensus 2012. BMC Pediatrics 2014; **14:** 48.

Cottrell EB, Chou R, Wasson N, Rahman B, Guise JM. Reducing risk for mother-to-infant transmission of hepatitis C virus: a systematic review for the U.S. Preventive Services Task Force. Ann Intern Med 2013; **158:** 109-113.

Koletzko B, Goulet O, Hunt J, Krohn K, Shamir R. Guidelines on Paediatric Parenteral Nutrition Journal of Pediatric Gastroenterology & Nutrition 2005; **41:** S1-S4.

Morgan C, Herwitker S, Badhawi I, Hart A, Tan M, Mayes K, *et al.* SCAMP: standardised, concentrated, additional macronutrients, parenteral nutrition in very preterm infants: a phase IV randomised, controlled exploratory study of macronutrient intake, growth and other aspects of neonatal care. BMC Pediatrics 2011; **11:** 53.

National Institute for Health and Clinical Excellence. NICE clinical guideline 93. Donor breast milk banks. The operation of donor breast milk bank services. February 2010.

Preer GL, Philipp BL. Understanding and managing breast milk jaundice. Arch Dis Child Fetal Neonatal Ed 2011; **96:** F461-466.

Chapter 15
Drugs and the neonate

Summary

- Pharmacokinetics of drug metabolism in neonates differ significantly from that of infants and children.

- Expression of drug metabolising enzymes alters with post-natal age.

- Because of the differences in pharmacokinetics and the immature physiology of the neonate, therapeutic drug concentrations differ to those of children and adults.

- Maternal medication may be a risk factor either for the developing fetus through placental transfer or post-natally if excreted in breast milk.

Introduction

Neonates are very different to older children and adults in their handling and response to drugs. Whilst only a relatively small number of drugs are regularly prescribed for neonates that number is increasing despite the vast majority being unlicensed for use in this age group . For the frequently prescribed drugs, the dosing and monitoring regimens are usually relatively well defined. For drugs that are prescribed infrequently, there is often little information to guide the prescriber although this has improved somewhat in recent years (British National Formulary for Children). The laboratory often has an important role in monitoring for direct or indirect evidence of both the efficacy and potential toxicity of these therapeutic agents. Infrequently used agents should be administered cautiously, with close monitoring during therapy.

As well as drugs that are administered directly, the neonate may also be exposed to drugs taken by the mother, either by transfer across the placenta before delivery, or via breast milk.

Pharmacokinetics

Routes of administration and bioavailability

ORAL

Liquid formulations of a variety of drugs can be administered to neonates. However, oral administration produces unpredictable variability in drug absorption, and hence in blood and tissue concentrations. Factors that affect absorption include milk, the higher neonatal gastric pH and slower rate of gastric emptying, differences in the neonatal gastrointestinal flora, gestational and post-natal age, and the presence of underlying illness when ileus, and therefore delayed absorption, may occur. Lower activities of gastrointestinal digestive factors, such as bile acids and lipase, lead to decreased absorption of lipid soluble drugs.

RECTAL

Absorption of drugs rectally is greater in the neonate than in either children or adults. Solutions of drugs such as paraldehyde, paracetamol and chloral hydrate are available for rectal administration. Calcium resonium can be administered as an enema to remove excess potassium in hyperkalaemia. This route of administration sometimes has slower absorption and may be less effective than oral dosing, but is occasionally useful, especially where intravenous access is not readily available or the infant is nil by mouth. Problems with rectal administration include variability in absorption due to depth of insertion available and/or retention of the drug in the rectum. Drugs enter the systemic circulation via rectal veins and are then subject to liver metabolism.

RESPIRATORY TRACT

Exogenous surfactant to treat the surfactant deficiency associated with prematurity is administered directly into the trachea if the baby is intubated. Other drugs such as corticosteroids and bronchodilators can be administered directly into the respiratory tract of ventilated babies using specific delivery devices. Theoretically this can provide high concentrations of drug in the respiratory tract with less risk of systemic toxicity, but in practice the efficacy of drugs administered in this way is variable (surfactant being a notable exception).

INTRAMUSCULAR (I.M.)

Lipid-soluble drugs can diffuse directly through capillary walls and are rapidly absorbed by this route. Drugs that are not lipid soluble are absorbed much more slowly via the lymphatic system, provided that they are water soluble at physiological pH. The unreliability of the i.m. route is accentuated in neonates, because of the small amount of suitable skeletal muscle available, the decreased contractility and poor tissue perfusion, especially during illness. Occasionally, this slow absorption produces a depot effect that is clinically useful, for example with vitamin K. The slower absorption rate results in lower peak serum drug concentrations. However, water soluble drugs do tend to show improved absorption with respect to that of children and adults due to a greater water content and increased density of skeletal muscle capillaries.

INTRAVENOUS (I.V.)

This is the main route of drug administration in emergency situations and to ill babies in neonatal units. Intravenous administration gives rapid action and complete availability of the drug to the body without first-pass metabolism. Dosage is easily controlled, which is especially useful when titration of drug concentrations to within a therapeutic range is required.

Distribution

Neonates, particularly those born prematurely, have a relatively larger total body water and lower body fat as compared with older children and adults. The proportion of total body water that is extracellular fluid is higher in neonates, especially during the first 48 hours of life (see Chapter 4). As a result, most drugs have a larger volume of distribution during infancy, and a larger dose related to weight is required. Extracellular fluid volume directly correlates with body surface area, therefore, theoretically, drug dosing based on surface area should be more precise. However, volume of distribution is only one variable influencing drug handling by neonates, and for convenience most drug doses continue to be based on body weight, together with gestational and post-natal ages. The lower total protein in neonatal plasma, together with the lower drug binding capacity of neonatal albumin, also contributes to a larger volume of distribution for drugs that are protein bound. It is unbound drug that is able to cross membranes in order to exert its biological effect. For example, theophylline has decreased protein binding in premature neonates, hence increased unbound concentrations compared to children or adults. As a result a lower total plasma concentration of theophylline will be required for efficacy and to avoid toxicity.

Metabolism

The most important site of drug metabolism is the liver. In general, enzymic biotransformation of drugs is markedly slower in the newborn, especially the preterm neonate. However, the various metabolic pathways differ in their maturity; glucuronidation, N-dealkylation and oxidation are important pathways that are especially immature in the neonate. There is also considerable variation between individuals, which can be compounded by enzyme induction or inhibition by other drugs given to the neonate, or even to the mother before delivery. Drugs that can induce enzymes include phenobarbital, phenytoin and rifampicin. Inhibitors include chloramphenicol and cimetidine.

Drug metabolism can involve two phases:

- Phase I metabolism is a modification of the drug by oxidation, reduction or hydrolysis, usually catalysed by microsomal enzymes. Oxidation is the most common phase I reaction, and involves a group of haemoproteins called cytochrome P450 (CYP) superfamily that act as the terminal oxygen carrier in the oxidation pathway. These drug metabolising enzymes in the neonatal liver develop at differing rates. For example, CYP2C19, which metabolises phenobarbitone and phenytoin, has low expression at 0-2 days of age, shows rapid increase in expression at one week of age and reaches adult values at two years of age. Development of the enzymes may be influenced by neonatal diet, for example, CYP1A2, which metabolises caffeine, matures more rapidly in formula fed neonates than those that are breast fed.

- Phase II metabolism is a synthetic reaction which involves conjugation of the drug or its metabolites with another molecule, e.g. glucuronic acid (UDP-glucuronosyltransferases – UGT), sulphate (sulfotransferases SULT) or glutathione (glutathione S-methyltransferases – GST) and thiopurines (thiopurine methyltransferase – TPMT). Some drugs pass through only one phase, whereas others must undergo a phase I reaction before a phase II reaction can take place. Drugs that are eliminated by both phase I and II reactions (e.g. diazepam, chloramphenicol) have particularly unpredictable pharmacokinetics in neonates.

Immaturity of drug receptors, or differing expression of the receptor, will also impact on drug efficacy, examples include increased sensitivity of mu (μ) opioid receptors (morphine), or low intestinal motilin receptors before 32 weeks gestation meaning that erythromycin at this point has little impact on gastrointestinal motility.

The following drugs exemplify the problems arising from slower drug elimination in neonates.

- Pethidine is hydrolysed by an esterase that is present in low concentrations in neonates.

The drug has an elimination half-life ($t_{1/2}$) of up to 22 hours, seven times that in adults. Pethidine used as an analgesic during labour can cross the placenta and cause prolonged respiratory depression in the newborn.

- The N-demethylation pathway for caffeine is deficient in neonates. A large proportion of the drug is excreted unchanged in the urine, and the half-life is four days, compared with around four hours in adults.

- Glucuronidation of chloramphenicol by UGT2B7 is an important elimination mechanism that is immature in the neonate. This leads to high circulating concentrations of chloramphenicol, which in turn can inhibit microsomal enzymes involved in phase I elimination. High circulating concentrations of chloramphenicol occur, which are toxic to mammalian cells. Without dose reduction and close monitoring of drug concentrations this can lead to the fatal 'grey baby' syndrome with shock and circulatory collapse. Chloramphenicol is rarely used in neonatal practice in the UK.

Excretion

Renal function is poor at birth, especially in the preterm or sick neonate. The glomerular filtration rate (GFR) can be as low as 2-3 mL/min in the 28 week baby, and increases only slowly in the first post-natal week. After the first week, the GFR increases steeply with a further sharp increase at the equivalent of 34-36 weeks gestation. Glomerular filtration, adjusted for surface area, only reaches adult rates at two years of age. As a result, the half-life of drugs that are excreted unchanged in the urine can be greatly prolonged, e.g. digoxin ($t_{1/2}$ 100 hours, compared with 30 hours in adults) and gentamicin ($t_{1/2}$ 18 hours, compared with two hours). Drugs, such as penicillin, are mainly eliminated by active tubular secretion. Tubular function is poor, particularly in the preterm or sick neonate, resulting in diminished tubular secretion of such drugs. Furosemide is excreted unchanged by both filtration and secretion. The mean half-life in neonates is seven hours, compared with 1.5-3 hours in adults. This is associated with a sustained diuretic effect and increased risk of electrolyte disturbance and loss of minerals. Nephrocalcinosis can occur in preterm neonates as a consequence of furosemide treatment.

Monitoring for the adverse effects of drugs

Adverse effects are usually concentration-dependent, resulting from an augmented pharmacological response to the drug. They are more common in neonates than in any other age group, both because drug pharmacokinetics are more unpredictable, and because of the immaturity of neonatal physiology. For example, increased sensitivity to opiates relates partly to markedly slower metabolism of the drug, but also to inefficiency of the immature blood-brain barrier. Adverse effects rarely produce characteristic physical signs until they have become serious. The laboratory, therefore, has an important role in both reducing the risk of adverse effects by monitoring blood drug concentrations (see later), and in detecting biochemical and haematological changes that may either affect drug handling or be directly drug-induced (Figure 15.1).

Drug	Suggested monitoring	Minimum frequency of monitoring	Rationale for monitoring
Aminoglycosides*	Urea and electrolytes	2-3 times weekly	Potentially nephrotoxic. Dosage adjustment required in renal impairment
Amphotericin B (systemic therapy)	Urea and electrolytes	2-3 times weekly	Biochemical disturbances predictable (especially raised urea and hypokalaemia). Less commonly, hypomagnesaemia
	Full blood count	1-2 times weekly	Haematological dyscrasias sometimes occur
β-lactam antibiotics (Penicillins, cephalosporins, carbapenems)	Urea and electrolytes	Twice weekly	Electrolyte disturbances (hypokalaemia, hyper-natraemia) may occur, especially with high doses
Digoxin*	Urea and electrolytes	Daily	Electrolyte disturbances (especially hypokalaemia and hypercalcaemia) may potentiate digoxin effect. Dosage adjustment required in renal impairment.
Furosemide	Urea and electrolytes	Every 1-2 days	Biochemical disturbances common (especially hypokalaemia and hypocalcaemia)
Indomethacin	Urea and electrolytes	Daily	Biochemical disturbances may occur (especially raised urea and hyponatraemia)
Phenobarbital*	Full blood count	Weekly	Risk of anaemia with prolonged therapy
Phenytoin*	Blood glucose Full blood count	1-2 times weekly Weekly	Risk of hyperglycaemia Risk of anaemia with prolonged therapy
Ranitidine	Urea and electrolytes	Weekly	Elimination is prolonged in renal failure
Theophylline*	Urea and electrolytes	1-2 times weekly	Risk of hypokalaemia, especially with concomitant diuretic or steroid therapy

*Laboratory measurement of drug concentrations is usually also indicated (see later)

Figure 15.1. Indications for biochemical and haematological monitoring in neonates receiving drug therapy.

Idiosyncratic drug effects are comparatively rare events that are unpredictable and not dose-related. Allergic reactions are rarely seen in neonates. Genetic abnormalities may lead to abnormal and unpredictable responses to drugs. For example, infants with glucose 6-phosphate dehydrogenase (G6PD) deficiency or hereditary methaemoglobinaemia are susceptible to oxidant drugs, such as sulphonamides.

Obstetric drugs and the neonate

Drugs administered to the mother late in pregnancy may cross the placenta to the fetus and produce direct drug effects in the baby. This particularly applies to drugs that are rapidly absorbed across membranes, that is, those with a low molecular weight, low ionisation and a high lipid:water partition ratio.

The neonate can be adversely affected by maternal drug therapy in a number of ways. Problems may be due to:
- a direct effect of *in utero* exposure to the drug,
- the effects of abrupt withdrawal of supply after delivery,
- an inability to eliminate the drug, leading to accumulation and toxicity,
- accelerated development of some hepatic elimination pathways as a result of prolonged fetal exposure to enzyme-inducing drugs, e.g. phenobarbital,
- idiosyncratic effects.

The effects of specific drugs that may adversely affect the neonate if taken by the mother late in pregnancy are shown in Figure 15.2. A more comprehensive list appears as an appendix in the British National Formulary for Children.

Drug withdrawal

This is the most commonly encountered problem in neonates relating to maternal drug exposure. Maternal drug addiction, particularly to narcotic agents, may lead to the development of a withdrawal syndrome in the neonate after delivery. Presentation is usually within four days of birth, but can be delayed until ten days and may last up to six months.

Symptoms and signs are variable, and are predominantly those of autonomic overactivity: cerebral irritability, nasal congestion, sneezing, yawning, runny eyes, photophobia, poor suck, hiccups and diarrhoea have all been described. In more severe cases there is an abnormal high-pitched cry, increased extensor tone, irritability, poor sleeping, tachypnoea, weight loss and convulsions. Treatment is with a reducing course of opiates, or with sedative drugs if the maternal drug was a benzodiazepine.

Drug	Effect on neonate
ACE inhibitors	Neonatal blood pressure control and renal function may be affected
Alcohol	Intrauterine growth retardation, fetal-alcohol syndrome
Amiodarone	Risk of neonatal goitre
Anaesthetics, general (high doses, or delivery prolonged by >20 minutes)	Neonatal respiratory depression
Anaesthetics, local	Neonatal respiratory depression Hypotonia and bradycardia after epidural block
Anti-coagulants	Risk of neonatal bleeding
Antidepressants	Tachycardia, irritability, muscle spasms may occur
Anti-convulsants	Risk of bleeding
Antipsychotics	Extrapyramidal effects occasionally occur
Aspirin	Impaired platelet function Kernicterus in jaundiced newborn
Benzodiazepines	Risk of neonatal withdrawal symptoms
Beta-blockers	Risk of neonatal hypoglycaemia or bradycardia
Carbimazole	Risk of neonatal goitre and hypothyroidism
Iodine and iodides	Risk of neonatal goitre and hypothyroidism
Lithium	Risk of toxicity
Opioid analgesics	Depression of neonatal respiration Withdrawal effects in dependent mothers
Sulphonamides, related drugs	Risk of neonatal haemolysis and methaemoglobinaemia
Thiazide diuretics	Risk of neonatal thrombocytopenia

Figure 15.2. Drugs that may adversely affect the neonate if taken by the mother late in pregnancy.

Drugs and breast milk

Many drugs given to the mother following the birth will be excreted to some degree in breast milk. Factors that affect the rate of excretion include maternal pharmacokinetics (blood flow to the breast, hormonal influence, etc.), the physiological composition of the milk and the properties of the drug. Drugs that are weak bases, highly lipophilic and/or have low protein binding are excreted in the largest amounts. However, the amount of most drugs available in breast milk for absorption is small (usually less than 2% of the maternal dose). For drugs with low to moderate potential toxicity, an exposure of up to 10% of the weight-adjusted maternal dose is generally regarded as acceptable. Thus there is only a small number of drugs where breast feeding is absolutely contraindicated (Figure 15.3). Laboratory tests are occasionally useful in monitoring the effects of maternal drug therapy on breast-fed infants, e.g. thyroid function tests when the mother is receiving anti-thyroid drugs. A comprehensive list of drugs that can be excreted in breast milk is provided as an appendix in the British National Formulary for Children.

Lithium	Cytotoxic drugs
Immunosuppressants (excluding corticosteroids)	Radiopharmaceuticals
Phenindione	Ergot alkaloids

Figure 15.3. Maternal drugs for which breast feeding is contraindicated.

Therapeutic monitoring

Monitoring drug concentrations is most valid when there is a direct relationship between the plasma concentration and the pharmacological and/or toxic effects. Sometimes there is no such relationship, e.g. when the drug has active metabolites, or where the drug action is irreversible and therefore unrelated to steady-state concentrations. Regular monitoring of blood concentrations in the neonate is indicated for drugs with one or more of the following characteristics:
- unpredictable half-life,
- toxic cumulative effects,
- narrow therapeutic index (i.e. the difference between effective and toxic concentrations is small),
- where inadequate dosage leads to loss of efficacy.

A list of such drugs, and their therapeutic ranges at the appropriate sampling times, is given in Figure 15.4.

Drug	Sampling time	Target range
Amikacin (multiple daily dose regimen)	Peak (30-60 min post-dose) Trough (<60 min pre-dose)	15-20 mg/L <10 mg/L
Amikacin (extended interval dose regimen)	Trough (<60 min pre-dose)	<5 mg/L
Gentamicin (extended interval dose regimen)[1]	Trough (<60 min pre-dose)	<2 mg/L (<1 mg/L if more than 3 doses administered)
Vancomycin	Trough (<60 min pre-dose)	10-15 mg/L (15-20 mg/L for less sensitive strains of methicillin-resistant staphylococci)
Chloramphenicol	Peak (1-2 hours post-dose)	15-25 mg/L
Digoxin	>6h post-dose	1-2 µg/L
Caffeine	>6h post-dose	15-30 mg/L
Theophylline	Peak (60 min post-dose)	5-12 mg/L
Phenobarbital	>6h post-dose	15-30 mg/L
Phenytoin	>8h post-dose	10-20 mg/L

[1]Consider measuring a peak (60 min post-dose) concentration in neonates with poor response to treatment, with oedema, with proven Gram-negative infection, or with birth weight >4.5 kg; consider increasing the dose if the peak concentration is <8 mg/L.

Figure 15.4. Therapeutic monitoring of drugs in the neonate.

Further reading

British National Formulary for Children 2015-2016.
https://www.medicinescomplete.com/mc/bnfc/2011/

Ku LC, Smith PB. Dosing in neonates: special considerations in physiology and trial design. Pediatric Research 2015; **77**: 2-9.

Jong G. Chapter 2. Pediatric Development: Physiology. Enzymes, Drug Metabolism, Pharmacokinetics and Pharmacodynamics In: Pediatric Formulations: A Roadmap, AAPS Advances in the Pharmaceutical Sciences Series 11   Bar-Shalom D, Rose K (eds) American Association of Pharmaceutical Scientists 2014.

Van den Anker JN, Schwab M, Kearns GL. Developmental Pharmacokinetics In: H.W. Seyberth *et al* (eds) Pediatric Clinical Pharmacology, Handbook of Experimental Pharmacology 205. Pub. Springer-Verlag Berlin Heidelberg 2011.

de Wildt,SN, Tibboel D, Leeder JS. Drug metabolism for the paediatrician. Arch Dis Child 2014; **99**: 1137-1142.

Appendix A
Routine specimen collection

Blood collection in neonates

Blood can be collected by capillary puncture, venepuncture or arterial sampling. The choice of sampling site will depend on the quantity of blood required, the analytes requested and the clinical condition of the infant. Whilst specimens collected by skin puncture from the heel can yield enough blood for routine testing, it is not without risk. Moreover, there is evidence that venepuncture, when done by a trained practitioner, causes less pain than heel lance. Venepuncture is indicated when larger volumes of blood are required for coagulation and bacterial culture.

Guidance on blood collection from neonates is contained in the WHO protocol on best phlebotomy practice.

Capillary blood collection

Most neonatal units have their own guidelines and training procedures for capillary blood collection. Practical video guidance for capillary blood collection is also provided by blood gas analyser manufacturers and suppliers of neonatal capillary blood collection tubes. Collections should be planned to coordinate for both haematology and biochemistry investigations. Blood for haematology investigations should be collected first to minimise the fall in platelet count from shed blood and to provide results similar to those from venous specimens. A site on the medial or lateral side of the heel should be chosen (Figure A.1). The collection site must be warmed and well perfused prior to lancet puncture. For neonates, the depth of the lancet puncture should not go beyond 2.4 mm to avoid penetration of the bone which has the potential complication of osteomyelitis. It should be possible to obtain the most commonly requested tests from a collection volume of 1 ml.

Specimens for blood culture

Care must be taken to avoid contamination of the sample with bacteria from the patient's skin, the phlebotomist or the environment. To minimise the risk of contamination:

- A sample collected from a fresh venepuncture through carefully prepared skin is always preferred. Chlorhexidine is commonly used as a skin antiseptic in NICUs, despite the small risk of chemical burns, especially with higher strength and/or alcoholic solutions. Be careful to use the preparation that is recommended in your hospital, and to avoid dripping or pooling of the product on or under the patient.

- Where the blood sample is going to be used for multiple tests always inoculate the blood culture bottle first, before inoculating any other tubes.

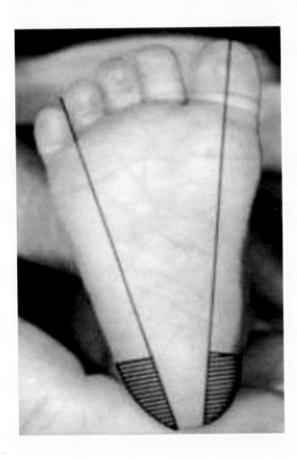

Figure A.1. Recommended capillary specimen collection sites on either medial or lateral side of heel.

Further reading

Shah VS, Ohlsson A. Venepuncture versus heel lance for blood sampling in term neonates. Version 4. Cochrane Data Base

Paediatric and Neonatal Blood Sampling. WHO Guidelines on Drawing Blood Best Practices in Phlebotomy. World Health Organization. Geneva; 2010

www.gosh.nhs.uk/health-professionals/clinical-guidelines/blood-sampling-neonatal-capillary Capillary sampling on neonates www.youtube.com/watch

Appendix B
Emergency specimen collection for the diagnosis of inherited metabolic disorders

In life-threatening situations where an inherited metabolic disorder is thought to be a likely cause (either from family history, results of preliminary investigations or clinical presentation) the specimens detailed below should be taken. At the earliest opportunity a specialist laboratory should be contacted to discuss appropriate investigations. If possible, urine and blood specimens should be taken before death. Appropriate policy and procedure for obtaining informed consent should be followed. If any of the samples are taken after death it is extremely important to record accurately both the time of death and when the samples were taken.

Specimen	Preservative	Volume	Storage (sample type and temperature)	Notes
Urine	None	5-10 mL	-20°C	If contaminated with blood centrifuge to remove cells. Freeze supernatant
Blood	Filter paper/newborn screening card	Blood spot	Whole blood, room temperature	
	Lithium heparin	5-10 mL	Plasma -20°C Packed red cells +4°C	
	Fluoride oxalate	0.5 mL	Plasma -20°C	
	EDTA	5-10 mL	Whole blood +4°C	For DNA
Skin	Culture medium (Ham's F10, Eagle's MEM, Dulbecco's medium) or sterile isotonic saline	2 punch biopsies from different sites (or 3 mm x 3 mm full thickness biopsies)	+4°C (DO NOT freeze as this will destroy any viable cells)	Best taken when baby is alive but may be collected up to 24 hours post mortem. Sterility is very important
CSF	Plain tube Fluoride oxalate	1 mL 1 mL	-80°C (deep frozen)	If cloudy or blood stained, centrifuge and store supernatant

Specimen	Preservative	Volume	Storage (sample type and temperature)	Notes
Tissue (liver, heart muscle, skeletal muscle, kidney)	Plain plastic tube	2-3 needle biopsies	Snap freeze in liquid nitrogen (or solid carbon dioxide). -80°C (deep frozen)	Only collect if there is a strong suspicion of primary defect of the tissue. Ensure clear labelling of tubes. Samples are only suitable for biochemical analysis if collected whilst alive or within 2-4 hours of death

Appendix C
Laboratory investigation of sudden unexpected death in infancy (SUDI)

SUDI is the unexpected death of an apparently well infant over one month of age, for which no cause can be found, in spite of a post-mortem examination. The precise cause of such sudden, unexplained death in infants under one year of age remains unknown in approximately 80% of cases. However it is recognised that a small but significant number of sudden deaths in infancy and occasionally in older children are a result of inherited metabolic disease. Therefore a specimen collection protocol analogous to that advocated for inherited metabolic disease (Appendix B) should be adopted (http://www.metbio.net/docs/MetBio-Guideline-RASU337946-27-11-2010). Additional body fluids proven to be of diagnostic value include bile and vitreous humour. A pre-prepared SUDI-BOX containing all the appropriate specimen collection tubes and advice has been demonstrated to be useful.

Appendix D
Reference ranges

The birth process and the adjustment of the newborn to independent life have a major effect on the production, metabolism and excretion of many metabolites, hormones and enzymes. Rapid growth and organ maturation further modify these parameters with increasing post-natal age. So not only do reference ranges for neonates differ from those in infants and older children, but many of them change significantly during the first four weeks of life. These differences are further compounded by prematurity and intrauterine growth restriction.

Mechanisms responsible for differences in neonatal reference ranges include:

- Birth stress. The stress response elevates endocrine parameters notably TSH and cortisol in the first twenty four hours of life.
- Vaginal delivery causes release of muscle enzymes resulting in elevated creatine kinase in the first week of life.
- Maternal contributions. At birth the baby's biochemical profile resembles the mother's and it may take several days for the maternal concentrations of for example creatinine to be cleared owing to lower neonatal glomerular filtration rates.
- Foetal accretion. This is most notable for calcium.
- Organ maturity. Both glomerular and tubular function is different in neonates.
- Feeding regime – formula milks may contain supplemented amino acids and phosphate.

Reference data provided in this book are intended to be only a guide and it is incumbent on all laboratories to have locally applicable reference ranges for neonates distinct from those employed for older children and adult. This is to avoid abnormal results being reported as normal or conversely normal results being reported as abnormal and prompting unnecessary further investigation. These reference ranges should be instrument and method specific and harmonised across laboratory networks.

Biochemical reference ranges

Blood/plasma	Unit	Reference range	Comments
Acid base status:			
Hydrogen ion	nmol/L	38-48	Arterial
pH		7.32-7.42	Arterial
pCO_2	kPa	4.0-5.5	Arterial
Bicarbonate (derived)	mmol/L	17-25	
Base excess (derived)		-4-+4	
pO_2	kPa	8.0-11.0	Arterial
Alanine aminotransferase (ALT)	IU/L	Up to 40	
Albumin	g/L	28-43	0-7 days
		30-43	7-14 days
		27-44	14-21 days
		32-44	21-28 days
			Concentrations increase by 15% over first 3 weeks. Concentrations are lower in preterm babies and correlate with gestational age.
Alkaline phosphatase (ALP)	IU/L	63-294	Neonate Higher concentrations in first week due to placental ALP. Preterm concentrations higher and may be up to 700 in the absence of active rickets. Range can vary widely with method. Hypophosphatasia should be considered where results are consistently below the reference range.
α1-antitrypsin	g/L	0.9-2.2	'Adult' concentrations at birth, with fall after 2 weeks. Gradual rise to adult concentration by one year. Genotype should be assessed if <1.6 g/L in infants with prolonged jaundice. Concentrations may be increased as part of an acute phase response.

Blood/plasma	Unit	Reference range	Comments
α-fetoprotein	kU/L	450-55,000 185-27,000 80-13,000	Birth 2 weeks 4 weeks After birth concentrations fall (t1/2 5.5 days) in first 2 weeks. Retest at 1-2 weeks to determine appropriate fall in concentration. Concentrations are method dependent.
Ammonia	μmol/L	Up to 125	Preterm and/or sick babies may have concentrations up to 200 μmol/L. Lower concentrations after one month (<40 μmol/L).
Amylase	IU/L	Up to 50	Reference range for children reached after one year
Anion gap i.e. $([Na^+]+[K^+])-([Cl^-]+[HCO_3^-])$	mmol/L	Less than 20	
Aspartate aminotransferase (AST)	IU/L	Up to 120	<14d May vary with method
Bilirubin Total Conjugated Direct reading	 μmol/L μmol/L μmol/L	 Up to 200 Less than 20 Less than 40	<10 days of age (peak 3-4 days) Total bilirubin >50 after 14 days is abnormal
Calcium	mmol/L	2.00-2.70	0-28 days There is often a marked fall after birth with lowest concentration (1.8) at around 24-48 h of age.
Chloride	mmol/L	95-110	
Cholesterol (total)	mmol/L	0.5-4.2	Gradual increase from birth
Copper	μmol/L	3-11	Rapid increase during first week.

Blood/plasma	Unit	Reference range	Comments
Cortisol	nmol/L	180-550 Lack of established diurnal rhythm means 9am and midnight levels are unlikely to have clinical utility. Appropriate dynamic function tests should be used instead.	Peak cortisol is difficult to measure accurately at birth because of cross-reacting steroids. Concentrations are high at birth. There is a marked fall within 24 hours following delivery – partly due to a falling maternally-derived cortisol.
Creatine kinase	IU/L	High levels up to 4-fold those in infancy/childhood	
Creatinine (modified Jaffe – IDMS traceable)	μmol/L	41-89 13-70 8-46	0-7 days 7 days-1 month 1 month – 2 years Method dependent. Sharp decline in concentration over first month. Also dependent on gestational age – see Figure A.2.
C-reactive protein (CRP)	mg/L	Up to 10	Plasma half life 5-7 h
Ferritin	mg/L	90-640	From two weeks (lower at birth). Falls to lower concentration by six months (upper limit 150).
Glucose (plasma fasting)	mmol/L	2.5-5.5 3.5-6.0	Birth From 1 week For discussion of hypoglycaemia see chapter 7 15% lower in whole blood than plasma

Blood/plasma	Unit	Reference range	Comments
17α-hydroxyprogesterone (17-OHP)	nmol/L	0.7-12.4	There is a rapid fall from the very high concentrations of 17-OHP (maternally derived) in the first 24-48 hours of life. This is therefore an inappropriate time to measure 17-OHP for diagnostic purposes. Premature and stressed neonates may have 2-3 fold higher concentrations of 17-OHP compared with values for full term infants.
Immunoglobulins IgG	g/L	5.2-18.0 5.0-17.0 3.9-13.0	Cord blood 0-2 weeks 2-6 weeks
IgA	g/L	<0.02 0.01-0.08 0.02-0.15	Cord blood 0-2 weeks 2-6 weeks
IgM	g/L	0.02-0.20 0.05-0.20 0.08-0.40	Cord blood 0-2 weeks 2-6 weeks
IgE	kU/L	<5 <11	At birth At 3 months
Iron	μmol/L	10-30	May be much higher at birth (up to 60 μmol/L)
Lactate	mmol/L	0.5-2.0	
Magnesium	mmol/L	0.6-1.0	
Osmolality	mmol/kg	275-295	
Phosphate	mmol/L	1.3-3.0	Affected by milk feed type
Potassium	mmol/L	3.4-6.0 3.5-5.5	Capillary blood. Venous or arterial blood and not haemolysed.
Protein (total)	g/L	54-70	Term baby. Gradual increase from birth. Preterm babies have lower values.

Blood/plasma	Unit	Reference range	Comments
Sodium	mmol/L	133-146	
Thyroid stimulating hormone (TSH)	mU/L	0.5-7.9 <10 (whole blood) <5 (plasma)	0-5 days At 6-14 days; pre- and full term infants show a rapid increase in TSH during the first 24 h.
Thyroxine (free, fT4)	pmol/L	18.3-44.8 10.7-21.8	0-5 days 5d-11 years
Triglycerides (fasting)	mmol/L	0.3-2.0	
Immunoreactive trypsin (IRT)	ng/mL	<70 (dried blood spot) <130 (plasma)	0-2 weeks
Urea	mmol/L	0.8-5.5	Infants fed on cows' milk formula may have higher concentrations than breast milk.
Urate	μmol/L	105-300	Values are higher at birth.
Zinc	μmol/L	9-22	0-5 days. Preterm infants have higher values

Urine	Unit	Reference range	Comments
Calcium	mmol/kg/24h	<0.4	
Calcium:creatinine ratio	mmol/mmol	<2.4	Term baby; first two weeks
Copper	μmol/24h	Up to 1.0	
Phosphate	mmol/1.73 m^2/24h	Up to 2.0	Term baby; first two weeks Higher in preterm babies.
Fractional phosphate excretion	%	1-6	Term baby; first two weeks. Higher in preterm babies.
Potassium	mmol/kg/24h	Up to 5	Depends on potassium intake and gestational age
Sodium	mmol/kg/24h	Up to 1 (full term) Up to 3 (preterm)	Depends on sodium intake and gestational age

Urine	Unit	Reference range	Comments
Fractional sodium excretion	%	<0.3 term 2-5 preterm	During week 1
Urate:creatinine ratio	mmol/mmol	Up to 2.0	

CSF	Unit	Reference range	Comments
Glucose	mmol/L	2.5-4.5	Normally 75% of blood glucose
Protein	g/L	<1.2	<8 weeks

Postnatal age	Gestational age (weeks)			
	28	32	36	40
2 days	23-206	9-160	<128	<102
7 days	5-130	<103	<82	<64
14 days	<102	<81	<63	<49
21 days	<88	<70	<54	<40
28 days	<79	<61	<47	<36

Figure A.2. Plasma creatinine concentration (µmol/L) (modified Jaffe adjusted for IDMS calibration) and gestational age.

Haematological reference ranges

Value	Gestational age (weeks)						
	24	34	Full-term Cord blood	Day 1	Day 3	Day 7	Day 14
Hb (g/L)	145	150	168	184	178	170	168
Haematocrit (L/L)	45	47	53	58	55	54	52
Red cells (x10^9/L)	4.0	4.4	5.25	5.8	5.6	5.2	5.1
MCV (fL)	120	118	107	108	99	98	96
MCH (pg)	40	38	34	35	33	32.5	31.5
MCHC (g/L)	310	320	317	325	330	330	330
Reticulocytes (%)	5-10	3-10	3-7	3-7	1-3	0-1	0-1
Platelets (x10^9/L)			290	192	213	248	252

MCV, mean corpuscular volume
MCH, mean corpuscular haemoglobin
MCHC, mean corpuscular haemoglobin concentration

Age (h)	Total white cell count	Neutrophils	Bands/metas	Lymphocytes	Monocytes	Eosinophils
Term Infants						
0	10.0-26.0	5.0-13.0	0.4-1.8	3.5-8.5	0.7-1.5	0.2-2.0
12	13.5-31.0	9.0-18.0	0.4-2.0	3.0-7.0	1.0-2.0	0.2-2.0
72	5.0-14.5	2.0-7.0	0.2-0.4	2.0-5.0	0.5-1.0	0.2-1.0
144	6.0-14.5	2.0-6.0	0.2-0.5	3.0-6.0	0.7-1.2	0.2-0.8
Premature infants						
0	5.0-19.0	2.0-9.0	0.2-2.4	2.5-6.0	0.3-1.0	0.1-0.7
12	5.0-21.0	3.0-11.0	0.2-2.4	1.5-5.0	0.3-1.3	0.1-1.1
72	5.0-14.0	3.0-7.0	0.2-0.6	1.5-4.0	0.3-1.2	0.2-1.1
144	5.5-17.5	2.0-7.0	0.2-0.5	2.5-7.5	0.5-1.5	0.3-1.2

Figure A.3. Leucocyte and neutrophil counts in term and premature infants (10^9/L).

Test	Older Child	Full-term newborn	Healthy growing premature infant
Platelets ($\times 10^9$/L)	100-400	150-400	150-400
Prothrombin time (secs)	10-14	11-15	11-16
Partial thromboplastic time (secs)	25-35	30-40	35-80
Fibrinogen (g/L)	1.75-4.0	1.65-4.0	1.5-3.25
Fibrin degradation products (mg/L)	<10	<10	<10

Figure A.4. Normal values for coagulation screening tests.

Index